JEFFREY T. CHECKEL

Ideas and International Political Change

SOVIET / RUSSIAN BEHAVIOR AND THE END OF THE COLD WAR

Yale University Press
New Haven and London

Set in Sabon type by Keystone Typesetting, Inc., Orwigsburg, Penn.
Printed in the United States of America by Vail-Ballou Press, Binghamton, New
York.

Library of Congress Cataloging-in-Publication Data
Checkel, Jeffrey, T., 1959–
    Ideas and international political change : Soviet/Russian behavior and the
    end of the Cold War / Jeffrey T. Checkel.
       p.   cm.
    Includes bibliographical references (p.   ) and index.
    ISBN 0–300–06377–6 (cloth : alk. paper)
      1. International relations — Methodology.   2. Peaceful change
(International relations).   3. Ideology.   4. Detente.   5. Soviet
Union — Foreign relations.   I. Title.
JX1395.C483   1997
327.47 — dc20   96–18149
                                               CIP

A catalogue record for this book is available from the British Library.

10 9 8 7 6 5 4 3 2 1

For Craig

Contents

Preface: Capturing Complexity, Explaining Change

The end of the Cold War and Soviet "new thinking" represented astounding, unprecedented, and largely unanticipated policy reversals that have led observers to reconsider their views on the nature of international politics. To many, this seems to be a case where new ideas won out against amazing odds, defying the inertial force of both great power rivalry and the domestic institutions and ideology of a well-entrenched regime. How could these changes have come about, and what do they tell us about the need to revise the way people have thought about international relations since Thucydides?

This book offers a simple answer to such puzzles: international political change is driven by ideas, as well as by power and interests. As will be discussed in more detail in chapters 1 and 7, the move to revitalize the study of ideas has become increasingly evident in the various subfields of political science; my own research has been inspired and guided by this work. Yet, like any young research program, that on ideas has left many key issues unresolved. In particular, much of the literature has tended to offer idiosyncratic explanations that do not lend themselves easily to generalization; moreover, it has largely failed to explore the process — the mechanisms and conditions — through which ideas affect state behavior.

To fill these gaps, I develop an institutional argument that allows for an exploration of the process through which new ideas are empowered. More-

over, I do not assume that political institutions and processes are unique to a particular national environment; instead, I explain in a systematic manner why variation in the broader structure of a state affects the role played by ideas. I thus lay the ground for comparative, cross-national work on the role and influence of ideas, a point to which I return in chapter 7.

Within the international relations literature, I seek to recast the debate over the sources of state behavior ("levels of analysis") away from an either/or orientation. I thus join with those who have argued that we must combine international and domestic variables for comprehensive explanations of state behavior.[1]

This is not to deny the importance of structural sources of state behavior. But systems-level explanations can only tell so much. They limit the universe of possible outcomes without explaining why particular outcomes occur. The challenge for theorists is to develop frameworks in which to explore the dynamic between international and domestic variables—a dynamic that ultimately determines the character, content, and timing of particular policy outcomes. Put another way, theories that analyze domestic "decision processes as well as [systemically influenced] decision outcomes are stronger theories than those which purport merely to explain outcomes."[2]

Behind scholars' newfound willingness to mix levels is a recognition that the boundary between domestic and international politics has become too fuzzy to maintain a clear distinction between comparative politics and international relations. This mixing of levels demands a greater tolerance of theoretical pluralism and synthesis as researchers attempt to understand and explain processes of change and other contemporary political phenomena.[3]

A basic theme of this book is that a commitment to theoretical synthesis should guide research on processes of international change; we need explanatory frameworks in which to examine the relations among independent variables operating across domestic and international levels of analysis. Such frameworks, by their very nature, must contain concepts and theories from both the comparative politics and international-relations literatures. My purpose is thus not general theory building; rather, I wish to advance a middle-range theory, which incorporates several independent variables, and explore more systematically the sources of change in international politics.[4]

My particular empirical concern is the process of change that led to the end of the Cold War, a concern that demands that we bring theoretical tools to bear in the study of the former Soviet Union. Yet scholars in the Soviet field rarely did so; rather, they tended to take a descriptive and narrative, or "area studies," approach.[5]

Indeed, because so much of the work on the former Soviet Union was atheoretical and driven by implicit assumptions, the level-of-analysis issue so hotly debated in international relations was rarely addressed in studies of the USSR's international politics. Analysts, for the most part, were content to adopt an either/or approach — stressing either international or domestic sources — to explain change in Soviet behavior.[6] Even more theoretically inclined scholars have tended to focus on systemic factors at the expense of domestic variables, or the reverse.[7]

This book seeks to push both international relations and the Soviet/post-Soviet field in new theoretical directions. Specifically, I consider the ability of ideas to promote change in international politics, by examining domestic as well as international variables. Exploring the interaction between ideas, political institutions, and the international system, I argue that the influence of ideas on state policy is mediated by structure and individual agents. Internationally, a changing external environment helps create windows of opportunity through which policy entrepreneurs — the carriers of new ideas — jump. Domestically, however, such entrepreneurs operate within an institutional setting that sharply affects their ability to influence policy.

My general argument is applied to case material drawn from the former USSR and post-Soviet Russia. Paradoxically, while the structure of the Soviet state hindered the adoption of new ideas, it also insured consolidation of those ideas that were adopted by the leadership. Thus, in the authoritarian Soviet political system, ideas could and did matter, and they had a far-reaching impact on its interests and policy. Nowhere is this seen more dramatically than in the Gorbachev years, when new ideas on international politics played a central role in bringing the Cold War to a peaceful end.

In making this argument, I draw upon several literatures that have received little attention in foreign and security studies. These include work on ideas in the field of comparative political economy, institutionalist approaches first developed in the subfield of international political economy, and research on policy entrepreneurs that was previously used in the American politics and public policy literatures. In casting my theoretical net so broadly, I am motivated by two concerns: (1) to demonstrate that international relations has much to gain by systematically employing approaches first developed in the broader fields; and (2) to develop explanations of change that combine both individual agency and structural (domestic and international) constraints.

I am fully aware of the trade-offs involved in such an approach. Explanatory richness is being purchased at the expense of theoretical parsimony. Indeed, many theorists would surely prefer a shorter list of causal variables than

I offer. Such parsimony, however, would be gained at the cost of failing to capture the full array of factors affecting a complex process of change.[8]

Part I of the book sets the theoretical context. In chapter 1, I develop an explanation of ideas-based foreign policy change that incorporates both agency and structure. I begin by arguing that the influence of new ideas on state behavior is mediated by domestic and international structures. In centralized polities, for example, the initial adoption of new foreign policy ideas is difficult; however, once adopted, they are likely to have an enduring impact on state behavior.

I also introduce the hypothesis that changes at the international level increase the likelihood that policymakers will search for new ideas as they redefine their foreign policy preferences. I address individual agency by using work on policy entrepreneurs that was first developed in the American politics literature. I argue that entrepreneurs play a key role in the process through which new ideas are empowered—especially in countries with centralized decision-making structures. But such individuals often operate in organizational settings that influence their ability to play the role of entrepreneur. Chapter 1 concludes by considering several alternative explanations drawn from neorealist, learning, and coalition theories.

In chapter 2, my approach is more inductive. I explore the expected relation of ideas to foreign policy change in an authoritarian polity such as the former USSR. While the broader structure of the Soviet state hindered the adoption of new foreign policy ideas, it also insured consolidation of those adopted by the leadership.

Chapters 3–6 present three case studies that describe and explain the process through which ideas have shaped Soviet and, now, Russian foreign behavior. Chapter 3 examines the failure of new ideas about international politics to take hold in the Brezhnev era—particularly during the early detente years. Chapter 4 sets the stage for the Gorbachev period by reviewing the supply and demand for new foreign policy ideas as the Brezhnev era drew to a close.

In chapter 5, I draw on interview data with Aleksandr Yakovlev and other key advisers to Gorbachev (as well as other primary sources) to explain the revolutionary change in the USSR's international behavior under Gorbachev and the role of new ideas in this process. I show how the nature of the Soviet state allowed these ideas to have a far-reaching impact on its interests and behavior.

Chapter 6 explores the post-Soviet future, explaining how and why an opportunity was lost in the early 1990s to consolidate a fundamentally new set of

foreign policy ideas in the "new" Russia. In particular, I explore how changes in the institutional structure of contemporary Russia have diminished — in comparison with the Soviet period — the ability of any one set of ideas to shape its foreign behavior.

In the concluding chapter I assess the implications of my research for several debates in the international-relations literature, including the importance of domestic politics and the role of transnational policy networks. I also suggest future directions for work on ideas and foreign policy, arguing for a greater cross-national focus and attention to theory building.

Acknowledgments

Through their comments and support, many colleagues and friends contributed greatly to this project. Much of the empirical material is taken from a Ph.D. dissertation I completed at the Massachusetts Institute of Technology. I thank my committee, and especially Don Blackmer, for guidance at those early stages. The data were considerably enriched by three research trips to the former USSR. In Moscow I owe special thanks to Georgiy Arbatov, Vladimir Benevolenskiy, Sergey Blagovolin, Oleg Bykov, Yuriy Fedorov, Nikolay Kosolapov, Ruslan Kumakhov, Aleksandr Naumenkov, Aleksandr Yakovlev, and Lyudmila Zonova, as well as to many other scholars at the Institute of the World Economy and International Relations of the Russian Academy of Sciences and personnel at the Russian Foreign Ministry.

In the United States, participants in a workshop on "Bringing Russia Back In: International Relations Theory, Comparative Politics, and the Study of the Former USSR" provided helpful comments on an early version of the theoretical argument presented here. The workshop was funded by the Social Science Research Council, co-chaired by myself and John Lepingwell, and held at the University of Pittsburgh in February 1993. In addition, Peter Almquist, Jeff Knopf, Ned Lebow, John Lepingwell, Ron Linden, David Lumsdaine, David Meyer, and Martha Snodgrass were models of professionalism as they carefully read and constructively commented upon various chapters. Particularly helpful were the insights and criticisms of Matthew Evangelista, Jack Snyder, and an anonymous reviewer, all of whom read the complete manuscript; the book is better for their careful reading of it. The students in my comparative politics–international relations graduate seminar on "Ideas and Political Change" provided helpful and critical insights on the ideas literature more generally.

Thanks of a different sort are due to Peter Katzenstein, Ned Lebow, Ken Oye, Simon Reich, Alberta Sbragia, and Martin Staniland. Their moral sup-

port and encouragement were crucial as a neophyte navigated the turbulent waters of the post–Cold War academic publishing world.

Finally, Martha Snodgrass deserves a second and more important mention. She has reminded me time and time again that while books, articles, and course syllabi may come and go, the more important things in life stay — and grow better with time.

Abbreviations and Acronyms

C.C.	Central Committee (of the Communist Party of the Soviet Union)
CIS	Commonwealth of Independent States
CPSU	Communist Party of the Soviet Union
FBIS	Foreign Broadcast Information Service
ISKAN	Institute for the Study of the USA and Canada
IMEMO	Institute of World Economy and International Relations
JPRS	Joint Publications Research Service
Kvs	*Kommunist vooruzhennykh sil*
Memo	*Mirovaya ekonomika i mezhdunarodnye otnosheniya*

Ideas and Foreign Policy

I

Ideas and Policy Change

In recent years, a number of works in comparative politics and international relations have studied ideas and knowledge as factors that influence domestic and international political outcomes. This research can be summarized under two headings: ideas and politics in comparative and international political economy, and the new transnationalism in international relations. A brief review sets the theoretical context for my own approach.[1]

The literature on ideas and politics argues that ideas can influence the content and direction of public policy. Of course, to declare that ideas matter is to beg the analytically more interesting question: How and under what conditions do they matter? Analysts at first emphasized the importance of individuals and the ideas they carried. Nowadays, however, we pay greater attention to institutional context, where an ideas-based approach is integrated with one emphasizing the importance of political institutions.[2]

While this new institutionalism is many things to many people, of primary concern to me is historical institutionalism. This is an approach that emphasizes the ability of institutions to limit over time the boundaries of policy choice. In recent years, analysts have demonstrated its utility in a number of national settings.[3] Within the literature on ideas and politics, this approach has provided a clear sense of how institutions can inhibit or promote the adoption of particular ideas.[4]

This latter work would be enriched by exploring the ideas-institutions nexus in different issue areas, as well as in countries where basic political institutions and actual policy are undergoing change. Such explorations would address a central criticism of the institutionalist approach: its emphasis on explaining continuities over time and consequent lack of attention to the equally important task of understanding policy change. Thus, explaining the sources of institutional dynamism, as it has been called, is an important challenge in the historical-institutionalist approach.[5] I address this issue by developing an institutional-ideational framework for understanding broad patterns of foreign policy change.

Attention to the transnational dimension of international politics has been renewed in recent years, with research on so-called epistemic communities — networks of professionals with recognized expertise in a particular domain — figuring prominently. Using the epistemic approach, analysts explore the interaction between domestic and international sources of state behavior and argue that ideas play a central role in shaping policy. Here, ideas are defined as "consensual knowledge," which is a shared set of beliefs about particular cause-effect and ends-means relations held by all members of an epistemic community. This community, which is usually transnational in character, plays a key role in bringing new ideas to the political process.[6]

Analysts using the epistemic framework see a three-part causal logic at work. The first two elements are the uncertainties faced by political decision makers and the interpretation of these uncertainties by experts (who may be members of an epistemic community). The third is institutionalization — the extent to which an epistemic community consolidates bureaucratic power within domestic or international institutions. The community's influence on policymaking will correlate with the degree of this bureaucratic consolidation.[7]

The strength of the epistemic approach is the integration of international-structural factors into its analyses. This helps us better understand the overall context in which new ideas influence policy choices. Where the epistemic research program requires further elaboration is in the final element, institutionalization. For many analysts in the epistemic literature, institutionalization is a domestic-level process. These same researchers, however, lack a theory of domestic politics that would explain the conditions under which an epistemic community might come to influence national policymaking.[8]

The work of Peter Haas, who has been prominent in developing the epistemic approach, is a case in point. Implicitly, he does advance a theory of domestic politics, arguing that a change in state interests is the result of actions by domestic political elites (members of a transnational epistemic community) who control key governmental organizations. The agencies themselves seem

passive — waiting to be hijacked by these elites. Institutionalization, then, is a matter of selected elites imposing their newly learned preferences on relatively compliant organizations.[9]

If this is the theory of domestic politics the epistemic approach aims to utilize, it needs to be tested explicitly. In particular, we must make cross-national comparisons where the approach is applied in polities with different political structures from those found in the Mediterranean littoral, which is Haas's focus. While several analysts in the former Soviet field have begun to explore how ideas conveyed by epistemic communities influenced policymaking in the USSR, their research, with no evident justification, employs the same implicit theory of domestic politics used by Haas.[10] As I argue in chapter 7, an explicit consideration of institutional variables within the epistemic framework allows for a more complete understanding of the conditions under which transnationally generated ideas bring about policy change.

Ideas and State Interests

The recent work on ideas — either domestically or transnationally generated — offers important insights on how nonmaterial factors help reshape elite preferences, state interests, and policy. My purpose here is to supplement this research, specifically by developing a middle-range theory, incorporating several explanatory factors, to explore the processes that bring new ideas to politics and to look at how such ideas can help redefine a state's interests.[11]

Specifically, my dependent variable is the foreign policy preferences of key political elites — in particular, the heads of governmental bureaucracies and top-level decision makers. Depending on the type of political (and constitutional) system, such decision makers may be presidents, prime ministers or general secretaries, as in the former Soviet Union.

Two important causal variables to consider at this point are ideas and political institutions. I define the former as broad concepts and basic beliefs that can play a central role in organizing politics and shaping public policy. For decision makers, ideas provide a policy paradigm or road map for interpreting international politics and shaping preferences, as well as a sense of the proper instruments to use in promoting state interests.[12]

In the foreign-affairs and national security-issue areas, ideas so defined would address, among other things, the fundamental dynamics of international politics (balance of power, say, versus interdependence); the role international organizations can play in mitigating competition and conflict; basic foreign policy orientations (multilateralism versus bilateralism, regionalism versus internationalism); and rightful participants in foreign policymaking

(the role of civilian versus military agencies, or the division of powers between executive and legislative bodies).

As for political institutions, both historical institutionalists and international-relations theorists employ a definition that includes not only formal rules and structures but informal procedures and norms. Theorists — comparativists and international-relations scholars alike — are concerned with how institutions constrain activity, regularize behavior, and shape the interests of political actors.[13]

This general definition can be refined by specifying three levels of institutions. At the broadest level, there are the basic organizing principles of a domestic polity (social norms and class structure, say) or of an international system (anarchy or international society, for example). Second are more specific institutions that allow state and society to interact within different countries (social actors, intermediate associations) or states to interact within a particular international system (the nonproliferation regime is a contemporary example). Third come the organizations and agencies that shape specific policy outcomes in the domestic (defense ministries, say) or international arenas (the International Atomic Energy Agency, for example).

The broadest level, while useful in setting the overall context of policymaking, tells virtually nothing about the content of particular outcomes. Indeed, an institutional approach at this level suffers the well-known drawbacks of structural theories of domestic and international politics — for example, the inability to explain change.[14] On the other hand, an institutional approach at the third level suffers from being context dependent and too focused on the particular agents who are attempting to influence outcomes within particular organizations.

This third level is the domain of organization theory and Allison-like studies of policymaking.[15] While useful, this work neglects the historically determined features of a given polity that structure the game of politics in ways that may benefit or hinder particular organizations and bureaucracies. In addition, an institutional approach focused exclusively on the third level hinders theory development because comparison across time and countries is difficult.

I seek to avoid these problems by developing an approach to foreign and national-security policymaking that combines elements of the second and third levels. This situates the analysis at a level sufficiently broad to facilitate cross-national comparison, while keeping the focus sharp enough to explain policy-relevant outcomes.

As defined here, institutions are thus both specific organizations and a broader set of historically constructed parameters that structure foreign policymaking. The latter address questions of legislative-executive interaction (separation of powers), the role of intermediate associations, and the auton-

omy of state actors. This combination allows me to study a less-explored middle ground between analyses that examine policy change over decades and those that consider bureaucratic pulling and hauling over particular issues.[16]

Empirically, I place the process of foreign policy change in particular countries in a broader frame. Those who study such processes — area specialists — have a tendency to become caught up in the details of the matter without addressing the larger context in which political outcomes are structured.[17]

What is the connection between institutions as defined here and the role of ideas in the political process? Simple logic suggests an inverse relation between the centralization and autonomy of institutional structures and whether new ideas influence the formation of elite preferences and state interests. As structures weaken, access to policymaking increases and the insulation of political elites decreases; this creates a greater number of pathways for promoters of new ideas. Furthermore, as institutions decentralize and become more penetrable, the likelihood that some of these pathways will be transnational increases. Thus, a greater variety of ideas from a greater number of sources has a higher probability of reaching key decision makers when domestic institutions are weakening.[18]

These general relations can be clarified if we distinguish between the adoption and the implementation of new ideas and appreciate the role of organizational ideologies. The adoption of ideas will be more difficult in states with centralized political institutions, where access to decision makers is restricted. Once these ideas are adopted (for whatever reason), however, the implementation of policies based on them is more likely. In contrast, less-centralized states are more likely to adopt new ideas but less likely to implement them successfully.[19]

Organizational ideologies are historically constructed sets of beliefs that act as filters — making particular organizations within the broader structure of a state more or less open to certain ideas. This fact complicates the framework presented above and introduces an element of contingency in it. Indeed, a challenge for those working within the historical-institutionalist literature is to develop generalizable theories that explore the conditions under which particular ideas come to influence policy.[20]

My approach differs in several ways from previous institution-oriented research. In his comparative study of state responses to international economic crises, Peter Gourevitch develops an explanatory framework of which a key part is a second-level institutional approach. In contrast, I pay more attention to third-level organizations because of a greater concern with the role of agency in shaping outcomes.[21]

In his work on domestic structures, Peter Katzenstein also employs a primarily second-level institutional approach. The domestic-structures frame-

work, to which historical institutionalists owe a clear intellectual debt, has been applied primarily to foreign economic policy.[22] I intend to build on this earlier work by exploring the role of agency more systematically, by considering the interaction between institutional and ideational variables, and by applying an institutional approach to the foreign and national-security policy arena.[23]

To this point, I have discussed the structural or "supply side" of my argument, analyzing the conditions under which new ideas are more likely to reach key political elites. The next step is to explore the preference formation or "demand side" of the equation. In particular, under what conditions are elite preferences likely to be in flux? This is an important question, for it is plausible to assume that at such times elites are more likely to be searching for new ideas and policies.

Standard realist theories take elite preferences and state interests as a given. Of course, realists do admit that preferences change — but only as a function of changing international structure. Elites modify their preferences in a rational way to accord with new structural realities; decision makers are above the fray of domestic politics. Free from broader societal and bureaucratic constraints and reacting to international power imperatives, they are in a position to define their state's interests in a rational, objective manner.[24]

I do, in fact, agree with the realists in two ways. First, elite decision makers and their preferences play a crucial role in defining state interests. This is especially likely to be the case in centralized polities where so-called intermediate associations (political parties, organized interest-group lobbies) that link government and society are missing or weakly developed. Second, elites often respond to external stimuli when defining state interests.[25]

To black-box this response with assumptions of rationality and unitary state actors, as realists do, however, is to obscure the various domestic-level factors at work. Rather, a changing international environment creates windows of opportunity by fostering a sense of crisis or uncertainty among elites or undermining previous policies and views. Put another way, the international setting can open policy windows that allow decision makers to engage in an information search as they define preferences and state interests; decision makers will be in the market for new ideas.[26]

Entrepreneurs and Policy Change

From a policy perspective, ideas in and of themselves matter little; more important is how they become empowered politically. In the previous section, I explored how domestic institutions and international stimuli affect the likeli-

hood of ideas-based policy change. That analysis set the broad structural context that explains how new ideas reach the top levels of political systems, but it is inadequate for explaining why certain ideas become politically influential.

To answer this last point requires a consideration of the particular agents of ideas-based policy change. Possible carriers of new ideas include individuals, domestic or international nongovernmental organizations (NGOs), and transnational coalitions.[27] Broader state structure, however, creates pathways that advantage some of these advocates over others. In states with highly centralized policymaking, individual policy entrepreneurs should be able to play a more important role in bringing about change. The structural logic of such states suggests that many of the "normal" pathways for affecting policy (public opinion, pressure from NGOs, transgovernmental coalitions) are either blocked or diminished in importance.[28]

In decentralized states, the situation is more complex. Such states certainly present entrepreneurs with a greater number of pathways and access points through which to influence policy. But although they may gain greater access in a less centralized state, so, too, will various other groups and forces. Thus, relative to the situation found in centralized states, individual entrepreneurs and their ideas will play a less important role in fostering policy change.

Because my empirical material is drawn from a prototypical centralized state (the former USSR), let me develop the argument on policy entrepreneurs at more length. Entrepreneurs are clever individuals with a "game plan"; endowed with certain resources, they apparently bring about policy change. I say apparently because the research on entrepreneurship, until recently, has been more descriptive than explanatory.[29] As a result, we lack a clear sense of what particular variables maximize the likelihood of successful entrepreneurship. The entrepreneur variable thus runs the risk of becoming a catch-all category — it explains as much or as little as one desires.

Entrepreneurs, to quote one straightforward definition, are "individuals who change the direction and flow of politics."[30] This definition, however, begs a more important question: What resources and conditions allow such individuals to change the flow of politics? The literature suggests that successful entrepreneurs possess one or more of the following: expertise and knowledge in their given field; substantial negotiating skills; persistence; connections to relevant political actors. The first category makes a bridge to the literature on ideas and politics: ideas may be key resources held by entrepreneurs.[31]

These resources, idiosyncratic in nature, are necessary but not sufficient conditions for successful entrepreneurship. Two situational factors are also essential. Are there problems whose resolution would be assisted by the implementation of the entrepreneur's ideas? Are there leaders in power who

recognize that such problems exist? Taken together, these two factors create an opportunity — a policy window — for the aspiring entrepreneur to sell a particular idea, intellectual outlook, or policy.[32]

In the foreign policy arena, policy windows create a crucial link between the domestic and international settings. In particular, for entrepreneurs addressing questions of foreign and national-security policy, external threats to the state and their removal or other changes in the international environment help form such a window. How wide it opens, however, is a function of the second factor: a political leadership willing to consider the new ideas purveyed by these individuals.[33]

The last point raises an important issue: politics matters. Entrepreneurs can be clever, persistent, and politically well connected, and they can offer solutions to many problems. But their goal of changing the direction and flow of politics will be extraordinarily difficult unless elites in positions of political power also recognize that such problems exist. Politicians in search of answers to these problems and the crises they face are thus a key link in my argument. This is simply another way of stating the truism discussed by Gourevitch and others: politics opens up, becomes more fluid, under conditions of crisis and uncertainty.[34]

Entrepreneurs, however, are not always free agents; they often operate within an organizational context that influences their behavior in important ways. How? If an entrepreneur carries ideas that are at variance with core aspects of the organization's ideology and mindset, his or her task will be doubly difficult. That is, the entrepreneur will face significant organizational obstacles in addition to the individual and situational factors discussed above.[35]

Within organizations, the ability of any one individual — even a capable entrepreneur — to modify basic missions is highly constrained. A process of selective recruitment usually insures that individuals with a mindset different from the dominant organizational ideology rarely join a particular agency. Moreover, once an individual has joined, an array of bureaucratic obstacles and power relationships minimizes the member's ability to affect policy.[36]

Thus, under conditions where there is a mismatch between ideas held at the individual (entrepreneurial) and organizational levels, the chances of successful entrepreneurship are significantly reduced. Following the same (organizational) logic, however, one would deduce that where there is a close fit between a particular entrepreneur's ideas and his or her organization's dominant ideology, successful entrepreneurship will be more likely.

I conceptualize organizational ideologies as sets of concepts that help organizations understand their interests.[37] Ideologies thus shape organizational behavior. The interests and behavior of the British Treasury in the post–World

War II period, for example, were dramatically influenced by the Keynesian economic ideology it adopted. Interests, in other words, are in part subjectively determined and ideas based.[38]

A critical question is how ideologies develop and become embedded in particular organizations — a point the ideas literature has only begun to address. From an institutionalist perspective, an important factor affecting the ideology-organization nexus is the broader structure of the state. When bureaucratic units and the elites who run them are insulated from broader societal forces — that is, in centralized states — there is a greater probability that organizational ideologies will become embedded. In less centralized states, this probability is reduced.

A second important factor is unit leadership. As one analyst puts it, "Pivotal institution builders often leave an ideological legacy" within their organizations.[39] This legacy, which helps shape the broader organizational ideology, can be propagated in a number of ways: training procedures, selective recruitment and advancement, and the dissemination of written materials.

Summary

I have outlined here a causal mechanism that explains why and how new ideas inform elite preferences and state behavior. Although I believe this mechanism to be deductively sound and logically coherent, it may be empirically false. I thus need to explore whether it actually exists, and to do this requires that a set of propositions or hypotheses be generated. In other words, if my argument is valid, how should the process of ideas-based foreign policy change occur in centralized polities (my empirical focus)? The following propositions, which I shall look at with regard to three cases of change in the international behavior of the former USSR, explain how ideas might come to affect foreign policy.[40]

- Under conditions of high international uncertainty or foreign policy crisis, decision makers engage in an information search and are thus more receptive to new ideas. Their foreign policy preferences, in other words, are in flux.
- Conditions of high international uncertainty or foreign policy crisis create policy windows. These windows link the international and domestic environments and motivate advocates of new ideas to promote them.
- In centralized states, there are fewer pathways by which ideas can reach elites; their initial adoption is thus more difficult. Once adopted, however, such ideas stand a greater chance of being implemented and thus of altering state behavior.
- In less centralized states, there are a greater number of pathways by which

new ideas can reach elites; their initial adoption is thus less problematic. Once adopted, however, such ideas are less likely to be implemented in a way that has a lasting effect on state behavior.

•Policy entrepreneurs will play a critical role in empowering new ideas in centralized states because many of the other pathways for affecting change are blocked or diminished in importance. In a decentralized state, entrepreneurs will see their comparative advantage diminish as elite insulation decreases.

Several observations are in order. First, this framework for understanding the formation/redefinition of elite preferences and state interests is purposely meant to be highly contingent. International and domestic structures set broad limits, but within these boundaries many possible state interests informed by different ideas are possible. Put another way, my framework admits the role of chance in this process. (Are entrepreneurs available? Are policy windows open?)[41]

Second, my framework differs in several ways from those advanced in the ideas literature. Most important, I elaborate a set of parameters for explaining cross-national variation in the mechanisms and pathways through which new ideas are empowered. In doing this, I also suggest a route through which international variables enter the domestic arena, creating windows for the promotion of particular ideas. The international setting, in other words, may trigger changes in state behavior, but a complex interplay among ideas, entrepreneurs, and institutions determines the content of the resulting policy initiatives.

Third, the argument advanced here (and the ideas literature more generally) does not simply reinvent the wheel. After all, it has been nearly two decades since Robert Jervis' pathbreaking study of perception and misperception in theories of international relations highlighted the importance of beliefs.[42] Yet the arguments of Jervis and the theorists who followed him are most often pitched at the level of individual cognition. The ideas literature, in contrast, is more concerned with explicating the political influence and mechanisms through which beliefs come to affect international politics. Thus, the argument about ideas advanced here is a considerably more "socialized" one, stressing the international and domestic institutional contexts through which particular beliefs are empowered.

The ideas literature should also be distinguished from recent constructivist approaches in international relations. The latter adopt an even more socialized view on the role of beliefs and ideas, seeing them as prior to and constituting state identity and interests. Those who research the role of ideas — myself included — typically argue that ideational arguments should supplement but not replace structural and interest-based accounts.[43]

Alternative Explanations

The plausibility of my argument is strengthened if we compare it with several alternative explanations for how elite preferences are changed and foreign policy is effected. Given my focus on the foreign and national-security area, the obvious place to start is with realist and neorealist accounts. I have argued that the process of changing preferences and the redefinition of state interests is partly subjective and ideas based. Domestic institutions structure this process, but ideas and policy paradigms "fill in the blanks" — that is, they reveal much about the content of the new interests.

Neorealists would applaud my attention to structure but note that it is misplaced. International structural constraints, in other words, are what really matter. In its most elegant form, the neorealist argument is that preference formation and interest redefinition are objective, rational processes driven by changing international circumstances. While there are many problems with this argument, I do share a common premise with it: when defining state interests, decision makers are responding to external stimuli.[44]

This response, however, cannot be "black boxed" with assumptions of rationality and unitary state actors. Although such abstractions may be analytically necessary for generating parsimonious general theories, they are of little use for the middle-range theory building to which this book contributes. Moreover, they obscure the various domestic-level factors that help shape interests.

A variation on the neorealist explanation is that elite preferences are modified in response to a broad array of international stimuli — including, but not limited to, international structure. Such an argument has been advanced to explain the foreign policy changes that occurred in the Soviet Union under Gorbachev. These changes, it is suggested, were a rational, largely inevitable, process of adaptation to changing external stimuli. Like neorealist accounts, however, this explanation is also underspecified. In particular, by dismissing the importance of domestic-level variables, it ignores the process through which preferences and state interests come to change.[45]

Although international environments clearly help induce changes in state interests, a focus on external stimuli alone is inadequate for explaining the timing and content of these new or redefined interests. Put another way, the challenge for theorists is to understand how international factors matter — under what conditions. This is an issue that must be empirically explored, not simply assumed away.[46]

Turning to the domestic level, there is a straightforward and parsimonious

alternative explanation for policy change: new leaders with new preferences come to power and proceed to act on them. In the case of the former Soviet Union, this interpretation would argue that such key elites as Brezhnev or Gorbachev arrived in office with new policy preferences. With Brezhnev, this was certainly not true.[47]

Gorbachev is a more interesting case. It is clear that by the early 1980s he was dissatisfied with many aspects of Soviet policy (domestic and foreign) and was consulting with a wide range of individuals outside the leadership.[48] So perhaps Gorbachev came to power in March 1985 with a new set of preferences that later became the central conceptual elements of his liberal foreign policy. Given the clear correlation between Gorbachev's accession to power and the promulgation of the "new thinking," such an explanation is appealing.

There is, however, little evidence to support it. Before late 1985, although Gorbachev had clearly hinted that he was open to new ideas on international politics, there is no indication that he had developed a comprehensive conceptual or policy framework for foreign policy reform. In fact, the evidence is quite clear that in the early years of Gorbachev's ascent to power his thoughts were concentrated on a different domain of public policy: domestic socioeconomic reform.[49]

Another alternative explanation at the domestic level argues that the foreign policy preferences of elites change as they acquire new knowledge (called cognitive-content learning). Yet even if one accepts that learning is the mechanism by which ideas come to alter preferences, such explanations overlook important questions. Proponents of this approach are typically interested in ascertaining whether learning has taken place; they often fail to address what accounts for learning among individuals at particular times. If preferences do change as a result of new knowledge, it is still important to ask who or what was the source of the knowledge and how this process occurred. Learning approaches, in other words, need to be supplemented with an exploration of the broader political context and process.[50]

The mention of politics brings me to a final alternative explanation at the domestic level. Perhaps domestic political maneuvering explains why elites change their preferences. That is, new ideas are seized upon in an instrumental manner by elites attempting to build a winning political coalition. In this way, the power of domestic "interests" wins out over "ideas." There are, however, several reasons for questioning such explanations—especially in their stronger forms.[51]

First, advocates of political coalition approaches are themselves often am-

biguous about the power of ideas versus that of interests. They assert the dominant influence of interests as (rationally) dictated by position in the domestic or international political economy. Yet ideas often seem to pop up in an independent role — shaping elite preferences or helping domestic interests understand exactly what their "interests" are in the first place.[52] While this ambiguity is troubling, it does not mean one should take the opposite tack and assert the absolute causal prominence of ideas. Rather, it suggests that ideas deserve a more central place in our explanations of political change.

Second, the importance of politics in shaping preferences may vary as a function of the stage reached in the process. While policy studies is torn by conceptual and empirical disputes as lively as those found in any other field, there is one thing upon which most analysts agree: policies do not emerge out of thin air. They have a history.[53] Indeed, a process perspective helps one better understand when ideas — as opposed to politics and interests — should dominate in the reshaping of elite preferences.

At early stages in the process, the degree of uncertainty surrounding an issue or problem will often be high. Decision makers are likely to be more open to new ideas and concepts simply because uncertainty and confusion will lead them to question whether policy options drawn from the standard repertoire are adequate for the issues at hand. Individual decision makers are thus engaged in their own cognitive search for answers to new sorts of problems.[54]

The skeptic could argue, of course, that politics and the power of interests will override this cognitive search. After all, political leaders have to worry about building coalitions for their policies. While this is true, it is important to recognize that the politics of policymaking may be quite different — and less important in shaping elite preferences — at other points in the process. A number of studies have shown that organizational, bureaucratic, and interest-group pressures are often minimized at earlier stages. Indeed, many actors and interests may not even be aware that the "game" is under way and as a result will not have mobilized their resources (intellectual, political or financial) to influence it.[55]

Applied to the former Soviet Union, the argument would not be that politics and conflict were unimportant. Rather, their importance and influence on elite behavior varied at different points in the process. Kremlinological studies of elite conflict and more theoretically informed studies of competition within the Soviet Politburo correctly assert that conflict was a key variable in shaping elite preferences and, ultimately, Soviet policies.[56]

These studies err, however, in ascribing too much explanatory weight to such conflict, largely because they adopt an overly narrow understanding of

the political process as Politburo politics. Clashes of interests and power may matter less at other points — a fact recognized in all too few studies of Soviet policymaking.[57]

Third, coalition politics may be more important in countries with certain types of institutional structures. Indeed, prominent advocates of interest-based and political-coalition explanations recognize that their usefulness varies as a function of domestic setting. Coalition dynamics should be less important in such states as the former Soviet Union that have more autonomous political institutions.[58]

In particular, one would expect the Soviet Politburo to serve as a "unitary oligarchy with relatively diffuse, encompassing interests. Though influenced by the parochial interests of institutional constituencies, its members' loyalties were largely to the Politburo itself." If the Politburo was indeed insulated from broader societal and interest-group pressures, it is certainly worth exploring the role that ideas played in determining those encompassing interests.[59]

As this discussion should make clear, I do not assert the absolute dominance of ideas over other explanatory variables in policy decisions. Rather, my concern is with exploring the role ideas play within the often-broad limits imposed by domestic institutions, politics, and international structure. Put another way, I am seeking a middle ground between two strikingly different understandings of the relation of ideas to preferences and policy. At one extreme, ideas are mere tools of convenience. Having chosen to change policy for instrumental, interest-based reasons, political elites need some legitimation or justification to still opposition. The adoption of new ideas reflects crass political calculation. At the other extreme, changes in preferences and policy are caused solely by changes in ideas. Dissatisfied with mental road maps that seem to be going nowhere, elites adopt new ideas that lead to new policies.[60]

Theoretically, the middle ground I stake out will not satisfy some. Empirically, however, it best captures the complex reality of political change — a process where ideas have both a political and cognitive role to play.

Methodology

Central to any institutional analysis is an assessment of political structures. For my Soviet case studies, I measured these in two ways. First, I examined how policymaking was mandated or constrained by laws or decrees (for example, the Party program of the Communist Party of the Soviet Union). These measures provided a sense of how the broader structure of the Soviet state was shaping foreign policy outcomes.

Second, I considered particular organizations involved in setting foreign

and national-security policy. Data on their history, ideologies, and degree of insulation were needed. In addition to my studies of relevant documents, I conducted interviews with officials and analysts.

Interviews were also essential for exploring how ideas reached decision makers.[61] Process tracing of this sort is a fairly straightforward method; it is also essential for establishing the plausibility of the multivariate, middle-range theoretical approach advanced here.[62]

The method of structured, focused comparison was used to organize the analysis. Based on the propositions advanced earlier, an identical set of questions is addressed in each of the case studies; this provides a similar structure for the primary narrative chapters of the book. The questions include: (1) Was a policy window open in the foreign or national-security issue area? (2) Were entrepreneurs present, and did they seek to advance particular ideas? (3) What was the institutional and organizational context in which the entrepreneurs operated? (4) Were the preferences of key political elites modified? and (5) If so, what role did new ideas play?[63]

A final methodological issue concerns not so much the collection and organization of data but the use to which they are put. The case studies that follow illustrate and seek to establish the plausibility of my argument; they do not constitute a crucial test of its validity. This is so because the argument was partly derived from the empirical material to which it is applied. It will be the task of future research to design rigorous critical case studies to validate the thesis advanced here, as well as others put forth in the ideas literature — points to which I shall return in the last chapter.

2

Policymaking in an Authoritarian State

To this point, my approach has been primarily deductive. Using insights from the international political economy, comparative politics, and American politics literatures, I have advanced an argument to explain the processes and mechanisms through which ideas come to shape the foreign policy preferences of national decision makers. My purpose in this chapter is to supplement the deductive argument with a more inductive approach that explores the expected relationship of ideas and foreign policy behavior in an authoritarian state like the former USSR.

Ideas and Soviet Institutions

A key source of ideas throughout the Soviet period was the network of research institutes associated with the USSR Academy of Sciences. But it was only beginning in the late 1950s — after the 20th Party Congress of the Communist Party of the Soviet Union (CPSU) — that the academy became a source of ideas on questions of foreign policy. The post-Stalin political elite, realizing that they needed expertise about the outside world, sanctioned the establishment of a number of international-affairs research institutes under the academy's aegis.[1]

As many analysts noted, these specialists and their ideas were outsiders.

They were nonactors in the policy process until the political elites granted them access. The nature of Soviet political institutions was such that policymakers were insulated, and access to the process was restricted.[2]

The Soviet state, in other words, was centralized and strong. Although few scholars discussed Soviet political institutions in such terms, they were indeed insulated and impermeable to broader societal influences. In addition, foreign policymaking was centralized in what might be called the executive branch — primarily the apparatus of the Communist Party Central Committee (secretariat and departments) and Politburo.[3]

This particular set of institutional parameters structured foreign policymaking in important ways and directly influenced the role ideas could play in the changing of policy. Certain beliefs about international politics, for example, had become embedded in influential and insulated agencies.[4] This was particularly true of the Ministry of Defense and the Central Committee's International Department. The Ministry, which had an important role in the formation of national-security policy, saw international politics primarily as a zero-sum affair and emphasized a narrow definition of national security that gave primacy to military instruments. It had, in other words, a pessimistic, Hobbesian vision of the world.[5]

The International Department, which oversaw key aspects of Soviet policy with regard to developing nations, also viewed politics in starkly zero-sum terms and, in addition, placed extraordinary emphasis on the class-based nature of the international system. Two believers in Soviet ideology — Mikhail Suslov and Boris Ponomarev — had overseen this unit since the early 1960s, and they deeply influenced its development.[6]

The point to emphasize is that key avenues for bringing new ideas to Soviet politics were blocked by these dominant ideologies. Soviet state interests, as articulated by top political leaders, seemed heavily influenced by this balance-of-power, Soviet Marxist vision of the international arena. Put another way, what made ideas politically powerful was a combination of elite support and organizational basis.[7]

If these ideas were so powerfully entrenched, then how did change come about? After all, both in the late 1960s and, especially, in the mid-1980s, elite preferences and foreign policy behavior did change in important ways. The answer, as I document in subsequent chapters, is that political leaders reached out and around these powerful organizations for new ideas. And as leaders reached out, aspiring entrepreneurs were ready with their solutions.

This end-around strategy, as it might be called, was successful precisely because of the broader structure of Soviet politics — most important, the extraordinarily centralized nature of foreign policy decision making. While this

made it difficult for new ideas to reach the top, their consolidation once there was easier because elites controlled key instruments for disseminating ideas.[8]

In sum, and as the historical-institutionalist literature surveyed in chapter 1 would predict, the adoption of new ideas was difficult in a centralized and insulated state like the former USSR. Once adopted, however, the implementation of policies based on these ideas was likely. Leadership, entrepreneurship, and new ideas were critical, but these idiosyncratic and ideational variables were mediated by a broader institutional context.[9]

Let me now address more specifically the likely roles played by political elites and policy entrepreneurs. One would expect entrepreneurs — given the institutional parameters of the Soviet state — to play an enhanced role in empowering a particular set of new ideas and thus changing the direction and flow of politics. Exploiting policy windows created by a changing international environment, entrepreneurs could serve as a critical conduit for transmitting ideas from academy research institutes to foreign policy elites.

These entrepreneurs from the academic world, however, were often affected by the organizational setting in which they operated. Depending upon a particular organization's history and ideology, these settings could either hinder or promote particular ideas or outlooks. In other words, these specialists responded to the "constraints and opportunities presented by [their] institutions."[10]

During the Brezhnev and Gorbachev eras, the most important international-affairs units within the academy were the Institute for the Study of the USA and Canada (ISKAN) and the Institute of the World Economy and International Relations (IMEMO). Organizational constraints were clearly at work within both units. Informal norms and rules dictated that research problems be approached in different ways. At IMEMO, the emphasis was on fundamentals and theory, while at ISKAN, the focus was more applied and policy oriented.[11]

These differing organizational norms were widely known in the Moscow policy and academic communities and were clearly evident in the institutes' respective publications. The differing organizational reputations also explain why the two institutes attracted different sorts of specialists. For example, ISKAN, with its greater policy focus, had typically recruited more retired military officers to its ranks than had IMEMO.

These informal organizational norms interacted with more formal ones to reinforce the sense that the two institutes had different missions. Indeed, when ISKAN was established in the late 1960s, its founding mandate covered a much narrower set of policy-relevant issues (focusing on the United States and the U.S.-Soviet relationship) than was the case for IMEMO. Over the years,

the differing organizational mandates at the two institutes were further formalized in a series of yearly and five-year plans with which they were required to comply.[12]

Researchers at these institutes were thus operating in an organizational context that affected their ability to play the role of entrepreneurs promoting policy change. As will be seen, these organizational norms and rules (both informal and formal), in combination with several other factors, allowed a particular set of ideas on international politics to take hold at one of the institutes, IMEMO. This embedded ideology helped shape IMEMO's understanding of its own interests; it also gave preference to those entrepreneurs within it whose ideas resonated with this broader normative basis of IMEMO's behavior.

Policy entrepreneurs, however, would be an unimportant part of the story were it not for political elites who were willing to consider their ideas. Moreover, for my explanatory framework to apply, these elites would have to be in a position of sufficient political power that a change in their preferences would lead to shifts in state interests and behavior. Elites in the USSR — especially those in the Politburo and Central Committee (C.C.) apparatus — were in such a position. Both theoretical logic and empirical data suggest this was the case. Theoretically, one would expect that in states without intermediate associations linking government and society (political parties, organized interest group lobbies, and the like), elite decision makers would play an enhanced role in shaping outcomes.[13] Such associations were clearly missing in the USSR.

Empirically, there is abundant evidence that the preferences of top elites played a crucial role in shaping Soviet policy, especially in the foreign and security issue areas. Indeed, the consensus among Western analysts was that to explain major foreign policy change, one needed to pay close attention to the shifting preferences of top leaders like the CPSU general secretary.[14]

I shall examine three periods over the past thirty years when elite preferences and foreign policy behavior were in the greatest flux in the former Soviet Union: the detente of the late 1960s and early 1970s; the new political thinking of the 1980s; and, in the post-Soviet period, the international political behavior of the Russian Federation during the early 1990s. Details of the third case are addressed in chapter 6; below, I provide an introduction to the earlier periods, with which readers may be less familiar.

My purpose here is not to give detailed histories. Rather, it is to explore the causal role of ideas in these periods of international political change. I consider one particular source of ideas, IMEMO, which was arguably the most important Soviet research institute specializing in international affairs. Empirically, the puzzle to explain is the change that occurred in elite preferences and state interests. For the first two cases, a key part of the puzzle is understanding the

differential rate of change: Why were beliefs and interests modified in the early 1970s but revolutionized in the 1980s?

The Detente of the Late 1960s and Early 1970s

Soviet foreign policy in the late 1960s was in a state of change as political elites sought a more cooperative and stable relationship with the West. In part, this was a quest for a solution to the USSR's China problem. It was also, however, a search for greater stability in Soviet-American relations — in particular, a more constrained and predictable competition in strategic weaponry. This reassessment culminated in the Anti-Ballistic Missile (ABM) Treaty and the Strategic Arms Limitations Talks Interim Agreement (SALT I), both signed in May 1972.[15]

These dramatic changes in Soviet policy of the late 1960s cannot be understood in isolation from their domestic and international contexts. Domestically, three important factors in the change were elite politics, the state of the economy, and shifts in the leadership's approach to policymaking. At the outset, it should be stressed that the early Brezhnev years were a time of dynamism and moderate change in various policy areas; the *zastoy* (stagnation) of later years was not yet in evidence.[16]

In the realm of elite politics, the years 1964–71 were marked by less political conflict than had been the case throughout Khrushchev's tenure as Soviet leader. This is not to deny the existence of conflicts within the leadership during Brezhnev's early years; they clearly existed. Two facts, however, moderated the degree of conflict: (1) a strong elite consensus to prevent the re-emergence of the kind of political regime that had developed under Khrushchev (perhaps best described as an attempt at one-man dictatorship without the use of terror); and (2) Brezhnev's personal leadership style, which emphasized a go-slow, consensus-building approach. These years also saw Brezhnev slowly consolidate his leadership position. By the 24th Party Congress in March 1971, he was recognized as the first among equals within the political leadership.

The Soviet economy continued to grow in the years after Khrushchev's ouster, but growth rates slowed and serious structural problems emerged. During this period, there was an increasing recognition among academic specialists and parts of the political leadership that the USSR faced serious economic difficulties. This realization was influenced by the elites' growing awareness of the importance of scientific-technical progress and technology's acceleration throughout the world. By the late 1960s, there was high-level recognition that weaknesses in the USSR's economic system were hindering

both the development of new scientific achievements and their rapid assimilation into the national economy.

There were two possible strategies for addressing these problems. One approach involved far-reaching reform of the economic system, including decentralization and a change in incentive structures. The Soviet leadership rejected this solution, assessing the economic reforms implemented after Khrushchev's ouster as limited in success and fearing, in the wake of the 1968 Czechoslovakia crisis, the political consequences of any radical restructuring. A second strategy involved the expansion of East-West trade and economic ties; this was the approach eventually adopted.

A final important factor in the domestic realm was a change in the Soviet approach to policymaking. There were two concerns at work here. Political elites had a strong desire to avoid the improvised method of policymaking that had been typical of Khrushchev. Brezhnev's leadership style, with its emphasis on stability and consensus building, was well matched to this new-found elite concern.[17]

Among specialists and some members of the leadership, there was also a desire to expand participation in Soviet policymaking. Toward this end, Brezhnev and others began to call for a "scientific approach" in various realms of social and economic policy; such calls began in the immediate wake of Khrushchev's ouster and continued intermittently through the early 1970s.[18]

There was clearly a political motive behind pronouncements of this sort. They distinguished the Brezhnev leadership from the subjective and "voluntaristic" governing style of Khrushchev. A practical consideration was also at work: the new leaders wanted more information on a broader set of public-policy issues from a wider variety of sources than they had received in the past.

In the international realm, two important factors behind the policy changes were U.S.-Soviet relations and the strategic balance of power. With the exception of the three years 1965–68, the Soviet-American relationship was oriented toward engagement between 1963 and 1972. In Khrushchev's last years (1963–64), the United States and the Soviet Union negotiated on a narrow set of security issues; achievements included the Limited Test Ban Treaty and the Moscow-Washington Hotline Agreement. Beginning in 1968, Soviet-American engagement was renewed and became more multifaceted. Security issues still dominated in the late 1960s, but matters of economic and technological interchange gained increasing attention, primarily because of changes in Soviet attitudes.[19]

The obvious lacuna in this story of modest cooperation is the period 1965–68, during which relations were tense and strained. Two factors were at work: the war in Vietnam and the political crisis in Czechoslovakia. During the

mid-1960s, Soviet spokesmen constantly denounced U.S. policy in Vietnam. Everywhere in the official press — be it *Pravda* or *Kommunist* — the tension and condemnation were palpable. Relations began to improve in early 1968, and by July the United States and the Soviet Union had agreed to a September 1968 starting date for the SALT negotiations. The invasion of Czechoslovakia in August, however, put a temporary end to this thaw and postponed the opening of the SALT negotiations for more than a year.

In the realm of the strategic balance, the 1960s were years of catch-up for the Soviet Union. By 1969 the country was approaching a state of quantitative parity with the United States — that is, the two had equal numbers of land- and sea-based nuclear missiles. However, the USSR still lagged behind in the qualitative arms race, where the United States held important advantages in MIRV (multiple independently targetable reentry vehicle) and BMD (ballistic missile defense) technologies.

New Political Thinking of the 1980s

Beginning in 1985, long-standing assumptions informing Soviet foreign policy were cast aside and the USSR's behavior in the international arena acquired a dynamism that had not been seen in more than sixty years. These policy changes were accompanied by equally important and radical reforms of the foreign policy process.[20]

Political elites and specialists debated the basic assumptions and beliefs shaping the USSR's understanding of its interests in the international arena, as well as the strategic prescriptions that informed its day-to-day policy. Changes in basic assumptions included a revised view of the international system, one that emphasized its non–zero sum qualities. Official statements on the inevitability of socialist-capitalist competition were supplemented and to some extent replaced by assertions that stressed the interdependence of the world and the danger posed by global problems like environmental degradation and resource depletion.[21]

Another change at this level was the introduction of a new goal structure for Soviet foreign policy. The previous emphasis on the primacy of class interests was downplayed, while universal interests (*obshchechelovecheskiy*) were stressed. This new hierarchy clearly suggested that Soviet state interests give priority to problems that affected all countries (for example, the nuclear threat and environmental decay) over class-based solidarity (the promotion of socialism in the developing world, say).

In the fall of 1987, the leadership revised yet another of the basic assumptions underlying Soviet policy: the image of capitalism as a relentlessly aggres-

sive, imperialist, socioeconomic order. This construct was replaced by a more benign image.

Gorbachev and other leaders used these changes in basic assumptions to redefine Soviet state interests in the international arena. The result was the legitimation of radical shifts in the strategic prescriptions underlying Soviet national-security policy. First, there was a change in the conceptualization of security. The previous emphasis on a unidimensional approach (which focused on military power) that was attained unilaterally was downgraded and replaced by a multidimensional approach (emphasizing political means as well as military power) that was to be attained by mutual consent.

Second, there was a change in the definition of how much security was needed by the Soviet state. The previous formulation, the principle of equality and equal security, was replaced by the concept of reasonable sufficiency. Third, since the new emphasis on political means for insuring security gave greater legitimacy to arms control, a different approach toward verification was feasible. The earlier emphasis on national technical means (reconnaissance satellites and the like) was supplemented by a willingness to consider intrusive forms of verification such as on-site inspections.

These radical changes in preferences and policy were conditioned by a confluence of domestic and external factors. At the domestic level, four factors were key: changing perceptions of the vitality and capabilities of the Soviet economy; a growing appreciation of the scientific-technical gap that separated the USSR from the developed capitalist countries; a breakdown in the elite consensus on the foreign policy strategy pursued during the Brezhnev years; and basic changes in the Soviet approach to policymaking.

By the early 1980s, there was clear evidence that members of the political elite as well as academic analysts were asking fundamental questions about the vitality of their socioeconomic system. Initially (during 1982 and early 1983), this concern appeared in a debate over the nature and status of developed socialism (a term favored by the Brezhnev leadership to describe Soviet socialism).[22]

By the middle of 1983, the now-famous Novosibirsk Report, written by the sociologist Tat'yana Zaslavskaya, was circulating among academics and segments of the political elite (only seventy numbered copies were produced). In essence, the report called for a major reform of the Soviet economic system. Zaslavskaya used a Marxist framework to argue that the system of production relations in the USSR was lagging behind the development of its productive forces.[23]

In addition, during the mid-1980s the elite became increasingly aware that the USSR was falling farther behind in the race for scientific and technical

progress. The third industrial revolution of computers and information technology had arrived, and the Soviet Union was unready for it. Recognition of
this fact was clearly demonstrated by the priorities established in Gorbachev's
initial economic program for 1985–86, whose emphasis was not consumer
welfare and consumption but investment — in particular, the commitment of
additional resources to overhaul Soviet industry. It is telling that one of Gorbachev's first major domestic-policy initiatives was to convene a meeting in the
CPSU Central Committee on a "fundamental" question of economic policy:
"the acceleration of scientific-technical progress."[24]

A third domestic factor was a breakdown in elite consensus over the foreign
policy strategy pursued during the Brezhnev era. This strategy had sought to
combine detente and East-West economic cooperation with continuing efforts
to increase Soviet military power and to expand the Soviet Union's influence in
the developing world. Brezhnev's death played a key role in undermining the
consensus; equally important, the strategy was simply not working very well
by the early 1980s. The USSR was over-extended in the developing world and
mired in an unwinnable war in Afghanistan. Moreover, its relation with the
United States was skidding to a post–World War II low.[25]

A fourth domestic factor was a fundamental change in the Soviet approach
to foreign policymaking. Under Gorbachev, there was a shift in the balance
between two competing philosophies. One approach, long favored by ideologues in the CPSU apparatus, employed a deductive framework based on
Marxist-Leninist principles. The other, favored by academics at such organizations as IMEMO, used an inductive-empirical framework of analysis. With
respect to leadership thinking on issues of foreign policy, one philosophy had
never dominated over the other; both approaches had coexisted uneasily for
many years.[26]

Beginning in late 1984, however, there was a clear shift in favor of the
empirical approach. In a series of speeches and articles, both Gorbachev and
his close adviser Aleksandr Yakovlev advocated basing foreign policy more on
facts and existing realities than on Marxist-Leninist dogma. This point came
across in various ways: calls to change Soviet foreign policy "views and practice" if "life requires it"; a recognition that the contemporary world was "constantly changing [according] to its own laws" (a bit of ideological heresy from
a Marxist-Leninist perspective); a recognition that the dynamism of the world
was forcing a reevaluation of "conventional ideas and approaches"; and a call
to bring the results of "scientific analysis" (conducted by academic research
institutes) to bear on the practice of Soviet foreign policy.[27]

This empirical approach mandated basic changes in the foreign policy process. By early 1986 Gorbachev was discussing policymaking in ways that

would please Western students of public policy. Policymaking, he argued, consisted of elaborating, formulating, and implementing policies. Elaboration involved a definition of what issues needed to be addressed; the CPSU played the key role here. Formulation meant discussions and, if necessary, a "struggle of viewpoints" on the issue; it provided the basis for taking political decisions. Implementation was when political decisions were turned into actual policy. As became clear in subsequent years, the Gorbachev leadership was committed to a broadening of participation in policymaking. It allowed, and indeed often encouraged, competing viewpoints on a wide array of domestic and foreign policy issues.[28]

Internationally, it is important to consider both changes in the global system and, beginning in 1980, the sharp deterioration in the USSR's international position. Soviet commentators, in explaining the origins of Gorbachev's liberal foreign policy, often explicitly linked it to a series of fundamental changes in the international system, including the appearance of nuclear weapons, rapid increases in international economic ties, and the growth of global problems.[29]

Soviet leaders and analysts, however, were more reluctant to address the impact of the second factor—a worsening international climate. There is no doubt, however, that it played a central role. By the early 1980s, the objective realities facing the USSR in the international arena were daunting. It was being condemned for its invasion of Afghanistan; the situation in Poland was highly unstable; and U.S.-Soviet relations were at a low that had not been seen since the early Cold War years. On top of all this, the Soviet leadership faced a U.S. administration whose stern anti-Soviet rhetoric and rearmament policies were a matter of great concern. By early 1984, some members of the elite were genuinely alarmed that international affairs were simply spinning out of control.[30]

This brief review confirms what most observers already know: the changes of the 1980s far outstripped those of the late 1960s and early 1970s. Elite preferences and state interests were at best modified in the earlier period, yet revolutionized in the latter one. Put another way, radically new ideas on international politics failed to take hold in the sixties, but triumphed a decade and a half later. Why?

From Detente to New Thinking and Beyond

3

Entrepreneurs Looking for a Window

The present chapter has two parts. In the first half, I examine one particularly important source of ideas about international politics during the early Brezhnev years: the Academy of Sciences' Institute of World Economy and International Relations (IMEMO). I show that by the late 1960s a particular set of ideas on international affairs was well on its way to becoming embedded at IMEMO; it would influence the institute's behavior in key ways as the Soviet debate over detente unfolded. In examining these ideas, I consider the mechanisms that allowed them to take hold at IMEMO, as well as their content. The second part of the chapter offers a case study of why such ideas failed to exert a marked influence on elite preferences and Soviet behavior during the Brezhnev years — despite close ties between the institute and key political leaders.

If the logic of my argument is sound, I would expect the following sequence of events to have occurred during an ideas-based foreign policy change in the USSR in the late 1960s. Changes in its international environment (worsening relations with China, accelerating arms race with the United States, rapid advances in technology), if sufficiently dramatic, should have created uncertainty in the preferences of key foreign policy elites like General Secretary Brezhnev. These international-level changes should then have created policy windows in the domestic-level foreign policy process.

Individual entrepreneurs should have played a key role in exploiting those windows to promote new ideas, especially given the centralized nature of Soviet political institutions at that time. Indications of elite uncertainty and a turbulent international environment should have stimulated such individuals to increase their entrepreneurial activity. The insulated position of Brezhnev-era foreign policy decision makers, however, should have made adoption of the entrepreneur's ideas an uphill struggle.

My treatment of this period will be briefer than my subsequent analysis of the Gorbachev years because the details of Soviet debates over strategic arms control (the SALT process) and relations with the West (the policy of detente) in the late 1960s and early 1970s are by now well known.[1]

Ideas and Institutions During the Brezhnev Era

To understand how a particular set of ideas would eventually take root at IMEMO, it is necessary briefly to review its history, leaders, and organizational development.

The origins of IMEMO date to the early Soviet period, when it was known as the Institute of the World Economy and World Politics and headed by an economist, Yevgeniy Varga. However, it was effectively disbanded in 1947 (a number of its researchers were arrested) after Varga angered the Stalinist leadership by publicly suggesting that the major capitalist countries, in the wake of World War II, would not be afflicted by the sort of socioeconomic crisis seen in the early 1930s.

In doing this, Varga and the institute essentially sought to place a new set of ideas concerning the political economy of capitalism on the Soviet agenda. But their attempt was successfully resisted by political elites, who enjoyed considerable power to keep new ideas off the agenda.[2] It also resulted in a severe penalty — organizational banishment — as the majority of the institute's work was transferred to the Academy of Sciences' Institute of Economics beginning in 1947.

The reconstitution of IMEMO in 1956 was directly linked with decisions taken by the political leadership at the 20th CPSU Party Congress to reinvigorate the social sciences. For the next ten years the institute was headed by Anushavan Arzumanyan. Under his leadership, it continued to emphasize research on contemporary capitalist political economy; it grew to include more than three hundred researchers. Arzumanyan shared several key traits with Varga. Both men were economists by training (Arzumanyan had previously been deputy head of the Institute of Economics); they also held similar beliefs and outlooks. Indeed, as Arzumanyan worked to reestablish IMEMO, he consulted regularly with Varga on both research and personnel matters.[3]

Thus, the institute's two leaders between 1927 and 1965 were economists who held similar beliefs. Given the important role of leaders in shaping organizational behavior, one would expect this fact to influence the development of IMEMO's basic missions. Evidence suggests that this was indeed the case. By the late 1960s, the institute's research agenda covered a wide array of topics, including the political economy of contemporary capitalism; imperialism; the world socialist system; revolutionary processes; international relations; the strategy, tactics, and ideology of Soviet foreign policy; policymaking in capitalist societies; international economic relations; the scientific-technical revolution; and disarmament.[4]

Not all these topics, however, received equal attention. The greatest emphasis by far was placed on the economics and political economy (domestic and international) of capitalism. Of the forty-six books published by IMEMO during 1966 and 1967, twenty-four examined various aspects of capitalist political economy. In addition, at this point the institute was staffed largely with researchers who had been trained as economists. Finally, the emphasis on economics and political economy was reflected in the institute's organizational structure.[5]

An important milestone in IMEMO's development occurred in 1966, when Nikolay Inozemtsev was appointed its director — a position he would hold for nearly seventeen years. Inozemtsev was a historian of international relations and foreign policy, not an economist. Reflecting his training and preferences, the institute paid greater attention to questions of international relations as the 1960s and 1970s progressed. Yet under Inozemtsev's leadership, issues of political economy still received top priority. This apparent anomaly is explained by Inozemtsev's own research interests, which throughout his tenure at the institute focused on the political economy of contemporary capitalism. Indeed, he received the Lenin State Prize in 1977 for research on capitalist political economy.[6]

By the latter half of the 1960s, Inozemtsev had made it clear that a particular set of topics within the institute's broader mandate was to be accorded priority status. This included studies of foreign policymaking, long-term patterns of economic growth or decline in advanced industrialized democracies, and the changing dynamics of international politics. The emphasis on foreign policy process was driven by two concerns: (1) gaining a better understanding of the domestic interests and actors influencing foreign policy behavior in capitalist countries; and (2) advocating a broadening of participation in Soviet foreign policymaking.[7]

The study of political economy included the exploration of the possibilities for economic growth in capitalist nations. While Inozemtsev still paid lip service to Leninist theory (for example, by noting the deepening of capitalism's

general crisis), his real theoretical and empirical interest was to explicate the complex of political, economic, and technological factors that fostered periods of growth in capitalist economies.[8]

The nature of international politics, for Inozemtsev, was a matter of empirical inquiry; the use of purely deductive logic based on the Leninist policy paradigm was not sufficient. A basic implication of his analyses was that a class-based interpretation of international affairs was too narrow; there were phenomena at work in the world political economy that cut across the traditional socialist-capitalist divide.[9]

In raising these issues, Inozemtsev was advancing elements of an alternative policy paradigm for interpreting key aspects of the USSR's international environment. The foreign policy process in Western countries, for example, was understood as just that — a process, where various interest groups and organizations competed in shaping policy outcomes. Moreover, international politics was not a zero-sum battle between opposing class-based alliances but an arena where states had common interests.

Inozemtsev's ideas are but one part of the story; the next step is to consider the mechanisms through which they would come to shape IMEMO's organizational ideology. Several existed. First, Inozemtsev was a forceful agenda setter. Second, by the late 1960s Inozemtsev was in no sense an uncommitted thinker, having developed a particular set of beliefs on capitalism and international politics.

Third, Inozemtsev was willing to employ the organizational means at his disposal to develop and advance these ideas. For example, he played a key role in making all top-level appointments at the institute, and he sanctioned bureaucratic innovations within it to advance the study of particular topics. These organizational tools, in combination with his vision and long tenure as director, allowed Inozemtsev to leave a significant ideological legacy at IMEMO.[10]

My discussion of organizational leadership is not meant to suggest that such individuals as Varga or Inozemtsev were all-powerful or free of constraints in setting organizational agendas. As the institute's (temporary) demise in 1947 indicates, these leaders operated in a highly politicized environment, one in which the Soviet state could exert significant influence on IMEMO's behavior.

Aside from overt political interference, this influence was felt in a number of ways. As noted in chapter 2, organizations like IMEMO had to adhere to a series of yearly and five-year plans, which were prepared by the Presidium of the Academy of Sciences. In preparing these plans, the Presidium often sought or was "offered" advice by various departments within the CPSU Central Committee. As institute head Arzumanyan was once told by C.C. Secretary Mikhail Suslov: "If you are going to write a paper, send it to us first — one

copy — and we'll decide whom to send it to!" In addition, until the reforms of the Gorbachev years, candidates for the directorship of IMEMO had to be formally approved by the C.C. — that is, the directorship was a *nomenklatura* position.[11]

With this background in hand, I turn to an analysis of the institute's ideology on the eve of the Soviet debates over detente. One thing that becomes immediately apparent when reviewing institute research of the 1960s is the relatively minor role accorded practical issues of international security. This is surprising given the precedents and opportunities that existed for discussions of such topics. The precedents were the agreements reached during Khrushchev's last two years in power on the limitation of nuclear-weapons testing and the creation of the so-called hotline. The opportunity arose from the U.N.-sponsored negotiations, held during the early and mid-1960s, for a nuclear nonproliferation treaty. Moreover, since 1964 the United States had been publicly proposing — to the USSR and other countries — measures of strategic nuclear-arms limitation.[12]

Various analyses of security issues were in fact produced by IMEMO during the early and mid-1960s. But they were all characterized by a paucity of detail and a clear adherence to the line set by the political leadership. In writings through 1967 institute scholars praised a policy of mutual example as an important arms-control measure and advocated partial measures of disarmament.

References to disarmament and arms control turned more polemical in 1966, with the focal point once again becoming "general and complete disarmament." This kind of propagandistic analysis was also evident in one of the few institute-sponsored books on East-West security issues produced during these years.[13]

This progression, in which guarded optimism over East-West security cooperation was replaced by a growing pessimism, is strikingly similar to the pattern of elite commentary during these years. While it is true that both General Secretary Brezhnev and the C.C. journal *Kommunist* evinced interest in various disarmament schemes that went beyond calls for general and complete disarmament, the tenor of analysis grew decidedly more pessimistic over time.[14]

The worsening of U.S.-Soviet relations because of American involvement in Vietnam goes a long way in explaining the evolution in elite behavior and the changing tone of commentary in *Kommunist*. As U.S. intervention in Southeast Asia escalated during the mid-1960s, official Soviet commentary became notably more harsh.

The story to this point is thus not terribly surprising. Political elites and their

preferences set the line, and organizations like IMEMO followed it. Put another way, the centralized and authoritarian Soviet state was able to dominate politics and policymaking in the national-security sphere. Such domination was perhaps all the more likely in a unit like IMEMO, which had suffered its own organizational repression once before.[15]

Such a structural explanation for IMEMO's behavior, while important, is not in itself adequate. It would predict similar behavior by the institute across various issues areas; yet, as I discuss below, this was clearly not the case. Rather, a complete understanding of IMEMO's behavior also requires a consideration of the power of ideas and their ability to shape the institute's understanding of its own interests.

By the mid-1960s, there were objective stimuli — the arms-control agreements of the Khrushchev years and the ongoing negotiations over a nonproliferation treaty — that might logically have led a large foreign policy research institute like IMEMO to pay greater attention to issues of national security. However, this did not occur — largely because the institute's emerging ideology accorded a relatively low priority to the study of such issues. Thus, researchers at IMEMO had little incentive to challenge the preferences of the political leadership on matters of international security.

My argument that ideas played an important role in shaping IMEMO's behavior is strengthened by a comparison with the USA Institute (ISKAN), which operated under the same structural constraints. In spite of these restrictions, ISKAN moved quickly after its establishment in late 1967 to make security studies a central part of its research program. In fact, the unsigned lead editorial in the first issue of the USA Institute's journal, *SShA,* specifically declared that national-security issues and military-strategic concepts should be subjects of study for its researchers.[16]

This picture of a tame organization changes dramatically when one examines IMEMO's behavior during these years on topics closer to its evolving organizational ideology. Here, the institute promoted a set of distinctive beliefs that was clearly not in step with the concerns of the political leadership and that did not reflect the worsening relations between the United States and the Soviet Union. These ideas advanced a more nuanced understanding of capitalism, specifically, of policymaking in capitalist countries; promoted a more complex view of the international system; and argued for a "scientific approach" to foreign policy.[17]

The image of capitalism advocated by IMEMO was complex and nuanced. Iosif Lemin, a leading researcher at the institute, argued that it was wrong to view monopolies as the chief actors in the U.S. foreign policy process, with the state appearing as only "the dumb agent" of big business. On the contrary, the

role of the state — and, especially, of the president — in foreign policymaking was increasing. Several years later, Lemin would again consider the role of agency in determining U.S. policy. Far from portraying this policy as dictated by large monopolies, he saw a considerable autonomous role for the president, who made use of foreign policy advisers and "consultative groups" within the State Department when making important decisions.[18]

Several analysts saw differentiation within the U.S. military-industrial complex; not all the agencies wished for a war to increase their profits. One analyst even claimed that certain parts of the military-industrial complex had developed a "known interest" in disarmament![19]

Scholars at IMEMO employed several additional methods to advance a more complex understanding of U.S. capitalism. Some noted that militarization was not completely dominant in the United States. Other analysts argued against the reductionism inherent in the Leninist theory of imperialism and claimed that capitalist foreign policy was more than the projection of the monopolies' economic goals onto the international arena. One researcher, in discussing the nature of capitalist foreign policy, went so far as to claim that Lenin himself had warned of the danger of reducing everything to economics. This is to turn Lenin on his head! In his theory of imperialism, Lenin had in fact overwhelmingly stressed the domestic economic roots of capitalist foreign policy.[20]

This advocacy of a more nuanced portrayal of capitalism also received forceful support from the institute's new director, Inozemtsev. Foreshadowing later arguments, he claimed that the aggressive nature of imperialism was mitigated by the "inevitable" strengthening of democratic forces within capitalist countries; that the relation between the economy and politics of capitalism was much more complex than previously thought (here, he explicitly attacked Stalin's *Economic Problems of Socialism in the USSR*); and that the capitalist system, in addition to its tendency toward stagnation, contained an opposing tendency toward progress and "rapid growth."[21]

By the late 1960s, one leading IMEMO researcher, A. Galkin, was openly and explicitly attacking a key element of the Leninist orthodoxy on capitalism. His topic was policymaking — in particular, traditional Soviet notions of ruling elites in capitalist countries. After stating his opposition to the official view that the capitalist ruling elite was composed of little more than the financial oligarchs of big business, Galkin argued for the importance of other ruling groups. It was not enough to study different tendencies within the ruling elite; other actors and interests had to be considered.

Galkin also sought to explain how these interests interacted to shape policy. Policymaking in the United States, he asserted, was a "complicated process

including preparation, discussion, the decision itself, and observation of its fulfillment." This description differed little from that of Galkin's Western contemporaries who studied policy cycles. According to Galkin, there are two primary sets of actors in the process: those who adopt decisions and those who, while playing a small role in making actual decisions, still exert influence on policy.[22]

The image of capitalism that emerges from these analyses had little in common with leadership preferences. Brezhnev and others continued to stress the traditional view, noting the militarism and growing aggressiveness of capitalism. The divergence between the two portrayals was at times so great that one could come away thinking that the object of their analyses was completely different.[23]

Throughout the 1960s IMEMO also promoted a conception of international politics that stressed its complicated nature.[24] Many analysts simply remarked on the growing complexity of the international system. In an editorial article published late in 1966, however, the institute was much more assertive — arguing that an "enormous number" of different factors influenced events in the international arena. Implicit here was a call to move away from the monocausal explanations of international relations so typical of official Soviet declarations.[25]

Inozemtsev and several other IMEMO analysts addressed the complexity issue by exploring the role of chance in international relations and nuclear war (that is, accidental-nuclear-war scenarios). One researcher argued that the international system was defined and shaped not only by permanently operating laws but also by chance and that war in the contemporary era could arise because of the latter. Analysis of this kind contradicted a central element of the prevailing Marxist-Leninist policy paradigm on international politics by suggesting that war occurred not only as the result of policies deliberately pursued by capitalist countries but by accident. It would be more than twenty years before ideas of this type reached the pages of *Kommunist*.[26]

The complexity of the international system was stressed by IMEMO analysts in several additional ways. Inozemtsev and one other researcher, Gennadiy Gerasimov, argued that international relations should be viewed in non–zero sum terms. In such an international system, Gerasimov declared, the interests of states are not absolutely counterposed, and, thus, there is a role for compromises, mutual concessions, and cooperation by the opposing sides. Nuclear weapons, according to this view, made it impossible to view "international conflict . . . as a zero-sum game."[27]

Inozemtsev also emphasized the complexity of the international system by discussing the growing internationalization of science, economics, and tech-

nology. He portrayed this internationalization as an objective process, which in Marxist-Leninist parlance was tantamount to declaring it a basic fact of life to which the Soviet state must adapt.[28]

One institute researcher, in an extraordinary analysis that foreshadowed ideas adopted only twenty years later by Mikhail Gorbachev, argued that the structure of world politics had come to resemble an apartment house where the "common interests of security" would prevail over the selfish inclinations of individual apartment dwellers. This was a non-Leninist and, in fact, supra-class view of the international system. It led the author to conclude that nuclear war was a universal (*obshchechelovecheskiy*) danger — one that would inflict equal damage on all countries, regardless of their social system or class structure.[29]

By 1969 a number of institute scholars were forcefully making the case for the validity of IMEMO's ideas about international politics. This message came across so strongly because the institute, in contrast with its earlier practices, was producing a series of related commentaries on the topic. This "round-table," as it was called, was entitled "Problems of the Theory of International Relations," and it occupied approximately forty pages in the September and November 1969 issues of *Memo*. It was co-sponsored by IMEMO's Sector for Theoretical Problems of Research and Forecasting of International Relations (which was a part of the institute's larger Department of International Relations) and the editorial board of *Memo*.[30]

Two basic themes emerged from the roundtable. Most important, the growing complexity of the international system required — indeed demanded — greater theoretical and empirical rigor in Soviet foreign policy research. The second theme (to be discussed below) was a logical extension of the first: given this increasing complexity, there was a need for more active participation by Soviet foreign policy specialists in the policy process.

Advocacy on the former was accomplished in various ways. Most important were the first explicit calls for a Soviet "science of international relations." The theoretical and empirical basis of this new science, it was strongly implied, should rely less on traditional Marxist-Leninist categories and more on Western theories and methodologies of international relations. Inozemtsev, for example, called for a "comprehensive theory of international relations" and argued that it should employ the data and methods of economics, sociology, military science, law, geography, demography, and social psychology, as well as make use of quantitative techniques. He also declared that Soviet scholars must make further studies of the systems and structures of the contemporary international arena.[31]

Several roundtable participants described in forceful language what they

saw as the realities of international politics — assessments that made a mockery of official Soviet ideology. For example, Dmitriy Tomashevskiy, head of the
International Relations Department, noted the globalization and increasingly
universal character of international relations and discussed the thesis — advanced by the USSR even before World War II(!) — on the "indivisibility of the
world." He went on to analyze the growing number of international problems
that objectively required interstate cooperation, "independent of differences
in social system." Several other scholars declared that the advent of nuclear
weapons had made clear the inadequacy of models of international relations
based on zero-sum approaches.[32]

It would be an understatement to note that these analyses bore little relation
to the assumptions and methodologies posited in the Leninist theory of imperialism or to leadership commentary on the nature of international politics.[33]
Indeed, the ideas taking root at IMEMO sounded less like a primer on scientific communism than like an introductory textbook on Western theories of
international relations.

The third idea promoted by IMEMO throughout the early and mid-1960s
was what the institute called a scientific approach in foreign policy. Early
analyses on this topic were general and simply equated a scientific approach
with a more comprehensive analysis of events in the international arena. The
implicit argument was that monocausal explanations of foreign policy behavior were inadequate.[34]

Later analyses called specifically for a broadened foreign policy research
agenda — one that included more interdisciplinary research and expanded the
topics addressed. On the latter, IMEMO asserted that beyond its traditional
topics of research, greater attention needed to be devoted to political interactions between socialist and capitalist states.[35]

While this topic seems innocuous, it in fact threatened the views of key
political elites. The emphasis on political interactions, that is, Soviet-American
cooperation and negotiation, came at a time when elites were downplaying
relations with the United States because of its growing intervention in Vietnam. Indeed, at a Central Committee plenum in September 1965, Brezhnev
had gone so far as to talk about a freezing of relations because of American
actions in Southeast Asia.[36]

In one case, a leading IMEMO scholar used a discussion of this scientific
approach and the scientific basis of Soviet foreign policy to advocate closer
links between institute-sponsored research and actual policymaking. As this
scholar pointedly noted, however, there was a lot of work to do before such
ties became a reality.[37]

By the late 1960s, IMEMO was aggressively promoting the idea of a scien-

tific approach to foreign policy. This topic was addressed in numerous contexts. Director Inozemtsev, for example, argued the need for foreign policy forecasting and noted that a group of researchers at IMEMO was devoting serious efforts to developing such forecasts. Several researchers used analyses of the growing role of specialist expertise in the capitalist foreign policy process to advocate the need for it in the Soviet Union. One analyst strongly hinted that such input had become a key feature of contemporary foreign policy and diplomacy — capitalist or socialist.[38]

At the 1969 IMEMO-*Memo* roundtable on international relations, Inozemtsev returned to the idea of a scientific foreign policy and gave it unambiguous and forceful backing. In particular, he argued for both an improved scientific basis for Soviet policy and an enhanced role for specialists in the foreign policy process. Observing that policymaking had grown very complex, Inozemtsev argued that capitalist countries had responded by raising the level of scientific research undergirding their foreign policy activity. The "brain trusts" that did this research were an important part of the policy process; they participated in the adoption of foreign policy decisions, and their reports influenced the thoughts of decision makers.

Inozemtsev's next comments made clear that the real purpose of his analysis of capitalist foreign policymaking was to establish a justification for how the Soviet policy process should operate. Arguing that a scientifically based policy was impossible without forecasting, he declared that such forecasting made no sense in the absence of a "scientific system for the utilization of expert evaluations." These experts were none other than "our scientific workers" — that is, researchers at IMEMO and other academy institutes. Inozemtsev concluded by noting that the creation of this "scientific system" would assist in the resolution of many practical foreign policy problems.[39]

Although Inozemtsev's advocacy was the most direct and his message the most clear, other IMEMO scholars and editorial commentary in the institute's journal made many of the same points throughout the year. These sources varied widely in their degree of advocacy, but they all were more direct and detailed than earlier institute writing on scientific foreign policy and specialist participation in the policy process.[40]

Taken as a whole, these analyses argued for a closer connection between academic expertise and ideas, on the one hand, and the Soviet state and its policies, on the other. Such an academia-policy connection was precisely what political elites meant when they, too, began to talk about a scientific approach to policymaking in the wake of Khrushchev's dismissal. However, it was researchers at IMEMO — not elites — who argued that such an approach should be applied in the foreign and national-security issue areas and that it should

lead to the systematic integration of these researchers into the policy process. Thus, here too one sees the institute defying the preferences of key policymakers.[41]

To conclude this review of IMEMO's organizational ideology, five points can be made. First, the dominant ideas held and promoted by IMEMO during the 1960s, when taken together, provided a radically different interpretative framework for Soviet foreign policy. In other words, they were key elements of an alternative policy paradigm. These ideas had much to say about the basic dynamics of international politics, the viability and likely behavior of the USSR's chief adversaries, and the workings of foreign policymaking in both capitalist and socialist countries.

If they came to shape the preferences of political elites, such ideas could contribute to a major redefinition of Soviet national interests and foreign behavior. The USSR might come to view its international political environment not in zero-sum terms but as a positive-sum game, thereby legitimating a greater cooperative dimension in both foreign-economic and national-security policy. Moreover, since the capitalist adversary would be economically viable for many more years than originally expected, it would be in Soviet self-interest to engage that adversary.

Second, the ideas promoted by IMEMO were strongest at the conceptual level. They said little about specific public-policy problems and how to resolve them (arms control or relations with the United States, for example). Given the abstract nature of such ideas, it is legitimate to ask whether they could ever matter much in terms of actual policy. In democratic polities, the answer is at best unclear.[42]

In the centralized and authoritarian Soviet state, however, the case was quite different. Broad concepts and categories mattered because political elites wanted them to matter, and these elites controlled a variety of instruments (central institutions, the mass media, security organs) that enabled them to make them matter. Moreover, ideas about class struggle, capitalism's general crisis, and the zero-sum nature of international politics had found organizational homes within the state and CPSU apparatus that gave them added staying power.[43]

These ideas mattered in two ways. In an instrumental sense, they were exploited by elites to legitimate CPSU rule. However, they also operated at a deeper level — providing decision makers with a framework for interpreting the USSR's domestic and international political environments. Thus, attempts to advance radically different concepts were often harshly suppressed (which was the fate of Varga and IMEMO in the late 1940s), and, as will be seen

below, efforts to introduce major changes to Soviet international behavior inevitably raised ideological issues as well.

Third, it was not just altruism (the development of a more sensible foreign policy, say) that led IMEMO to promote certain ideas during the 1960s. Self-interest was also at work. All three ideas—and especially the third (the scientific approach)—would, if adopted by the political leadership, accord IMEMO a greater role in Soviet foreign policymaking. The important point, however, is that the institute's understanding of its interests was heavily shaped by these dominant ideas. Topics that it would have been rational for IMEMO to address (arms control, for example) were virtually ignored, while other topics (a complex image of capitalism) were promoted despite significant incentives not to do so.[44]

Fourth, my account should make clear that individual leadership played a critical role in shaping the organizational ideology at IMEMO. The particular set of ideas that began to take hold at the institute sprang from the beliefs and preferences of assertive leaders—especially Inozemtsev. However, as will become clear below and in chapter 5, these leaders needed organizational support in the form of an embedded ideology at IMEMO to make their new ideas matter in Soviet politics.

Fifth, by the late 1960s IMEMO's behavior was beginning to change in important ways, as the institute became more assertive in promoting particular ideas. Why this was so is largely a story of policy entrepreneurs looking for an open policy window. Why these entrepreneurs and their ideas ultimately failed to influence elite preferences and policy is the subject of the case study that follows.

Windows and Entrepreneurs

As the 1960s drew to a close, a number of policy windows appeared to be opening in Soviet politics. The stagnation of the later Brezhnev years had not yet developed; debates were under way on several issues of domestic economic, foreign economic, and national-security policy. Below, I examine the degree to which these windows ever really opened, as well as the opportunities and constraints they created for entrepreneurs promoting new ideas and the limited impact the ideas had on policy. This is a case, in other words, where new ideas ultimately mattered little in shaping Soviet behavior. I begin with a brief review of the background and outcomes of these debates of the late 1960s.

By 1968 Khrushchevian optimism had diminished considerably among key

members of the political elite. Prime Minister Kosygin and General Secretary Brezhnev, in particular, portrayed the Soviet economy in increasingly pessimistic terms and stressed the importance of qualitative economic growth — that is, growth resulting from higher productivity rather than additional material inputs. The change in Brezhnev's commentary was especially striking. By the latter part of 1968, he was frankly admitting that the USSR faced severe economic problems.[45]

There was also a noticeable increase in elite concern over the economy's ability to generate significant advances in Soviet science and technology. Brezhnev and Kosygin portrayed the race in scientific-technical progress as a major arena of the socialist-capitalist competition. In a speech to the December 1968 plenum of the Central Committee, Brezhnev all but conceded that the United States was winning the race, and he called the acceleration of scientific progress "not only a central economic [task] but a most important political task."[46]

An additional factor in undermining confidence in the economy was a clash among competing priorities in the Soviet national budget. The basis for this resource crunch was laid when the leadership, following Khrushchev's ouster, committed itself to both an expensive program of agricultural investment and an increase in defense spending.[47]

The fiscal picture was further complicated when Brezhnev called in the latter part of 1967 for a significant increase in expenditures on consumer welfare. In particular, he declared that 1968 would see the largest commitment of resources to the consumer sector in the history of the USSR. This enhanced concern for the Soviet consumer was reflected in various other official sources. It also came at the same time that the most important Party military journal, *Kommunist vooruzhennykh sil,* began stressing the need to economize on military expenditures.[48]

As the 1960s drew to a close, the USSR's international environment was also changing in ways that contributed to increased pessimism among elites. Particularly important — and disturbing from a Soviet perspective — was the American decision of September 1967 to proceed with ballistic missile defense development and deployment, which threatened to undermine the strategic balance. The leadership's newfound respect for American technological prowess heightened concerns that such deployments would actually be carried out.[49]

In addition, during the late 1960s there was an increased level of instability in Eastern Europe (the Czech crisis and its aftermath) and a worsening in the USSR's relations with China. In 1969 clashes along the Soviet-Chinese border effectively militarized what had been an ideological dispute and made more likely the worst-case scenario developed by Soviet planners, in which the

country would have to prepare for a two-front war (Central Europe/NATO and Asia/China). The Nixon administration's determination to play the China card in the Soviet-American bilateral relationship only increased such fears.

This brief review suggests that one or more policy windows could have been opening for entrepreneurs by the late 1960s. Recall from chapter 1 that two factors are key in opening such a window: (1) there are problems whose resolution would be assisted by implementation of an entrepreneur's ideas; and (2) there are politicians in power who recognize that such problems exist. On matters of foreign policy and international affairs, one could certainly argue that the first factor was operative. The effects of the scientific-technical revolution on the world political economy, the continuing ability (surprising from an orthodox Soviet perspective) of the capitalist adversary to adapt to this revolution, the militarization of the Sino-Soviet conflict, and changes in American strategic policy were creating a turbulent and problematic international setting for the USSR.

It is more difficult to make a case for the presence of the second factor. Key elites did have concerns over several issues affecting the Soviet domestic and international political environments. But it is not at all clear that they perceived themselves as operating in uncertain or crisis-ridden environments. And it is the latter that truly open windows, as politicians engage in cognitive-information searches, seeking new ideas to solve the problems they face. The logic of my argument would thus suggest only a limited causal role for ideas in modifying elite foreign policy preferences in the Soviet Union of the late 1960s.

The evidence supports this interpretation: fundamental changes in elite preferences and Soviet interests did not occur during the debates over detente and SALT. Elements of the alternative-policy paradigm articulated by IMEMO would find their way into the speeches of Brezhnev and other elites, but one cannot talk of a radical shift in elite preferences. The Soviet state had exercised, once again, its considerable "gate-keeping" powers, limiting the role and influence of new ideas. It is to this story that I now turn.[50]

How wide a policy window was open in the late 1960s? Memoir and interview data suggest that, at best, a window was ajar.[51]

By the late 1960s, Brezhnev had assumed prime responsibility within the leadership for foreign policy. His official position (CPSU general secretary), his status as first among equals within the elites, the frequent references to foreign policy in his speeches, and the recollections of close advisers all indicate his importance. Thus, to assess how wide the policy windows in the foreign and national-security issue area were, it is essential to evaluate Brezhnev's receptivity to new ideas.

Several points can be made. First, in the early years after Khrushchev's dismissal, Brezhnev did show interest in new ideas — seeking alternative viewpoints from different sources on a number of issues. This interest, however, was limited and motivated by political concerns rather than by any genuine cognitive search to resolve the foreign policy dilemmas the Soviet Union faced. Put another way, Brezhnev sought new ideas not because of a desire to learn and therefore to puzzle better; rather, this search occurred because he was afraid that others in the leadership might be trying to ensnare and mislead him when they promoted their own orthodox and conservative ideas.[52]

Second, those close to Brezhnev in the mid-1960s are virtually unanimous in arguing that he came to power without any foreign or domestic policy agendas of his own. Thus, one could say that Brezhnev was an uncommitted thinker, and he may have been open to new ideas. Yet the range of acceptable ideas was severely limited by a fundamental feature of the new general secretary's personality: a deep aversion to radical change. Brezhnev was not an intellectual — former close advisers describe him as a man who "did not like reading," had a "limited vision," and was a "weak theoretician." He was a career party official who was good at "organizing things" (a favorite phrase of Brezhnev's).

Third, Brezhnev — despite his aversion to radical change — clearly did not favor the sharp conservative turn in policy that was championed by influential elements in the post-Khrushchev leadership. Some officials openly favored a neo-Stalinist restoration, under which domestic and foreign policy reforms implemented since the 20th Party Congress would be completely reversed. By opposing (or at least not siding with) these forces, Brezhnev sent an encouraging signal to policy entrepreneurs who were carrying new ideas.

Entrepreneurs, then, faced an ambiguous situation as the 1960s drew to a close. Changing circumstances in the USSR's international environment were opening one or more policy windows in the foreign and security policy arena. On the other hand, key elites — most notably General Secretary Brezhnev — were receptive to new ideas only in the limited sense described above. Given this state of affairs, my argument would predict increased incentives for entrepreneurs to promote their solutions, but it would not guarantee them success.

By the late 1960s, a small group of specialists had gained access to top-level foreign policy decision makers. As might be expected in the centralized Soviet state, this access resulted not from pressure or advocacy on the part of the individuals but through a conscious decision taken at a high level in the political hierarchy.

Two Brezhnev aides, Andrey Aleksandrov-Agentov and Georgiy Tsukanov, played especially key roles here — serving as conduits for bringing the ideas of Inozemtsev and others to the general secretary. Why they created such a pathway for the ideas of this group is not entirely clear. Both men were worried

about the number of conservative ideologues with access to Brezhnev, and thus they probably acted as they did to counteract this influence. Even for highly placed individuals like Aleksandrov-Agentov and Tsukanov, however, this behavior was not without risk. Tsukanov, in particular, gained many enemies in the C.C. apparatus as a result.[53]

In creating a pathway for specialists to reach decision makers, Aleksandrov-Agentov and Tsukanov were beginning to develop the "end around" strategy that would be exploited to such dramatic effect twenty years later. Not satisfied with the policy advice Brezhnev was receiving from official sources, they used the significant powers at their disposal to create an alternative, unofficial pathway for new ideas and expertise.

One carrier of new ideas was Inozemtsev. Was he a policy entrepreneur — a person in a position to change the flow of politics? Evidence suggests that he was. Most important, Inozemtsev was an individual with a "solution looking for a problem." Recall that by the late 1960s he was forcefully articulating key elements of an alternative foreign policy paradigm for the USSR. In addition, he had the connections to relevant political actors (Brezhnev) and the organizational resources at his disposal (IMEMO) that were essential elements of successful entrepreneurship in states with highly centralized decision-making structures.

These entrepreneurial assets, however, were offset by a basic feature of Inozemtsev's character: his innate sense of caution. This characteristic was certainly reinforced by the political context of those years — where the articulation of unorthodox views was not easy. This context was especially important at IMEMO, which had suffered for its earlier espousal of new ideas.[54]

Whatever one's net assessment of Inozemtsev's entrepreneurial strengths and weaknesses, it is clear that by late 1968 he was motivated to act by opening policy windows. In particular, he mobilized IMEMO to influence the emerging Soviet policy debate over arms control and relations with the West. This debate had two dimensions. One was ideological and conceptual in nature and focused on the basic framework for Soviet relations with the capitalist West. The other was more narrow, dealing with the specific issue of how Soviet national security could be promoted by arms-control agreements with the United States. Let us look at this debate and the role of ideas in it over the years 1968–72.

IDEAS AND INTERNATIONAL POLITICS

Images of international politics and, especially, of the USSR's capitalist adversary played central roles in the debates of these years. Inozemtsev was well situated to play the role of entrepreneur peddling ideas developed and nurtured at his institute to key elite participants in these discussions.

Inozemtsev mobilized IMEMO in several ways in an attempt to influence this debate. First, he organized conferences to promote IMEMO's ideas to a broader audience. This was most dramatically seen in the 1969 roundtable on international relations theory.[55] Second, Inozemtsev encouraged analysts at IMEMO to produce (and publish) very unorthodox research. Third, he took the lead in forcefully reiterating key ideas about international politics and capitalism that he (and other IMEMO researchers) had developed over the previous decades.

Concerning the roundtable on international-relations theory, several additional points can be made. A preliminary question is whether there was really any elite-level debate over the fundamental dynamics of international politics. Evidence suggests that this was the case. In his memoirs, Georgiy Arbatov, who like Inozemtsev had access to Brezhnev's inner circle during these years, recalls such a discussion. Moreover, at virtually the same time as the IMEMO-sponsored roundtable, where Inozemtsev and other analysts were arguing a need to study and learn from Western theories of international relations, *Kommunist* ran articles harshly attacking such theories and their non-class interpretation of international politics.[56]

Another point to consider is whether the roundtable was anything more than a chance circumstance. After all, social scientists at IMEMO (and elsewhere) during the late 1960s certainly had an interest in freeing their scholarly studies from the dogma and constraints of Marxist-Leninist ideology — hence, their promotion of a decidedly non-Marxist worldview. From this perspective, publication of the articles simply reflected a desire for intellectual autonomy and demonstrated that superiors within the institute agreed with such a goal.[57]

The manner in which the analyses were published and their overall content, however, suggest that other factors were at work. The articles, it will be recalled, were grouped together in a roundtable format. It was almost as if the institute wished to declare itself the repository for such expertise. This seemed to be precisely Inozemtsev's intent as he strove to embed at IMEMO the ideas on international politics and capitalism held by himself and other researchers. Moreover, scholars in the roundtable combined advocacy in favor of a more complex, empirically based vision of the international system with calls for a greater institute role in the foreign policy process. In other words, organizational interests — interests shaped by IMEMO's dominant ideas — were also at work.

Beyond the IMEMO-sponsored roundtable on international politics, Inozemtsev also encouraged his researchers to advocate aggressively ideas that undercut key elements of the current Soviet portrayal of contemporary capitalism. Abandoning the deductively derived categories of the Leninist theory

of imperialism, scholars at IMEMO adopted an inductive research strategy that took as an open question the likely future course of capitalism in the 1970s and beyond.

There are numerous examples of this approach. Several scholars, for example, elaborated what they termed "the principle of complexity" in the study of capitalist political economy. With it, they examined the growth of bureaucratic structures and the "mutual influence" of economic and political factors in capitalism's development, among other topics. These researchers did not hesitate to link the study of this principle to the intellectual legacy of Yevgeniy Varga, a strategy that suggests the extent to which these ideas had become embedded at IMEMO.[58]

Other scholars advanced unorthodox ideas on capitalism by returning to a topic that had been sporadically addressed by IMEMO for several decades: the role of the state in capitalist society. In particular, they argued that the state could be an arbiter between different social groups; they thereby rejected standard Soviet portrayals of the state as a tool used by monopolies to promote class interests at the expense of overall economic welfare. These scholars in fact saw a "relative independence" of the state that allowed it, under certain circumstances, to promote economic growth. In making such arguments, analysts were once again informed — if not inspired — by ideas first advanced by Varga nearly twenty years earlier.[59]

One IMEMO scholar took the discussion of the state and capitalist political economy a daring step farther by advocating the creation of a new category of research: adaptation. He argued that such adaptation was a law-governed (*zakonomernyy*) trait of the contemporary capitalist state. Capitalism's ability to adapt and avoid socioeconomic crises, in other words, was something that Soviet policy had better consider.[60]

The emphasis on an empirical-inductive approach to the study of capitalism was also seen in analyses of the U.S. foreign policy process. Building on ideas advanced by institute scholars in earlier years, researchers examined, among other things, groups within the political elite and how their presence complicated U.S. foreign and security policymaking, as well as the role of the public (*obshchestvennost'*) and public opinion in American foreign policy. The image of U.S. policymaking that emerged from such analyses was not that of an all-powerful state beholden to certain narrow interests. Rather, it was of a government that was often split internally and that was influenced by factors outside the state apparatus.[61]

In another case, an analyst talked not so much of the players in the process but of the socioeconomic factors influencing it. His particular concern was the phenomenon of militarism in contemporary capitalist society. In a radical

departure from the prevailing understanding of capitalist political economy, he argued that reducing military expenditures would not cause an economic crisis in the United States but rather would have an "enormous positive effect" on its economy. Indicative of the article's empirical emphasis were its twenty-four footnotes—a large number for a scholarly article of those years. The references themselves were drawn from a wide range of popular and academic American sources, including *Business Week, Fortune,* and the *American Economic Review.* By drawing upon Western sources, the author was able to avoid the dogma and orthodoxy typical of official Soviet discourse.[62]

A third way Inozemtsev mobilized IMEMO to participate in the foreign and security policy debates of the late 1960s was more direct and personal. In his speeches and writings, he addressed and attempted to advance novel, key ideas. The important point here is that Inozemtsev's commentary grew more assertive as the SALT/detente policy debates intensified in 1969–71. In a way that is consistent with the theoretical logic of my argument, Inozemtsev the entrepreneur was exploiting an opening policy window to promote institute ideas; these were presented as solutions to problems confronting the Soviet leadership.

Several examples of Inozemtsev's bolder commentary illustrate the point. Early in 1970, he returned to the topic of capitalist political economy and argued that Soviet scholars could not study only its economic and social dimensions. They also needed to examine the politics of capitalism because they were playing "an enormous, ever-growing role" in its development. The lack of such a multivariate analysis, according to Inozemtsev, had hindered the USSR from properly evaluating capitalism, particularly its "significant capabilities." These remarks, it should be noted, were carried as a lead article in the institute's journal, *Memo.*[63]

Inozemtsev was equally outspoken in remarks made in late 1969. At a workshop dedicated to the legacy of Yevgeniy Varga, he called for "sober evaluations" of capitalism, joined other IMEMO analysts in arguing for the state's "relative independence" from monopolies, and heavily attacked a recently published book—written by a scholar affiliated with a Central Committee research institute—that presented an overly simplistic and pessimistic view of capitalism. Several months later, Inozemtsev argued the need for "concrete analys[es] of concrete conditions" in the United States that examined both its weaknesses and strengths.[64]

To conclude this analysis of Inozemtsev's entrepreneurship and the new ideas he and other institute scholars were advancing, three points can be made. First, these ideas were less the result of any transnational diffusion process and more the product of more than forty years of research and thinking within

IMEMO (and its predecessors) on the nature of international politics and contemporary capitalism. Contacts between the institute and the international scientific community were, in fact, sporadic and tightly controlled through at least the mid-1960s. The use of Western source material, evident in several of these examples, while important, was not the same as personal contacts between Soviet and foreign scholars.[65]

Second, the ideas advanced by Inozemtsev and others must be viewed within the social and political context of the times. From a Western perspective, they seem simplistic and unsurprising, and they provide no rigorous model or theory of international politics or political economy. In the Soviet context, however, such weaknesses were in fact a source of strength. When taken together, these ideas did provide something important: the beginnings of an alternative framework — a new policy paradigm — for redefining Soviet interests in the international arena. Moreover, these concepts battled the prevailing Leninist class-based paradigm, itself a rather simple construct, on its own terms.

Third, these ideas did matter. As will be seen below, key elites adopted several of them over the course of the SALT/detente policy debates. While the influence of such ideas was clearly limited by a number of factors, an understanding of their role serves as an important corrective to portrayals of Brezhnev-era policymaking as simply the clash of vested political interests within the Politburo. Such clashes did indeed occur, but the interests and preferences at play were themselves being reshaped by new ideas on international politics.

IDEAS AND INTERNATIONAL SECURITY

The picture in this policy area is dramatically different from the one described above. The ideas of IMEMO and Inozemtsev were marginal to the debates — despite partially open policy windows and Inozemtsev's own ties to Brezhnev's inner circle. The institute's lack of influence is in part explained by IMEMO's lack of expertise in national-security matters. But we must also consider the dominant ideas within the institute and how they led it to interpret national security in ways different from other key players in the policy debates.

A review of the national-security analyses produced by researchers at IMEMO during these years makes clear the importance of the latter point. These analyses were of three types: conceptual explorations of a new approach to Soviet national security; analyses providing descriptive overviews of various national-security issues (U.S. nuclear forces or strategic arms control, for example); and research that advanced new — in the Soviet context — ideas

on specific and technical issues of national security (the concept of deterrence, say). The last received by far the least attention — despite a policy environment that provided objective incentives for IMEMO (and other organizations) to address such issues.

A number of researchers advanced understandings of national security that were inspired by ideas that had long been resident within the institute. One such idea was that international politics was not in all cases a zero-sum game between opposing social systems. Implicit here was an understanding of state interests that foresaw the possibility of cooperative efforts to promote national security. This line of reasoning was made explicit in numerous instances by prominent institute researchers as the SALT policy debates progressed.[66]

Inozemtsev advanced a similar argument when he noted that nuclear war had become a universal danger. This observation, along with Inozemtsev's discussion of the "internationalization of economic life" and "common international policy" that were needed to preserve the world's environment and resources, was clearly meant to signal that similar joint efforts were necessary to promote Soviet national security. Bilateral nuclear arms control, in other words, was possible.[67]

A second type of analysis provided informational overviews on specific issues raised by the prospect of strategic nuclear arms control. These included general discussions of the socioeconomic costs of the arms race, the role of military force in U.S. foreign policy and military doctrine, nuclear proliferation, and the danger of accidental nuclear war. Other analyses provided more specific information about the SALT talks themselves.[68]

In several instances, IMEMO scholars grappled for the first time with the nuts and bolts of strategic analysis. These researchers provided information — and lots of it. Using a broad range of Western source material, they gave Soviet readers facts and figures on key U.S. strategic programs of the late 1960s (the Safeguard BMD system and MIRVed warheads), as well as information on other aspects of arms control. Never before had institute researchers provided such data.[69]

Research such as this, however, was exceptional. These analyses were highly descriptive (providing no assessment, for example, of how MIRVs might affect the strategic balance) and devoid of any sense of advocacy; at times, they got their facts wrong. Moreover, most of the work was conducted by recent recruits to the institute.[70]

Two comparisons highlight the inferior quality of this strategic research. One comparison is to research by IMEMO in other issues areas, where its analysts were not content simply to describe phenomena. Instead, they assessed, explained, and promoted new ideas about the issues. Consider, for

example, institute research and writing on U.S. foreign policymaking. On this issue, researchers not only described changes in policymaking; they also assessed their implications for U.S. external behavior—arguing, for example, that the growing complexity of policymaking made it harder for conservative elements to exert decisive influence on American policy.

Another comparison holds issue area constant but looks at the research output of other players in the Soviet SALT process—most notably, the military. When discussing U.S. strategic programs, military writers of the 1960s not only presented more descriptive detail; they provided assessments of how the new systems would modify U.S. nuclear strategy and what missions they would carry out.[71]

A third type of institute analysis advanced new ideas on technical issues of national security like strategic stability or deterrence. In spite of an evident need among important segments of the political elite for research of this sort, IMEMO scholars conducted little of it. Indeed, during the peak years (1970–71) of the SALT policy debate, the institute sponsored only one article on U.S. strategic policy that went beyond description to assessment. It was produced, however, by a former General Staff officer, Mikhail Mil'shteyn, who was then affiliated not with IMEMO but ISKAN. Mil'shteyn not only defined such American concepts as assured destruction and strategic sufficiency; he also assessed what criteria they provided for sizing the U.S. strategic nuclear-force posture.[72]

My argument that analyses of this third type were a low priority for IMEMO researchers is strengthened if we consider an instance of failed entrepreneurship within the institute during the late 1960s. By 1968, as it turns out, there was one individual who thought that IMEMO should conduct strategic research on technical ideas and concepts that would directly bear on Soviet national security. The story of this researcher, Aleksey Nikonov, again shows how dominant ideas within IMEMO were influencing its behavior during the SALT debates. It also confirms a theoretical point made in chapter 1: entrepreneurship is hindered when there is a mismatch between an individual's ideas and the ideas dominant in the organization as a whole.[73]

In early 1969 Nikonov, a researcher in IMEMO's Department of International Relations, went public with his entrepreneurship. He published an article in the institute's journal calling for research by civilian analysts on such topics as military strategy and science, international security, and arms control. Nikonov, in essence, was attempting to move IMEMO beyond its traditional understandings of security and international relations (with their theoretical focus) to applied studies of national security.[74]

This amounted to an extraordinary challenge to the prerogatives and role of

one particular organization: the Soviet military. For many years, and especially after Khrushchev's interventions into security affairs in the early 1960s, the military had deliberately developed a branch of knowledge — military science — in order to insulate the very topics listed by Nikonov from outside interference.[75]

Although Nikonov's analysis is extraordinary, the evidence indicates it did not lead IMEMO to significantly rethink or expand its understandings of security or international politics. No other institute writing during these years addressed security issues in this way, and the editorial commentary in *Memo* offered no support for the ideas expressed in the article. This behavior stands in marked contrast to that on issues closer to IMEMO's core set of ideas. In those cases, advocacy was not limited to one researcher, and commentary by Inozemtsev as well as editorial remarks in *Memo* lent further support to the ideas of individual writers.

How, then, to interpret the appearance of Nikonov's article? It seems best explained as a case of failed policy entrepreneurship. That is, Nikonov the entrepreneur was attempting to make his own ideas an integral part of IMEMO's broader organizational agenda. To understand why Nikonov's entrepreneurship failed, one must consider several factors.

First, he did not have a strong bureaucratic base within IMEMO. Sometime in 1969, a "section" on military-political problems of international relations was established at the institute; it was headed by a former military officer, Colonel V. M. Kulish.[76] In terms of resources and manpower, however, this new military-affairs section came a poor second to IMEMO's existing departments. These departments typically comprised between twenty to thirty researchers; the new military section, in contrast, had fewer than ten. Moreover, the new section did not have the status of a full-fledged department and was, in fact, subordinate to the institute's Department of International Relations. This state of affairs was not corrected until 1986, when IMEMO created a Department of Disarmament and International Security.[77]

Second, Nikonov lacked supporters within the institute — particularly among its leadership. Director Inozemtsev, who consistently emerges during these years as a strong supporter and molder of IMEMO's organizational ideology, had little interest in seeing the institute expand into strategic studies. In fact, throughout the SALT policy debate, he never supported — in public or private — the ideas advanced by Nikonov; if anything, he downplayed their importance. The need to study what Inozemtsev called capitalism's military potential was invariably listed toward the end of his articles and speeches and after many other subjects. These other topics, it might be added, reflected the set of ideas already dominant within IMEMO (on the political economy of capitalism and international relations, for example).[78]

Third, outside the institute — among the Brezhnev leadership — there is no evidence of support for Nikonov's desire to allow civilians to develop ideas on military-technical and other strategic issues. All these factors meant that Nikonov, the entrepreneur, faced a vanishing policy window — one that made it difficult for his ideas to have any influence on actual policy debates.

An alternative explanation to my reconstruction of this episode would argue that Nikonov's ideas had Inozemtsev's full support but that in light of military and elite opposition, Inozemtsev was being cautious, building a research potential in the area slowly and modestly. The main problem with this explanation is that at the time of Inozemtsev's death in 1982, strategic studies still occupied a low rung on IMEMO's ladder of organizational priorities.[79]

Moreover, if this alternative explanation is valid, the other main academic research unit addressing international affairs — ISKAN — should have been similarly quiescent on issues of national security during the early 1970s. But this was not the case. Throughout the SALT policy debate, researchers at ISKAN were much more aggressive in introducing and promoting a range of new (in the Soviet context) ideas on national security — concepts like assured destruction and sufficiency, among others. While these analyses were still inferior to the ones prepared by military professionals, they went well beyond the studies produced at IMEMO.[80]

The institute's behavior in the national-security policy area, then, was marked by seeming indifference; IMEMO tended to resemble the pliant organization one might expect, given the authoritarian Soviet polity of those years. But as I have shown, the institute was an aggressive player in the policy debates where it had strong and long-standing beliefs.

An interaction between two causal variables — ideas and leadership — best explains this contrasting behavior. As I have argued throughout this chapter, by the late 1960s a particular set of ideas was well on its way to becoming embedded at IMEMO. These ideas led the institute to interpret national security in certain ways that help explain these contrasting patterns of behavior. But the importance attached to this set of ideas had much to do with a particular individual, Nikolay Inozemtsev. Moreover, as a policy entrepreneur, Inozemtsev was clearly more aggressive and bold when it came to promoting ideas that resonated with his own understanding of the institute's interests.

In addition, the ideas on the technical dimensions of national security produced by IMEMO had, in contrast to those addressing capitalist political economy or international politics, a distinctly foreign flavor. There is little evidence that they were the result of research and thinking among Soviet scholars; rather, they were clearly borrowed from Western scholars and strategic analysts. Some of this borrowing was simply a reflection of careful reading: a number of Western journals and documents were available to Soviet

researchers. It is quite likely, however, that it also reflected the efforts of trans-national policy networks in which some Soviet specialists participated (Pug-wash or the Dartmouth meetings, for example).[81]

Finally, these ideas about national security played a minor role in the Soviet debates. Such concepts as sufficiency or assured destruction had little bearing on Soviet strategic policy, even after the SALT agreements were signed in May 1972. Indeed, through the early 1980s, Soviet policy seemed predicated on a war-fighting nuclear strategy.[82]

ELITE PREFERENCES AND POLICY

Elite debate focused less on the strategic details of arms control with the United States and more on fundamental understandings of capitalism and international politics. Put another way, the debate was about a new policy paradigm for Soviet foreign policy. The source of the dominant paradigm was the Leninist theory of imperialism, which stressed the deep roots of capitalist hostility toward socialism, as well as capitalism's fundamental inability to generate needed levels of economic growth. These understandings were fine so long as the USSR followed a more or less autarkic strategy of economic development and strove to maintain its security by unilateral means; the cooperation of the imperialists was not needed.

These traditional understandings, however, raised problems for policies premised on a more cooperative relationship with the United States. After all, why expand economic and scientific-technical ties with a doomed economic system? Why negotiate Soviet security with an inherently aggressive adversary? Given the nature of the Soviet system, such policy issues as these inevitably raised questions about the validity of the Leninist paradigm.

This was an anomalous situation for researchers at IMEMO. The good news was that a debate of this sort increased the potential importance of their ideas. But this was offset by the difficulty such ideas had in penetrating the Soviet state. The problem was not only Brezhnev's at best partial receptivity to new ideas; in addition, powerful agencies and individuals within the state and party apparatus had strong views about such traditional concepts and understandings.

Evidence of a wide-ranging debate among the elite first appears in the latter half of 1968. Ideas — or, better said, differing ideas — about the USSR's capitalist adversary played a key role. At the outset, I should note that reformist discussions of capitalism — for example, of splits within its ruling class — were not really new. Khrushchev had spoken of reasonable circles within the capitalist ruling class on several occasions in the early 1960s.[83] Now, however, these discussions were taking place among various members of the political

elite and were tied to the broader issues raised by SALT. Could the USSR cooperate and negotiate with a capitalist United States on questions of national security? Was an enhanced degree of economic and scientific and technical cooperation possible?

By mid-1969 several Politburo members — most notably, Brezhnev and Kosygin — were offering a tentative "yes" to these questions. Brezhnev in particular had begun to talk about capitalism in a manner that suggested the impact of new ideas. Most important was a speech he gave to a major gathering of international communist and workers' parties held in June 1969. There, Brezhnev discussed American foreign policy as if there were actually a process behind it, one where moderate actors and institutions (favoring "mutually acceptable solutions" of complex international problems) competed for influence with more conservative organizations.

Soviet foreign policy, Brezhnev declared, must take into account the existence of this moderate tendency and be prepared to negotiate with the West. In a later speech, the general secretary elaborated on these thoughts — arguing that plans for cooperation with the capitalist West were not marked by naïveté; rather, they were "ever more achievable."[84]

This portrayal of capitalism differed in important ways from earlier leadership pronouncements. Brezhnev was in fact adopting ideas advanced by numerous IMEMO scholars since the early 1960s. That is, his starting point was not the Marxist notion of class struggle but the empirically verified existence of differing views within the U.S. foreign policy establishment. Moreover, that the general secretary had spoken of "the formation of foreign policy" would surely please institute researchers who for years had argued that there was such a policy process behind American foreign behavior.

By the late 1960s, Brezhnev had also begun to evince a newfound respect for capitalism's ability to promote scientific and technological progress. In his address to a December 1969 plenum of the Central Committee, the general secretary noted that the Soviet Union had caught up with Western economies in a quantitative sense (the amount of steel produced, for example). The final result of the competition with capitalism, however, would be defined by "other indicators" — such factors as productivity and the level of scientific achievement. The capitalist West, Brezhnev frankly admitted, was doing quite well in these regards.[85]

If the above establishes a correlation between ideas developed at IMEMO and a change in elite preferences, then additional evidence indicates a causal role for them as well. That is, Brezhnev's understanding of capitalism was modified at least in part because these ideas existed within the USSR, and they were able to reach him.

As noted earlier, by the late 1960s a small group of specialists had gained access to top-level policymakers. Inozemtsev was one of them, and he was clearly in a position to disseminate new ideas from academic circles to top elites. This happened in two ways. Most important, Inozemtsev was one of several specialists who were often consulted by Brezhnev's advisers; on a few occasions, he was even asked to write portions of the general secretary's speeches. An indication of his privileged status was his selection for candidate membership of the Central Committee in early 1971.[86]

In at least one instance, however, Inozemtsev played a more open role as a carrier of new ideas. During a plenary session of the Central Committee in late 1971, Inozemtsev was invited to address the group. This was unusual (candidate members rarely if ever addressed the full committee) and, in retrospect, it is clear that his task was to state the case for a more cooperative relationship with the capitalist West.[87]

Changes in central press commentary confirm that Brezhnev's understanding of capitalism was undergoing modification. Recall that in the Soviet state, top elites exercised monopoly control over press organs; thus, it is likely that these media would reflect changing elite preferences — especially of a general secretary who was in the process of confirming his role as top leader.[88]

The changing pattern of commentary in *Pravda,* the daily newspaper of the Central Committee, best exemplifies this truism of Soviet politics. An authoritative article published in early 1970 was extremely cautious — both in its interpretation of American capitalism and on the more specific issue of strategic arms control. A second, equally authoritative analysis, appeared fifteen months later. It abandoned the caution and neutral tone of the earlier article; the capitalist West was portrayed as a partner with whom the USSR could do business.[89]

The story to this point is consistent with the theoretical argument I outlined in chapter 1. Changes in the USSR's international environment had created uncertainty in the foreign policy preferences of key elites like Brezhnev; they had also opened domestic-level policy windows that motivated entrepreneurs to act, bringing new ideas to the fore. However, broader Soviet state structure insured that the adoption of these ideas proved difficult. After all, the beliefs Inozemtsev brought to Brezhnev's inner circle were new only for the elites; they had been developing within IMEMO since the time of Varga's directorship. As expected, the centralized nature of the Soviet state allowed these ideas to be more easily consolidated. Elites controlled a number of powerful mechanisms (especially the media) for disseminating these new understandings about capitalism.

This account, however, fails to address a crucially important issue: politics.

By the time Brezhnev attempted to introduce the new ideas noted above, a wide-ranging debate was under way among the elite and other agencies. Its subtext of political maneuvering dramatically diminished the ability of new ideas to shape elite preferences and subsequent Soviet policy. Put another way, Inozemtsev the entrepreneur had effectively reduced the size of his policy window by failing to act early. In a manner that is again consistent with the theoretical arguments outlined in chapter 1, the causal role of ideas diminished as the process became overtly politicized.[90]

Indeed, by late 1969 signs were already appearing that Brezhnev's modifications to traditional elite beliefs about capitalism and international politics would be opposed. Indeed, the consolidation of any new ideas was undercut by the fact that different parts of the party and state apparatus were partial to differing sets of ideas.[91] *Kommunist,* for example, became a forum for both new and old ideas. One month after Brezhnev's speech to the June 1969 international communist meeting, the journal echoed the general secretary's new and more nuanced understanding of capitalism. By October, however, *Kommunist* was aggressively attacking these ideas; one article declared that the basic thrust of capitalist foreign policy remained the all-out preparation for "total nuclear war."[92]

By early 1970, key members of the Politburo were openly and vigorously disagreeing with Brezhnev and Kosygin's more positive assessments of capitalism's economic-scientific-technical prospects and the nature of its foreign policymaking. Politburo hardliners Mazurov, Suslov, Shelepin and Shelest' all publicly disagreed with such benign portrayals. Their implicit and at times explicit argument was that the USSR should think twice before widening its economic or security relationship with the capitalist West.[93] As the debate intensified in 1970–71, Brezhnev and Kosygin became more hesitant to advance new ideas on either capitalism or international politics.

In their defense of prevailing ideas, Politburo conservatives had a powerful institutional resource to which they could turn: the USSR Ministry of Defense. Throughout the SALT/detente policy debates, numerous Ministry spokesmen argued not only that a capitalist United States was inherently aggressive but that the level of its aggression was likely to grow. Indeed, the prospect of rapprochement with the West greatly disturbed the military. In particular, any move away from a unilateral approach to insuring Soviet national security would have adverse implications for its resource allocations and hinder the goal of attaining strategic superiority over the West.[94]

The military's response to the appearance of new ideas in the political arena was twofold. Criticism of the specific policy issue — SALT — was combined with an ideological campaign to undercut such ideas by portraying the United

States as increasingly aggressive. An Army colonel berated the authors of a Soviet monograph on war and peace for underestimating the difficulties of disarmament, for example. In a direct allusion to SALT, the officer attacked the concept of negotiated arms control, claiming that it was impossible to have "a calm discussion of this acute and complex question by representatives of opposing social systems."[95]

Given the tenor of the evolving Soviet debate, the ideological criticism was perhaps even more important. While it is true that the Soviet military had always portrayed the United States as aggressive and militaristic, commentaries appearing in the late 1960s were notable both for their ominous and polemical tone and for their increasing divergence from the views of Kosygin and Brezhnev.[96]

In addition, senior military officials continued to present an extremely aggressive image of capitalism. For example, Defense Minister Grechko and Main Political Administration head Yepishev both portrayed the capitalist system and its intentions toward the USSR in stark terms. Yepishev went so far as to claim that the West was "feverishly preparing for a new world war."[97]

There is a final, telling example of the important role ideas played in the policy debate. This occurred when the semi-classified General Staff journal *Voyennaya mysl'* served as the forum for new ideas on both security issues and contemporary capitalism. A mid-1969 article forcefully made the case for SALT, coupling its analysis with a moderate vision of capitalism and international politics. The content alone — given the journal and times — was extraordinary. Even more unusual, the article was not written by a General Staff officer; rather, the author was a civilian researcher at ISKAN. The political leadership, it is clear, was sufficiently worried about the staying power of old ideas to sanction such an unprecedented intervention in the most authoritative military journal.[98]

In the increasingly politicized atmosphere surrounding the Soviet debate, the ideas of Inozemtsev and others fared poorly. As the political battle heated up, Brezhnev's tenuous commitment to new ideas was sacrificed to the more pressing need of consolidating his position within the leadership. The result, as is widely known, was at best a modification to preferences and interests. The Leninist policy paradigm had been altered but not replaced. The goals of Soviet policy remained largely unchanged while some of the instruments were altered, allowing for some degree of economic and security cooperation with the West. "Normal policymaking" had won out over a "paradigm shift."[99]

But why had normal policymaking won out? This question is best addressed by explicitly considering the questions raised at the beginning of this chapter.

Were policy windows open in the foreign and national-security issue area during the late 1960s? Were entrepreneurs present and seeking to advance particular ideas? What was the institutional context within which the entrepreneurs operated?

On the first question, I have argued that one or more policy windows were indeed open. However, two important factors limited their size. For one, there is little evidence that leaders like Brezhnev felt themselves to be in a crisis-ridden or highly uncertain environment. They also clearly did not see previous Soviet foreign and security policy as marked by a series of failures. Thus, from the start, these leaders were not engaged in the wide-ranging information search that makes their preferences more susceptible to the influence of new ideas.

Furthermore, the heated debate among elites during 1969–71 made Brezhnev, always the political animal, even more cautious and less willing to innovate, thus further dampening his receptivity to new ideas. This open debate also sent signals to powerful organizations with vested interests in the prevailing foreign policy paradigm — notably the military — to mobilize their resources in an attempt to influence the course of policy.

The answer to my second question — the presence of entrepreneurs — is less ambiguous. I have identified at least one such individual: IMEMO head Nikolay Inozemtsev. Motivated by emerging policy windows, he was clearly a person with a solution in search of a problem. The "solution" in this case was an alternative interpretative framework for Soviet foreign policy. Inozemtsev also had several of the traits earlier identified as facilitators of entrepreneurial success: a high degree of expertise and knowledge (on international relations and the global political economy), and connections to influential political actors (Brezhnev's inner circle).

Yet Inozemtsev was by nature a cautious individual. Nor was he by instinct political. These traits clearly hindered Inozemtsev's entrepreneurship, for an entrepreneur must be willing to gamble and engage in political give-and-take in order to succeed. Studying Inozemtsev's behavior during these (and later) years and interviewing those who were close to him yields a paradoxical image. Within IMEMO, he was a strong and assertive leader — one willing to sanction bold and innovative research. Outside the institute, in the broader political process, he was more passive. If a policy window opened, he was willing to exploit the opportunity. At the same time, he seemed leery of taking initiative and actively seeking to force open such windows. Given the political context of those years and IMEMO's own organizational legacy (the Varga affair), it is easy to understand his caution. Politics was simply not Inozemtsev's forte — a point that would become painfully clear in the early 1980s.[100]

With regard to the institutional context within which entrepreneurs operated, things are even more clear. Inozemtsev's organizational environment was a factor that assisted his entrepreneurial activity. By the late 1960s, a distinctive set of ideas on international politics was well on its way to becoming embedded at IMEMO. In part, these were Inozemtsev's ideas; yet it is equally clear that his ideas resonated with beliefs long resident at the institute. Thus, Inozemtsev had a clear organizational resource at his disposal as he sought to bring new ideas to Soviet foreign policy.

At the same time, the institutional level — the broader structure of the Soviet state — did little to facilitate his entrepreneurship. Given the highly centralized nature of foreign policymaking in Soviet Russia, policy entrepreneurship, I argued in chapter 1, was a likely pathway for new ideas to reach key decision makers. This does not mean that the task was easy. Insulated agencies like the Ministry of Defense, which had an influential say in the process, had become organizational homes to very different ideas about international politics and contemporary capitalism. Brezhnev and his allies could not or would not ignore these agencies, and this resulted in an open and politicized debate. In such a climate, new ideas could take hold only if they benefited from the kind of top-level support they never received.

It is thus not difficult to see why ideas played only a minor role in the Soviet SALT/detente policy debates. Indeed, if anything, the outcome (the minor causal role of new ideas) was overdetermined. As Georgiy Arbatov has noted, by the early 1970s he and Inozemtsev were thoroughly discouraged. They had come to the sad conclusion that the political leadership simply "was not ready [to consider] serious and complex matters" of domestic or foreign policy.[101]

4

Windows Opening?

This chapter sets the stage for an exploration of the unexpected and dramatic international political changes that led to the end of the Cold War. Consistent with the book's theoretical and empirical concerns, my focus is the supply and demand for new foreign policy ideas in the former Soviet Union — in this case, as the Brezhnev era drew to a close. The demand for ideas by the top Soviet elite (Politburo members and members of the C.C. Secretariat) remained low until close to the end of Brezhnev's tenure in late 1982. This testifies to the staying power of the Leninist foreign policy paradigm. Indeed, what emerges strikingly from the analysis in this chapter is how little had changed from ten years earlier when the SALT/detente policy debates were drawing to a close. This period (1972–82) is the one to which the now-familiar term *zastoy* (stagnation) is truly applicable.

A Demand for New Ideas?

The Brezhnev foreign policy strategy had been to combine limited East-West economic and security cooperation with a continuing effort to expand Soviet global influence, especially in the developing world. By the early 1980s, elite consensus on the feasibility of such a strategy was weakening; more-over, Brezhnev himself was showing some signs of doubt as to its continuing

validity. The early rhetoric of the Reagan administration sharpened this emerging elite cleavage. Soviet hardliners, in particular, seized on Reagan's policies and statements to argue that — of all things — Brezhnev's strategy had been too soft on "imperialism."[1]

Whatever the impact of these changes, the early 1980s saw Brezhnev continue as the chief spokesperson for Soviet foreign policy. The preferences and strategies he articulated were at best a minor adaptation of those of the 1970s. Brezhnev's speech to the 26th Party Congress in February 1981 provides a good example of the combination of little new and much old in Soviet policy.

With regard to the new, Brezhnev's comments on Soviet relations with the developing world were more restrained than they had been at the previous Party Congress in 1976. Yet the broader interpretative framework behind his remarks was still clearly informed by the Leninist policy paradigm — especially his assertion of a "union of class interests" between socialism and national liberation movements. Brezhnev also indirectly referred to so-called global problems; he discussed various issues that were global in scale (disease and illiteracy, for example), without actually calling them global or assessing their importance for Soviet foreign policy.[2]

The remaining part of the foreign-policy section of Brezhnev's speech was basically a repetition of long-standing assumptions and policies. The general crisis of capitalism was portrayed as worsening; the activities of U.S. monopolies were seen as stimulating further inter-imperialist contradictions; U.S.-Soviet relations were portrayed as deteriorating because of American policies and actions; and the Peace Program elaborated at the 24th and 25th Party congresses was seen as a "reliable compass" for Soviet security policy.

Brezhnev's conceptual framework for Soviet security interests also broke no new ground. This was especially evident when he declared that any security cooperation with the West had to be conducted on the basis of "equality and equal security." This principle had been a part of Soviet discourse since the early 1970s; taken to its extreme, it allowed the USSR to retain armed forces that were as powerful as those of all its opponents combined.[3]

Overall, the general secretary's report to the congress strongly implied that the best strategy for the present was more of the same. Although Brezhnev and other elites recognized that Soviet foreign policy had encountered some problems ("storm clouds were rising" in the international arena), these were seen as temporary; thus, no fundamental changes were needed to correct them.[4]

This same message of adherence to preferences informed by the old policy paradigm was evident in other elite-level speeches and analyses of the early 1980s. Even in the few cases where conservatives made veiled attacks on the Brezhnev strategy, what they offered in its place could best be characterized as

more of the same plus: they sought a continuation of the Brezhnev strategy, but with greater emphasis on its military component.[5]

The last six months or so of Brezhnev's life brought not change but a perceptible hardening in foreign-policy pronouncements. In part, this was a reaction to the Reagan administration's continuing anti-Soviet rhetoric. But it was also a natural reaction for a system approaching its first leadership change in close to twenty years. The evident difficulties associated with the long-postponed succession would make any elite think twice before he created problems — for example, by tampering with the core ideas of the Leninist policy paradigm. Moreover, to the extent that the elites were maneuvering for the future leadership of the party, it would be disadvantageous for any of them to be seen as soft on questions of foreign or security policy.[6]

During Yuriy Andropov's tenure as general secretary (November 1982– February 1984), the trend evident in Brezhnev's last years continued. While Andropov and other elites clearly saw that Soviet foreign policy faced problems, their words and actions suggested a continued belief in the foreign policy strategy pursued under Brezhnev. Indeed, the overwhelming impression one gets from Andropov's ten healthy months in power (he first fell seriously ill in August 1983) is that changes in domestic policy were the clear priority of the leadership.[7]

There were numerous examples of this essential continuity in the Andropov leadership's approach to foreign policy. In 1983 the Soviets continued to make inconsequential concessions at the intermediate range nuclear forces (INF) talks in Geneva. There were also new proposals for sweeping political agreements — for example, a Warsaw Pact-NATO treaty on mutual nonuse of force. These simply echoed proposals made during Brezhnev's years in power.[8]

Other elite speeches and commentaries exhibited the same sense of continuity. There was praise for the Soviet Peace Program and calls for a return to detente. The importance of peace offensives was reiterated, while the class essence of Soviet policy was extolled. The policy of peaceful coexistence was rediscovered, with the explicit recognition that it was "a specific form of the class struggle" between capitalism and socialism.[9]

This same basic pattern prevailed during Konstantin Chernenko's year as general secretary (February 1984–March 1985). If one needed a phrase to capture the essence of foreign policy under Chernenko, it might be "damage control plus more of the same." The damage-control element aimed at preventing a further deterioration in Soviet-American relations, with leaders clearly hoping to rescue policy from the dead end (best exemplified by the USSR's decision to break off all arms-control talks in late 1983) it had reached during Andropov's last months in power.[10]

On other foreign policy questions, however, elite commentary during 1984 was more of the same. One of the May issues of *Kommunist*, for example, carried a lead editorial that presented an orthodox analysis of the nature of capitalism; it discussed the crisis of state monopoly capitalism and the growing influence of the military-industrial complex, among other Leninist verities. The article went on to attack those who used an empirical approach for understanding capitalism (this would include virtually all researchers at IMEMO), instead of relying upon the laws uncovered by Lenin. A stern warning was then issued: "The nature of imperialism is unchanged, its interests are incompatible with mankind's interests. The inspiration and growing topicality of these Leninist thoughts should find full reflection in our literature."[11]

Other examples of the lack of change abound. The principle of equality and equal security was reaffirmed as the conceptual basis for Soviet national security, as was the importance of a class approach for understanding international affairs. In one case, Chernenko actually used the subversive—for a Marxist-Leninist—phrase "global problems." However, he linked both the existence and resolution of such problems to "the development of the class struggle."[12]

This review clearly points to a good element of zastoy in Soviet foreign policy on the eve of the Gorbachev era, both in behavior and interpretative framework. Foreign-policy problems (Afghanistan, U.S.-Soviet relations, China) and crises (Poland, the Korean airliner incident) mounted; yet faith in the prevailing beliefs and preferences was reaffirmed. If any policy window existed in this environment, it was vanishingly small. The objective circumstances (to borrow some Sovietspeak) for opening a window were in hand; missing, however, were leaders looking for a solution. Put another way, the demand for new ideas was not terribly high.

The Supply of New Ideas

By the early 1980s, there was a voluminous and ever-growing scholarly literature in the USSR that made a mockery of the Leninist paradigm. Much, but certainly not all, of this research was centered at IMEMO. Indeed, the supply of new ideas was large and growing. Aside from research conducted at IMEMO, work at other academy institutes during the 1970s had examined topics (for example, global problems) that had clear relevance for the Soviet understanding of international politics.[13]

Of equal importance, during 1979–80 the Academy of Sciences established two scientific councils to coordinate work among various analysts and academic institutions on international policy issues, as well as on the

interpretative-theoretical context for Soviet behavior. The first new body was the Scientific Council for Research on Problems of Peace and Disarmament. It was established in June 1979, chaired by Nikolay Inozemtsev, and based in IMEMO's Department of International Organizations.[14]

In addition to researching such policy issues as arms control and international cooperation, the council had a clear propaganda function. For example, its main publication series — *Mir i razoruzheniye* — was published in five languages: Russian, English, French, German, and Spanish. Moreover, it is quite possible the council was established at the behest of political elites worried about the USSR's growing image problem abroad.[15]

The second new body established in the early 1980s was the Scientific Council on Philosophical and Social Problems of the Scientific-Technical Revolution. It was attached to the Presidium of the Academy of Sciences and chaired by Ivan Frolov, a reformist Marxist philosopher who later became one of Gorbachev's closest aides. This council had a section on the Global Problems of the Scientific-Technical Revolution. That global problems were being studied by a group that examined issues of philosophy was itself a breakthrough. In the Soviet context, philosophy meant Marxism-Leninism. In other words, one of the purposes of the council and its section was to study the effects of global problems on the Leninist policy paradigm.[16]

During the early 1980s, IMEMO evinced greater interest in the subject matter and activities of this second council than they had in the first (on peace and disarmament). This seems odd considering that the first council was chaired by Inozemtsev. Part of the answer to this seeming riddle was that both Inozemtsev and IMEMO researchers were more at home with basic conceptual issues of international relations (global problems, the nature of the international system, the nature of security) than with specific issues of international security (nuclear strategy or verification).[17]

As argued in earlier chapters, this preference for the abstract over the applied was clearly rooted in IMEMO's own organizational history and was by now reflected in its ideology. It is also probable that the second council evoked greater interest among scholars at IMEMO because it was seen as a more serious enterprise, one less devoted to propagandizing Soviet policy abroad.[18]

By the early 1980s, IMEMO was a well-established organization, with a stable structure and distinctive beliefs about international politics. Half of its top leadership (which included a director and five deputy directors) were holdovers from the early 1970s and before; director Inozemtsev had held his position since May 1966. Continuing a trend evident since the late 1950s, a majority (four) of IMEMO's six top leaders were economists or political economists by training.[19]

Moreover, IMEMO's bureaucratic structure differed little from that of a decade before. The institute had ten research departments and three sections: eight of the thirteen units examined issues of international economics and political economy, while four conducted research on various aspects of international relations. But IMEMO had grown during the 1970s, increasing in size by nearly 50 percent (from six hundred to more than nine hundred research and support staff). These numbers made IMEMO by far the largest of the academy's international-affairs institutes. Indeed, the academy continued to view IMEMO as the "leading scientific center" for research on contemporary capitalism and international relations.[20]

The institute's dominant areas of expertise also continued much as they had been in the 1960s and early 1970s. The emphasis was in economics and political economy (both at the national and international levels) and, to a lesser extent, foreign policy and conceptual questions of international relations. During 1981, for example, 60 percent of the articles published in its journal, *Memo,* examined the political economy of capitalism and developing countries, as well as general issues of economics, while 34 percent examined questions of foreign policy and international relations. Institute-sponsored book monographs published in 1980 showed a similar distribution by subject matter (70 percent on political economy and economics; 20 percent on international relations and foreign policy). The bias in favor of books on political economy is similar to that seen in the late 1960s.[21]

In addition, continuing a trend seen in the 1960s, the Scientific Life section in *Memo* was typically dominated by reports of conferences and appearances related to political economy and conceptual aspects of international politics (for example, global problems).[22]

Finally, between October 1979 and July 1983, a total of eighty-four dissertations (twelve doctoral and seventy-two candidate) were defended at IMEMO: of these, seventy concerned the political economy of capitalism and the developing world and other economic topics, while fourteen explored issues of international relations and foreign policy. In the latter category, none of the dissertations dealt with applied questions of international security (military strategy or conventional arms control, say).[23]

This brief review suggests that the IMEMO of the early 1980s held a sense of mission markedly similar to the one it possessed in the 1960s and 1970s. Research on political economy, contemporary capitalism, and international relations remained its central area of interest and expertise. These were clearly the issues about which it most cared and to which it devoted the most organizational resources. These interests were influenced little by the Soviet state and its leaders; more important was an ideology of international politics now firmly rooted in the structure, ethos, and personnel of the institute.

Before examining the institute's ideology, it is important to discuss exactly how the Soviet state still did matter. After all, the state seemed unwilling or unable to curtail the supply of new ideas from academic researchers at IMEMO and elsewhere. But it did have clear powers to keep such ideas off the political agenda, as the following story demonstrates.

Throughout 1982, IMEMO was the target of a pressure campaign that had backing at high levels within the CPSU.[24] The campaign began in the early months of the year, when an institute deputy director was arrested on trumped-up allegations of corruption. Although these charges were eventually dropped, IMEMO's troubles were just beginning. In fact, soon thereafter the KGB began a formal investigation of the institute, arresting two of its researchers for purported dissident activity.

The true purpose behind this campaign became clear when a CPSU commission was formed to investigate IMEMO's work. It was headed by Politburo member Viktor Grishin, a figure known for his extremely conservative views. The commission accused IMEMO of "ideological failings" and of providing the country's leadership with flawed interpretations of international political phenomena. If that was not enough, the institute was then accused of harboring Zionists among its staff. In the Soviet context, these were serious charges.

Throughout the summer months, there was a lessening of the pressure on IMEMO. The damage, however, had been done. Morale within the institute was shattered; more important, Inozemtsev was devastated. In August he died unexpectedly of a heart attack at the age of sixty-one, ending a sixteen-year tenure as institute head.

As argued earlier, Inozemtsev by nature was not politically adept. Not surprisingly, then, political intrigue of this sort left him, according to one close friend, broken and passive. Indeed, at a key session of the CPSU investigatory commission, Inozemtsev declined to defend himself or his institute. Whatever the actual connection between these events and Inozemtsev's broken spirit and subsequent death, IMEMO had lost not only a highly competent scholar but an ardent promoter of its distinctive set of ideas.[25]

With Inozemtsev's death, the pressure was once again turned up. Plans were announced for yet another party investigation of the institute's affairs. This investigation was terminated only after Georgiy Arbatov and the journalist Aleksandr Bovin personally appealed to an ailing Brezhnev to stop the campaign against IMEMO.[26]

The fall of 1982 thus marked the end of an extraordinarily difficult year for IMEMO. It had lost its respected leader and been subjected to considerable political pressure. Why? Two factors were key. First, "it is no accident" — as the Soviet press agency TASS used to declare — that these events transpired in 1982. The long-postponed succession to the Brezhnev elite was clearly under

way. Mikhail Suslov, a powerful C.C. secretary and Politburo member, had died early in the year, and Brezhnev, his health steadily deteriorating, died in November. It is clear that powerful elements in the CPSU hierarchy took advantage of the uncertainty generated by these events to unleash a long-overdue (from their perspective) attack on the liberal foreign-policy ideas championed by IMEMO. The Leninist policy paradigm, it would seem, still had influential supporters.

Second, there are persistent if unconfirmed rumors that during the early part of 1982 Inozemtsev was in line for a high-ranking position in the C.C. International Department. Suslov had overseen this unit for more than twenty years, a period in which it had championed the class-based paradigm.[27] With his death, such an appointment as Inozemtsev's was at least in the realm of the possible. Had this promotion been under consideration (by Andropov?), it would have provoked a strong and negative reaction from the conservative elements of the CPSU hierarchy noted above.

Whatever the reasons for the attack on IMEMO, one thing is clear. It was partly successful, and it had a tremendous influence on the institute's behavior throughout 1982. The institute's remaining access channel to the political process, aside from personal connections to top leaders and their staffs and occasional reports sent to the Central Committee (many of which were never read), was its publications — especially the monthly journal *Memo.*

Yet because of the political interference, *Memo,* for the first and only time in a twenty-year period, virtually lost its voice during 1982. The institute's strident advocacy of the need to study global problems, for example, which would be so evident in the early 1980s, nearly disappeared from the pages of *Memo* during 1982 and early 1983.[28]

Although not as damaging as the Varga affair in the late 1940s, these events had demonstrated yet again — and, as it turned out, for one of the last times — the coercive abilities of the Soviet state. At a more fundamental level, the episode suggests the critical importance of ideas in Soviet politics. But what kinds of ideas were so worrying to influential elements of the CPSU? This question is best addressed by considering IMEMO's own ideology of international politics as the era of zastoy drew to a close.

Ideas and International Politics

By the early 1980s, ideas on the interdependent and non-class nature of contemporary international politics, which had begun to take hold a decade earlier, were firmly rooted at IMEMO. We can see this in numerous sources: statements of the institute's research agenda by Inozemtsev and others, bu-

reaucratic innovations, IMEMO's research publications, and retrospectives by several prominent institute scholars.[29]

In the early 1980s, Inozemtsev himself was still forceful in articulating his and the institute's beliefs on international relations. For example, in his introductory article to the first of the volumes on peace and disarmament research, Inozemtsev promoted ideas long held by numerous IMEMO researchers. These included the "chance" factor in international politics (that is, the growing danger of accidental nuclear war) and the non-class nature of the international system. On the latter, he noted the world's "global integralness" and argued that global problems could be resolved only via the "collective efforts of people . . . independent of their social system."[30]

More important was what Inozemtsev had to say inside the institute. In a speech to its scientific collective in early 1981, he forcefully reiterated how the dominant set of ideas within the institute should guide its research. At a general level, he argued that IMEMO should give priority to such topics as the Soviet economy, world economic ties, capitalist economies, and the political economy of contemporary capitalism.[31]

More specifically, Inozemtsev made it clear that IMEMO had a basic interest in developing research on global problems and international relations. The institute, he declared, had given research on global problems a high priority, creating a series of special groups within the institute for their study. Inozemtsev's widow, Margarita Maksimova, confirms the extensive bureaucratic innovation undertaken to promote research on global problems, describing a "definite reorientation" of research and the creation of new departments and research groups.[32]

In the speech, Inozemtsev provided additional evidence that he sought to strengthen the bureaucratic base for the institute's ideas on international politics. In the field of international relations, IMEMO could only award graduate degrees on the *history* of international relations and foreign policy. This clearly rankled Inozemtsev, especially because he considered international relations an "independent scientific discipline" that undertook more than simply historical studies. He argued that degree categories other than the historical were needed in international relations. In fact, the idea that there could be a science of international relations had been present within the institute since the late 1960s.[33]

In the 1990s, two senior scholars long associated with IMEMO — Yevgeniy Primakov and Oleg Bykov — provided authoritative overviews of the ideology of international politics developed there during the 1970s and early 1980s. Both argue that by the end of the Brezhnev era, IMEMO had become home to several distinctive foreign policy ideas, including those on the evolutionary na-

ture of contemporary capitalism; the interdependent nature of world politics; and the belief that class values should be subordinated to universal values.[34]

Primakov, who has since gone on to play an important policy role in post-Soviet Russia, also provides fascinating evidence of how important ideas—both old and new—were in Soviet politics. More than once during the 1970s, Inozemtsev was summoned to high-level CPSU meetings to make the case for a new conceptual understanding of international relations. Primakov recalls one instance, a meeting on Soviet foreign trade and international economic policy, where Inozemtsev tried unsuccessfully to remind his audience that the simple fact of interdependence required fundamental changes in these policies (which were premised on the USSR's isolation from the global political economy).[35]

An analysis of IMEMO's research publications in the late 1970s and early 1980s provides further evidence of the ideas that were clearly resident within the institute. At a most general level, in this period IMEMO aggressively promoted—as it had in the late 1960s—a complex, empirical and non-class vision of the international system. When it came to discussions of global problems or the structure of international politics, the institute had clear beliefs. That such beliefs resonated with those of Inozemtsev does nothing to devalue their importance. Rather, it suggests the sort of ideological legacy that organizational leaders can impart in a centralized, authoritarian polity.[36]

During these years, the institute devoted an extraordinary amount of attention to one particular aspect of the international system: global problems. *Memo* ran a special rubric (section) on the topic that serialized key chapters from an institute monograph on the same subject. The ideological advocacy in these articles was cautious, but clearly present. For example, Margarita Maksimova (a senior institute scholar) presented a "very conditional" definition of global problems that stressed their "planetary" and non-class character.[37]

In less conspicuous arenas than a journal article, however, institute scholars were considerably less restrained. Maksimova herself provides a good example of their behavior. At a meeting on global problems, she argued that their comprehensive study was dictated by the decisions of the 26th Party Congress, which was simply not true. Maksimova then declared that there must be further study of such concepts as "world science," "interdependence," "universal values," and a "single world economy." Each of these ideas implied the existence of a single global political economy and thus neatly undercut the essence of the Leninist policy paradigm.[38]

The commentary was clearly at odds with the foreign policy beliefs and preferences of Brezhnev and other elites during the early 1980s. While the general secretary, for example, was willing to admit the existence of problems

of a global scale, researchers at IMEMO explored their implications for basic tenets of the Leninist worldview. They did this despite significant disincentives not to do so — most important, the increasingly conservative political climate of those years. As the KGB-party investigation of 1982 would demonstrate, the promotion of such ideas could entail painful costs — for individuals and the institute as a whole.

Two comparisons strengthen my argument that IMEMO now had a dominant set of ideas clearly informing its interests and behavior. One holds the unit — IMEMO — constant but varies policy area; a second comparison holds policy area constant but varies the unit, contrasting IMEMO's behavior with that of similarly situated organizations.

The behavior of IMEMO in the national-security issue area stands in stark contrast to that described above. Although it is true that the institute entered the 1980s with a slightly higher level of interest and expertise on security issues than it had shown in the late 1960s, some adaptation was virtually inevitable. This was especially likely given that security issues had been central to the Soviet-American relationship for over a decade.[39]

Overall though, the study of security issues remained a low priority for the institute. There are numerous indicators of this. The military-affairs section was still dwarfed in size and prestige by the institute's full-fledged departments (for example, those on international relations, international organizations, and the political economy of developed capitalism). The institute also continued to show little interest in establishing ties with other organizations — within or outside the USSR — that addressed questions of international security. These included the Independent Commission on Disarmament and Security (the so-called Palme Commission), the Committee of Soviet Scientists in Defense of Peace and Against the Nuclear Threat, and the Stockholm International Peace Research Institute (SIPRI).[40]

In addition, when Inozemtsev, during the early 1980s, discussed IMEMO's research tasks in the security realm, his proposals sounded strikingly similar to those outlined a decade earlier. His address to the institute's scientific collective in early 1981, which is indicative in this regard, included calls for research on the following security topics: the military-industrial complex; the goals Western countries sought in increasing their "military potentials" (a favorite phrase of Inozemtsev's since the 1960s); and the basic tendencies in Western military preparations. This was not exactly a call for serious strategic research. Furthermore, this discussion came — as it always had — after Inozemtsev had outlined the institute's research tasks in the international-relations sphere.[41]

Thus, there appears to have been no attempt to update and expand IMEMO's research on security to account for new issues like conventional

arms control or verification. In contrast, on issues that were closer to the institute's core set of beliefs, research agendas had been expanded — for example, in the fields of interdependence studies and global problems.

The lower priority accorded to security issues was also evident in the overall tone of the articles published in *Memo*. Much more so than on other issues, institute researchers were content to cite rather than to challenge the established dogma, such as the belief that arms control could be verified by national technical means (satellites and the like) alone. This was simply taken as a given by numerous IMEMO analysts. Another dogma was that U.S. policy was undermining strategic stability. Here again, most IMEMO analysts — including Inozemtsev — used the phrase without questioning the validity of the assertion, let alone defining the concept.[42]

As seen earlier, a key conceptual element of Soviet national-security policy during these years was the principle of equality and equal security. Many IMEMO analysts cited this principle, but none attempted either to criticize or to define it.[43]

It is instructive to compare their behavior with how IMEMO analysts treated other principles informing elite preferences and Soviet foreign policy — for example, this policy's class basis or the militaristic nature of contemporary capitalism. Here they took issue with official concepts and preferences, putting a different spin on them in the process. They had done this in the 1960s and were still doing it in the early 1980s, despite a more conservative political climate.

What ideas were promoted by similarly situated units, most important, the Academy of Sciences' USA Institute? By the early 1980s, ISKAN and IMEMO were the two most prestigious and influential of the academy's international-affairs units; both also operated in the same structural context defined by the authoritarian Soviet polity and the military's dominant role in national-security decision making. Yet ISKAN was a much more forceful promoter of ideas on security policy than IMEMO during the late Brezhnev years. A structural analysis, by itself, is therefore insufficient; agency, in the form of organizational leadership, and beliefs — that is, ideas — must be invoked to explain the variance in behavior of the two organizations.[44]

By the early 1980s, ISKAN — under the aegis of its long-serving director, Georgiy Arbatov — had developed an ethos and sense of mission that differed from IMEMO's in several important ways. First, Arbatov continued to speak out forcefully on security — both its conceptual basis and specific policy issues.[45]

Arbatov's agenda-setting clearly influenced ISKAN's behavior; during these years its journal, *SShA,* carried a number of articles that addressed security

and other military policy issues. There was even a rubric for articles on foreign policy and questions of military strategy. The institute also established ties with the Soviet foreign policy apparatus, military officials, and several committees and organizations (both within and outside the USSR) that were addressing security issues. On both scores, ISKAN's behavior differed dramatically from IMEMO's.[46]

Second, because of the recruitment policy pursued by ISKAN's leadership, a number of its researchers had technical training or degrees (for example, Candidate of Technical Sciences). Several of these analysts would play key roles as ISKAN sought to promote new strategic concepts for Soviet security policy during the 1980s.[47]

In sum, by the early 1980s Arbatov had begun to make good on his claim that ISKAN, from its founding, had undertaken "pioneering efforts" to create a new type of civilian expert on military-strategic issues. Indeed, in terms of both quantity and degree of sophistication, ISKAN's research on strategic issues during these years greatly surpassed that of IMEMO. One type of analysis provided information solely on U.S. military programs.[48]

Researchers at ISKAN, however, also conducted more sophisticated military-technical studies, analyzing various aspects of U.S. military strategy or the technical details of different weapons systems. These included overviews of space-based ballistic missile defenses and of U.S. plans for conducting strategic anti-submarine warfare, detailed assessments of the Strategic Defense Initiative, and analyses that distinguished between declaratory and operational levels of U.S. strategic concepts.[49]

Moreover, ISKAN analysts — in contrast to those at IMEMO — did not hesitate to introduce new ideas into Soviet strategic discourse. They provided specific analyses of such concepts as common security, strategic stability, deterrence, and nonprovocative defense, among others. Operating under the same (structural) constraints as IMEMO, ISKAN and its researchers behaved differently, their interests and behavior informed by the ideas of an assertive organizational leader.[50]

As the Brezhnev era drew to a close, there was a growing disjuncture between the supply and demand for foreign policy ideas in the USSR. The Leninist policy paradigm continued to inform elite preferences in important ways, even as a growing body of research and analysis made a mockery of it. Indeed, diverse ideas about international politics were now firmly rooted at different levels of the Soviet polity. But as the crisis of 1982 had demonstrated, the Soviet state — because of its authoritarian and centralized nature — still possessed a number of coercive instruments for maintaining this division.

In a sense, my argument here is similar to the one comparativists have made about a nascent pre-Gorbachev civil society: the roots and ideas of later reforms were present under Brezhnev (and in some cases even earlier). Missing, however, were the international pressures and domestic political processes necessary to empower these new ideas. How this "knowledge gap" would be closed is the subject of the next chapter.[51]

5

Open Windows, New Ideas, and the End of the Cold War

By the early 1980s, a policy window was ajar in the Soviet Union, but not fully open. That is, although the USSR faced a number of daunting international circumstances and pressures, its ruling elites did not perceive them as such. In the present chapter, I explore the process through which this window opened fully; the incentives this created for entrepreneurs; the political empowerment of a new set of foreign policy ideas; and how the broader structure of the Soviet state facilitated such empowerment. I should thus be able to offer an explanation for the unexpected, dramatic, and peaceful changes that led to the end of the Cold War; as well as the causal role of ideas in this process.

According to my argument, there should be a particular sequence of events in any process of ideas-based foreign policy change. International pressures and changes (the debacle in Afghanistan, growing complexity of global political economy, confrontational U.S. policy toward the Soviet Union, threat to strategic balance), if sufficiently dramatic, will create uncertainty in the foreign policy preferences of key elites. Equally important, these international-level changes will create policy windows in the domestic-level foreign policy process.

Given that Soviet political institutions were still centralized and autonomous in the early Gorbachev years, I would expect individual policy entrepreneurs to play a key role in exploiting these windows to promote new ideas.

Moreover, indications of elite uncertainty and a turbulent international environment should motivate such individuals to increase their entrepreneurial activity. If entrepreneurs and their foreign policy ideas succeed in shaping the preferences of key elites, then — given the institutional characteristics of the Soviet state — the likelihood of international political change is high.

I begin with a brief overview of the liberal foreign policy that, in the USSR, came to be known as new political thinking. By late 1986, several Western analysts had recognized there was something different about General Secretary Gorbachev's foreign policy in comparison to that of Brezhnev and Khrushchev. In particular, Gorbachev, in reforming Soviet policy, did not simply bring in new people (Eduard Shevardnadze as Foreign Minister, for example, in July 1985) and articulate new policies (the unilateral nuclear test moratorium in August 1985); he also brought in new ideas and concepts.[1]

Indeed, by early 1986 Gorbachev was articulating a dramatically different worldview and set of foreign policy preferences. In the language of Western social science, he was advancing a new policy paradigm; the ideas and conceptual frameworks underlying it would eventually lead to radical changes in Soviet international behavior.[2]

As noted in previous chapters, the conceptual basis for these new preferences — captured in such phrases as "universal values," "global problems," "interdependence," "mutual security," and "reasonable sufficiency in defense" — was not new at all.[3] Such concepts had been articulated by various academic specialists and organizations in the USSR since at least the mid-1960s. Yet it was only beginning in 1985–86 that they came to influence both the basic assumptions informing Soviet international behavior and the strategic prescriptions for the USSR's national security.[4] The revised basic assumptions could be stated thus:

- an understanding of international politics premised on notions of interdependence and global problems
- a goal structure for state interests that ranked non-class over class values and interests
- a portrayal of capitalism that questioned the Leninist orthodoxy concerning its inherent aggressiveness and militarism.

The revised strategic prescriptions were the following:

- a conceptualization of national security that gave first priority to mutual efforts at insuring it
- a criterion for the development of military forces that placed limits on their size (the principle of reasonable sufficiency).

The specialists at IMEMO were instrumental in bringing several of these ideas to the Soviet political agenda. To understand why these researchers were

influential in some cases but not in others, we must consider the institute's own history and ideology, how agency and structure played out within it, the role of policy entrepreneurs and windows, and — most important — the ties it was able to establish to a reformist political leadership.

Open Policy Windows

Today Mikhail Gorbachev is disparaged by many in the West and, especially, Russia, for his conservatism and inability to reject basic tenets of Marxist Soviet dogma on economic policy and doctrine. Yet at the same time many see him as a visionary when it came to redefining Soviet interests in the international arena. Indeed, it often seemed that there were two Gorbachevs: the radical foreign policy innovator and the cautious economic reformer. Part of the difference can be explained by political considerations: he had fewer, albeit still powerful, entrenched domestic interests to confront when attempting to redefine Soviet interests and policy in the international sphere.[5]

One needs to look beyond politics, however, to explain the difference, with an important factor being Gorbachev's greater openness to new ideas on foreign as opposed to domestic policy.[6] Gorbachev was a career official who had spent much time as a local party leader, where he devoted virtually all his attention to domestic issues. And it was precisely such questions that received the overwhelming amount of attention in CPSU ideology. When it came to domestic political economy, it is clear that Gorbachev had inculcated key parts of these beliefs. As evidence, there is his extraordinarily stubborn conviction — one he still held in late 1991 — that a more humane form of socialism was the proper framework for Soviet economic reform.[7]

In addition, as of the mid-1980s Gorbachev clearly did not see the domestic problems facing the Soviet leadership as having reached crisis proportions. In fact, the initial economic reform program articulated under his guidance in 1985–86 differed little from previous efforts. He proposed a number of changes to the existing command-administrative system but did not seek to alter it in any fundamental sense.[8]

In foreign and national-security policy, however, a different pattern emerged. By late 1985, Gorbachev and his allies in the leadership were beginning to outline a dramatically different vision of international politics and foreign policy preferences. It was a vision that rejected key elements of Marxist-Leninist ideology. Systemic theories of international relations are inadequate to explain this extraordinary change in elite preferences and, more fundamental, the normative context of Soviet international behavior. Rather, we must explore how systemic stimuli interacted with domestic politics — and, in particular, how they helped open policy windows.

By the late spring of 1984, Gorbachev was the clear heir apparent to a faltering Chernenko, and as second secretary was overseeing international affairs within the Central Committee Secretariat. Thus, anything he had to say from that time forward on foreign policy should be accorded special attention.[9] Through most of the year, however, Gorbachev did little more than reiterate the need for an improvement in Soviet-American relations, as had Chernenko. He combined calls for an improvement in East-West relations with a reiteration of many of the assumptions that had informed Soviet policy for decades.[10]

In two important speeches given in December 1984, however, Gorbachev publicly broke with the prevailing Leninist orthodoxy on foreign policy. The first was to an ideology conference and was devoted mainly to domestic matters. The foreign policy section of Gorbachev's report introduced an important nuance. In particular, he argued that "if life requires it," the CPSU should "in a timely way introduce one or another corrective to our views and practice." Indeed, earlier in the speech Gorbachev noted that a more thorough study of the processes of world development was needed and that the social sciences should undertake this task.[11]

The second speech, given a little more than a week later, was before the British Parliament. This was Gorbachev's first trip to the West after it had become clear he was a leading candidate for the top position in the Soviet Union; the trip received extensive coverage in the Soviet media.[12] The speech itself was a synthesis of old verities and new assumptions, and his description of the international system marked an important departure from the prevailing orthodoxy.

Most notable was Gorbachev's claim that the world was "constantly changing [according] to its own laws." This statement neatly undercut the assertion — long a staple of Soviet pronouncements — that the main moving force in the international arena was the class contradiction between capitalism and socialism, and it gave legitimacy to his later discussion of such non-class notions as global problems and the "interconnected" nature of the contemporary world. In the address, Gorbachev also used, for the first time, the phrase "new political thinking" — although he was vague on what it meant. The clear strength of the speech was precisely its conceptual innovation; at the level of concrete policy prescriptions, it had little new to offer.[13]

In articulating an agenda for foreign policy reform, Gorbachev had started from what a physicist would call first principles — the basic beliefs and assumptions underlying policy and behavior. Put another way, he was outlining a new policy paradigm for interpreting the USSR's international political environment.

What explains this shift in Gorbachev's beliefs and preferences? Politics is certainly not the answer. If anything, political factors should have made Gorbachev more prone to accentuate the verities of Soviet ideology. Given the overwhelmingly conservative nature of the ruling elite, it would have been risky for a new leader to portray himself as an ideological heretic. The shift is also not explicable by reference to the power of particular domestic interests. These interests — from the Ministry of Defense to the defense-industrial sector — had a great deal invested in the prevailing conflictual, balance-of-power worldview, for it gave them priority access to increasingly scarce resources.

Rather, this shift was a result of cognitive change; Gorbachev modified his foreign policy preferences as he acquired new knowledge. I am less interested in analyzing the cognitive mechanisms underlying his learning, however, than in exploring the political processes through which it occurred. This process, we now know, started in late 1983 or early 1984, when Gorbachev began consulting with individuals and institutes on foreign policy issues.[14]

The learning process, however, cannot be understood in isolation from the pressures and circumstances that defined the international context of Soviet foreign policy in the early 1980s. These realities were daunting and included a foreign adventure (the invasion of Afghanistan) that had gone wrong and brought the Soviets international condemnation; destabilization in Poland that created the greatest threat to Soviet interests in Eastern Europe since the 1968 Prague Spring; and a new Republican administration in the United States that backed its confrontational policy toward the USSR with such programs as the Strategic Defense Initiative (SDI).

In addition to this array of problems, in the last months of 1983 there was a noticeable worsening of the USSR's international position. In particular, the destruction of a Korean commercial airliner by Soviet fighter jets and the deployment of new U.S. nuclear weapons in Europe led the Soviet leadership to sharpen its attacks on the United States, while concern mounted in Moscow that international tension had reached a dangerous level. On the key issue of nuclear weapons, Soviet efforts to mobilize the Western European public against the new U.S. deployments had failed. The Soviets had left themselves little choice but to break off all arms-control talks, which they did in late November 1983. The pattern of elite commentary and Soviet behavior suggests a policy immobilized.[15]

In sum, by 1984 Soviet foreign policy had reached perhaps its lowest point in the entire post–World War II period, and at least one top elite — Gorbachev — had indicated an openness to new types of solutions to address the country's problems. An extraordinary array of international pressures had combined to create uncertainty and flux in the foreign policy beliefs and pref-

erences of Gorbachev. The cognitive search this stimulated, however, is the least interesting part of the story. To understand what it would eventually uncover—how new foreign policy preferences would be crafted—we must explore the role of ideas, the entrepreneurs who carried them, and the open policy windows they used.[16]

Ideas and Entrepreneurs

Aleksandr Yakovlev is best known for his contributions to Gorbachev's domestic political strategy, especially the policy of glasnost. Less well known is Yakovlev's critical role in shaping the new general secretary's beliefs about international politics.[17]

In the early 1980s, Yakovlev was Soviet ambassador to Canada. He was effectively in exile, having been posted to Canada in 1973 after losing a battle with conservative Russian nationalist elements within the CPSU. Before that time, he had spent most of his adult life working in the central apparatus of the party, mainly in its propaganda, science, and culture sections. In notable contrast with most career party officials, Yakovlev was well-educated, having earned a doctorate in historical sciences and the academic rank of professor. He had also spent a year as an exchange student at Columbia University in the late 1950s.[18]

In September 1983 Yakovlev was appointed head of IMEMO, an appointment that was largely a product of chance. Gorbachev had met Yakovlev during the summer of 1983 while touring Canada and the two men had hit it off. Deciding he wanted Yakovlev back in Moscow, Gorbachev inserted him into a convenient and relatively safe position (that is, not a high party or government post) that happened to be open: the directorship of IMEMO.[19]

At this point Yakovlev the entrepreneur, responding to the incentives created by the opening policy window, began to mobilize the institute to advance several radical ideas—ideas that within eighteen months began to find their way into Gorbachev's speeches. How did Yakovlev effect such mobilization? As institute researchers and Yakovlev himself recount it, he brought a more open atmosphere to IMEMO and encouraged serious, scholarly research. Indeed, within weeks after arriving at the institute, Yakovlev held a meeting of its scientific collective—the core group comprising IMEMO's intellectual and administrative leadership—where he urged researchers to be guided by "strictly scientific principles" and not by Marxist-Leninist dogma. These were bold instructions given the prevailing conservative political mood in Moscow.[20]

Equally important, during 1983–84 Yakovlev repeatedly clashed with high-

ranking CPSU officials (leading members of the C.C. Science and Education Department and Moscow City Party Chairman and Politburo member Viktor Grishin) over his stewardship of the institute. Their confrontation was all the more notable because it came less than two years after the notorious KGB-party investigation at IMEMO — an event that epitomized the CPSU's ability to interfere in institute research. By challenging both Grishin and the Central Committee, Yakovlev was reinforcing the message that Marxist dogma must not be a restraining factor within IMEMO.

The sense of renewal at the institute took other, more concrete forms. Under Yakovlev's leadership, several new sections specifically intended as forums for unorthodox, controversial views were introduced in *Memo*. In addition, Yakovlev claims that by early 1984 he had succeeded in eliminating the sole classified unit at IMEMO: the Department of Technical-Economic Research. (This department, which had existed since at least the early 1960s, conducted work for the Soviet General Staff and the KGB on the military-economic potential of the West.) These changes suggest that Yakovlev, the acknowledged mastermind of Gorbachev's later policy of glasnost, first implemented reforms in this spirit within IMEMO.[21]

Those familiar with Yakovlev's published writings before 1985 might well question these observations. Many of the writings were vitriolic, propagandistic, and anti-American. But Yakovlev himself and many IMEMO contemporaries are unanimous in asserting that his tone and approach within the institute were completely different. Moreover, a careful review of his writing during this period reveals several instances where he adopted an unorthodox approach on matters of foreign and domestic policy.[22]

Yakovlev's initial months at IMEMO suggest several factors that would be instrumental in his later success at policy entrepreneurship. First, he had direct access to a political leader whose stature was growing. As Yakovlev himself admits, this connection not only allowed him to serve as a conduit for ideas developed at IMEMO; it also provided crucial political protection for Yakovlev (and the institute) as he battled the C.C. apparatus.

Second, as the difference between Yakovlev's private and public behavior in 1983–84 suggests, he was politically adept. Yakovlev understood that given the conservative politics of those years, he could best protect IMEMO and revitalize it by public conformity. These instincts, it might be added, were surely developed during the 1960s and 1970s, when he worked in the C.C. apparatus.[23]

The point here is that Yakovlev was not just an intellectual and academic. As the literature on policy entrepreneurship might put it, he was not only

smart but clever. This key difference between Yakovlev and an earlier institute leader, Inozemtsev, also partly explains why the latter was so much less successful as an entrepreneur — even though he had strong ties to the Brezhnev leadership.

Third, the specifically Soviet organizational context of Yakovlev's entrepreneurship mattered. Students of Western organization theory might be skeptical of the above account — where a new leader, an outsider, takes charge and quickly mobilizes and revitalizes an organization of more than nine hundred research and support staff. After all, in the West, we know of endless instances where new leaders do not make a difference. In the USSR, however, the structure of the state (its autonomy and centralization) insulated organizations like IMEMO from a broad array of outside forces and consequently allowed leaders of these outfits great influence in shaping their structure and culture.[24]

In one sense, however, Yakovlev does not fit the standard description of a policy entrepreneur. He did not have a ready-made solution in need of a problem; instead, he was open to a range of new ideas and approaches on foreign policy. His only proviso was that they proceed from the realities of the contemporary world. This is a point he made publicly in several articles and speeches.[25]

More important, this public message was strengthened and reinforced by his actions within IMEMO. Sergey Blagovolin, a senior institute scholar who was close to Yakovlev, notes that he was open to new foreign policy "values." Yakovlev himself has said that he arrived at IMEMO "convinced [that] the system had to change," but his most important message was the emphasis on scholarly work free from the constraints of Marxist-Leninist dogma. As a deputy director put it, Yakovlev's most significant contribution was giving researchers carte blanche to develop new solutions for the USSR's foreign policy problems.[26]

Yakovlev's success, despite his lack of a clear vision for resolving foreign policy dilemmas, reinforced the importance of the organizational context within which he was operating. As will be seen below, he did indeed mobilize the institute and made it influential in the advent of the new thinking; but IMEMO was most mobilizable and influential only on those issues that best fit with its own long-standing ideology and beliefs about international politics.

A key to understanding Yakovlev's impact on IMEMO, then, is that he mobilized the institute to address issues that were compatible with its own embedded ideology. He was not trying to change the institute as such. Rather, he was urging a relatively competent organization to improve. This allowed Yakovlev the entrepreneur to play a greater role in shaping organizational behavior than might otherwise have been the case.[27]

Ideas and International Politics

As we have seen, beginning in late 1983 IMEMO began forcefully to advocate a radical change in prevailing Soviet understandings of international politics. Two issues, in particular, received significant attention: the correlation between class and non-class values in the world arena and interdependence. In many instances, this advocacy came in the work of senior institute scholars who were writing lead articles for *Memo*.

The clear message that emerged from the institute on class versus non-class, or universal (*obshchechelovecheskiy*); values was that the former should be subordinated to the latter. For example, two researchers noted that together with class and national interests, a new "objective category" had appeared in world politics: the interests of "the development of mankind as a whole." In the Soviet context, to call something an objective category was to denote a reality to which the USSR must adapt.

The authors clearly recognized the extent of their ideological heresy, as they managed to cite not just Marx or Engels or Lenin but all three as the source of this newly (re)discovered insight. Lenin, in particular, had purportedly recognized the priority of "the interests of social development" over "all remaining" interests. The authors hinted at the pragmatic significance of this insight for Soviet policy by declaring that it had acquired special topicality because of the scientific-technical revolution and the nuclear threat.[28]

Throughout 1984 institute scholars professed to have found an "organic connection" between socialism's class interests and interests common to humankind. This point was made by Oleg Bykov, a deputy director of IMEMO and head of its Department of International Relations, in early 1984 and was repeated word for word later in the year by a senior scholar in his department. In addition, two scholars who were not affiliated with the institute made virtually the same point (albeit in a more cautious way) in articles they contributed to *Memo*.[29]

While these distinctions might seem to have little practical significance for Soviet behavior, this was not the case. Beginning in 1986 the policy preferences of Gorbachev and other leaders shifted in ways that suggest the influence of these new understandings and concepts. In particular, support for national-liberation movements — a key class-based element of the foreign policy inherited from the Brezhnev leadership — was downgraded in both leadership statements and actual policy.

The boldness of the institute's advocacy in late 1983 and early 1984 can be appreciated only when one recalls the extremely poor state of Soviet-American relations, which were virtually frozen by the time of Andropov's

death in February 1984. Although the Chernenko leadership made efforts to bring an end to this freeze by renewing the policy of detente, these actions by no means sanctioned the ideological heresy in which institute scholars were now engaging.

On the second issue — the specific nature of the international system — the institute was equally outspoken throughout 1983–85. Here, the key concepts were interdependence and a single world economy that operated on economic laws common to both socialism and capitalism. Such concepts and their non-class framework were not new to the Soviet scene; scholars at IMEMO (and elsewhere) had accepted them for years.[30] The difference is that the language was more forceful. Furthermore, at a time when East-West relations were extremely poor, thinking and writing in such non-class terms required particular strength of conviction and/or support.

Institute researchers employed the concepts of interdependence and world economy with increasing frequency during this period. One article in March 1983 simply asserted the interdependence of states as a fact but offered no supporting commentary. Later in the year, however, Margarita Maksimova returned to a favorite topic of hers — a single world economy. Using forceful language, she explained why the concept should be understood in supra-class terms, attacked its Soviet opponents, and argued that the world had become "ever more interconnected."[31]

The lead article of the May 1984 issue of *Memo* declared that in the final account all states were "interconnected and interdependent" and that such interdependence had become "ever more stable and multi-sided." Several months later, an institute researcher returned to the concept of a single world economy and argued for a vision where "certain common economic laws" operated under both capitalism and socialism. In this aggressive, indeed combative, piece, he named and then bitterly attacked a Soviet opponent of the concept.[32]

During these years, the institute's advocacy of a non-class and empirical vision of international politics was clearly more outspoken than its interest in a revised view of national security. On the former, the advocacy was pronounced; articles favoring this vision were often written by leading IMEMO scholars and many times were placed as the lead article in *Memo*. On security, the advocacy was much less forceful, and there was less of it. Yakovlev, it would seem, had been fully able to mobilize the institute only behind a certain subset of foreign policy issues. Yet Second Secretary Gorbachev was apparently open to new ideas on a range of foreign policy questions, including security.[33]

Although the evidence on this last point is not definitive, there is a clear

correlation between Gorbachev's growing stature and power within the party leadership in the spring of 1984 and signs, which first appeared at that time, of a serious reevaluation of the Soviet approach to security.

In April and May, two middle-ranking members of the Central Committee apparatus wrote articles on the nature of contemporary security; both were published in academic journals. The articles made essentially the same point: that nuclear overabundance had rendered traditional views of security obsolete, and attempts to attain security unilaterally were no longer viable. Three months later, a book entitled *New Thinking in the Nuclear Age* advanced similar views on the changing nature of security. Regardless of whether Gorbachev was the instigator of the book or articles, he was clearly aware of the arguments they employed. As already noted, by December 1984 he was speaking in public of the need for "new thinking" in foreign and security policy.[34]

This brief digression indicates that a complete understanding of the institute's behavior as a purveyor of ideas requires an examination not only of Yakovlev's entrepreneurial role and the window available to him but of the organizational context within which he operated. Theoretical and empirical analyses of international politics were basic issues for IMEMO. It had a wealth of expertise in these areas and the promotion of a complex vision of the world had been a central element of its own ideology of international relations since the late 1960s.

It was natural that the institute would most vigorously promote those issues that allowed it to protect and extend this core sense of mission. Security questions like conventional arms control or verification had always taken a second place to broader issues of international relations. IMEMO was not a strategic studies center (like the Rand Corporation, say) but a foreign policy and economics think tank. Its understanding of its interests and its actual behavior were strongly shaped by the particular ideology embedded within it.

While this academic argumentation and bold analysis offers fascinating reading, one must still ask, Did it matter? In this case, yes. By October 1985 Gorbachev's beliefs and preferences had begun to shift dramatically, as he described the international system in language virtually identical to that employed by many of the institute scholars—often repeating parts of their analyses verbatim. Such concepts as interdependence, global problems, and non-class values had become integral to the new general secretary's ideology by October 1986.[35]

Indeed, a review of Gorbachev's commentary during these years reveals a striking change in his understanding of the dynamics shaping international politics. In the fall of 1985, he expanded upon the revisionist foreign policy concepts he had first (vaguely) articulated while visiting Great Britain a year

earlier. During a trip to France, Gorbachev portrayed the international system in essentially non-class terms, using forceful terminology. There was a "reality" all people had to accept: the world had become "ever more closely interconnected and interdependent." He then explained that this condition had arisen because of the development of international economic ties, scientific-technical progress, and the accelerating exchange of information.[36]

These innovative views served as a prelude for the bold and forceful speech Gorbachev gave to the 27th Party Congress in February 1986. In the opening moments of his report, Gorbachev declared that the changes in the contemporary world were so profound that they required a "rethinking and comprehensive analysis" of all the factors influencing global development.

Later in the report, Gorbachev expanded upon concepts articulated in previous months; his comments indicated a clear shift in preferences. He forcefully reiterated that global problems were a reality to which Soviet policy must adapt and that cooperation among states to resolve such problems had become a "categorical demand" of the times. Gorbachev again stressed the complex, interdependent nature of the contemporary international system.[37]

At the Congress, Gorbachev also addressed the nature of security. Here as well, his comments were bold and detailed. In particular, he argued that reliance on military means for insuring security was no longer possible and that political methods therefore had growing significance. Moreover, in the context of U.S.-Soviet relations, security could be maintained only if it was mutual.

As if to make clear that he was articulating a new paradigm for Soviet international behavior, Gorbachev followed his innovative comments on interdependence, the nature of security, and the like with a strong attack on the foreign policy pursued by his immediate predecessors. Continuity in foreign policy, he declared, has "nothing in common with the simple repetition of what has been done before, especially in the approaches to problems that have been mounting up." Implicitly drawing a contrast with the approach favored by Brezhnev and others, Gorbachev argued in favor of a new framework for understanding international politics, one that proceeded from the "realities of the contemporary world."[38]

Gorbachev's address to the Congress was meant to signal a clear shift in the dominant paradigm informing Soviet foreign policy. Significantly, his comments were made to the highest tribune of the CPSU, not to a foreign audience. Equally important, most of Gorbachev's comments on foreign and security policy were reflected in the resolutions of the Congress.[39]

As of mid-1986, however, this new paradigm was still coexisting uneasily with elements of the old Leninist worldview. While its class-based essence had

been implicitly weakened by references to interdependence and global problems, notions of class and class conflict had yet to be refuted explicitly. This changed in the fall of 1986, when Gorbachev publicly and pointedly addressed the correlation of class and non-class values in Soviet foreign policy.

Echoing many analysts at IMEMO, Gorbachev gave precedence to non-class values as the guide for Soviet international behavior. He asserted the priority of universal values (that is, non-class values) over the interests of any particular class. In making this claim, Gorbachev even managed to cite Lenin in support. Central Committee Secretary Dobrynin and Politburo member Ligachev soon echoed the general secretary on the priority of non-class values, thus reinforcing the impression that a sea change was under way in Soviet foreign behavior.[40]

My analysis to this point suggests the importance of a historical institutionalist approach, which is crucial for understanding the content of the new policy paradigm adopted by Gorbachev. Yakovlev, the entrepreneur, served as the conduit for transmitting a set of ideas historically embedded at IMEMO to the new general secretary.

Yet to explain the process through which this paradigm was being empowered politically, we must also consider the centralization and autonomy of the Soviet state. In particular, once Gorbachev had adopted the new political thinking, its diffusion and dissemination were more readily accomplished (than in a more pluralist setting) because of the extraordinary agenda-setting powers and control over media resources held by the top elites.[41]

Thus, throughout 1986 Gorbachev and his allies in the political leadership employed the significant resources at their disposal to diffuse these principles of a radically new policy paradigm.[42] This was accomplished through a number of mechanisms. First, Gorbachev, as well as other members of the leadership, continually reiterated, in the months after the Congress, the key themes of the new political thinking. Second, the central press mounted a vigorous campaign to promote the need for new approaches and new thinking in foreign policy.[43]

Third, in the wake of the Congress, the two ranking party members who oversaw foreign policy forcefully argued the need for new thinking. In late April, Foreign Minister and Politburo member Eduard Shevardnadze spoke on the anniversary of Lenin's birth, an occasion traditionally reserved for important statements by the party leadership. The speech, which was published on the front page of *Pravda,* served again to disseminate the key themes of the new thinking.

Shevardnadze also mobilized the broadest possible audience with his declaration that Soviet foreign policy should take a scientific approach toward

various international problems. As we have seen, for scholars at IMEMO (and elsewhere) such an approach was synonymous with a greater empirical emphasis in Soviet policy that required greater inputs from the academic community into the policy process. Shevardnadze, in other words, was seeking the community's help in elaborating a new foreign policy paradigm.[44]

Far less indirect than Shevardnadze's attempt at mobilization was the address given approximately a month later by C.C. secretary and International Department head Anatoliy Dobrynin. Speaking at a specially convened conference of academic analysts, Dobrynin made it explicit that the leadership wished for researchers at IMEMO and elsewhere to elaborate and advance the new thinking. He praised various institutes within the Academy of Sciences for developing expertise on a wide range of foreign policy and military problems but noted that there was a need for even more research. His language was particularly forceful: "The Party and government expect from Soviet academics — especially those who study international relations, foreign policy and military-political problems — new, serious works. Life itself demands that this entire branch of science be raised to a qualitatively new level." Dobrynin then spent several minutes outlining a research agenda that signaled the leadership's willingness to sanction studies by social scientists on a broad range of foreign policy and security issues, which he said were in need of "rapid scientific analysis." Dobrynin was clearly not just speaking his own mind; his contribution to the conference proceedings was reprinted as one of the lead articles in a June issue of *Kommunist*.[45]

The above suggests that leadership — in the centralized and authoritarian Soviet state — was therefore indispensable in the consolidation of a new set of ideas. Here I differ from Kathryn Sikkink, who suggests that individuals play a key role only in the initial adoption of new ideas. The difference stems from the institutional structure of the countries we studied. Sikkink looked at strong presidential systems in Latin America; I explored an extraordinarily insulated authoritarian polity.[46]

Ideas and (Capitalist) Political Economy

As of mid-1987, however, a key element of the old foreign policy paradigm had yet to be questioned by the leadership. Gorbachev and other leaders continued to speak of capitalism in much the same way as the leadership had in the bad old days of zastoy under Brezhnev. Gorbachev, in particular, seemed curiously dogmatic on this subject, continuing to talk of imperialism's inherently aggressive nature and the growth of militarism in capitalist societies.[47]

A dramatic change occurred in late 1987. At a major party gathering, Gor-

bachev turned the Leninist theory of imperialism on its head by suggesting that, yes, contemporary capitalism could free itself of militarism and its neo-colonial tendency to exploit the developing world. How is one to understand the dramatic shift in the general secretary's beliefs and preferences? Several explanations come to mind. One is that Gorbachev acted in a rational, self-interested manner: he needed a benign portrayal of capitalism (and, by implication, of America) to legitimate the more cooperative approach to insuring Soviet national security he had announced at the 27th Party Congress. After all, why attempt a more cooperative approach if your chief adversary is inherently prone to aggression and reliance on military force?[48]

There is a second possible interest-based reason for Gorbachev's embrace of a new image of capitalism. Simply put, by 1987 Gorbachev had finally lost his naive optimism concerning the state of the Soviet economy and was looking for ways to pare the burdensome Soviet defense budget. A benign image of the capitalist adversary would certainly make it easier to implement such reductions. In either case, ideas would be mere tools of convenience, which Gorbachev adopted for instrumental reasons that reflected political calculation on his part.

While self-interested behavior may have contributed to the introduction of the revised image of the capitalist adversary, there are problems with these explanations. For one, they cannot explain the content of Gorbachev's new beliefs and preferences regarding the capitalist adversary. Why were these particular ideas adopted over others? More important, interest-based explanations posit a logic and rationality that were not present in the increasingly tumultuous sociopolitical atmosphere of the USSR. This state of unrest, in which ideas, policies, and attacks came from all parts of the political spectrum, applied to the evolution of Soviet foreign policy as well.[49]

In other words, both domestic and international circumstances were inducing Gorbachev and other elites to make wide-ranging cognitive searches. In such situations, ideas are likely to have greater influence over the formation of preferences and beliefs as individuals "puzzle"; they are not merely epiphenomena.[50]

According to my argument, such a turbulent policy environment should provide continuing incentives for entrepreneurs to act. This is precisely what happened. And a key entrepreneur was the new head of IMEMO, Yevgeniy Primakov. Exploiting an open policy window and his close personal ties to Gorbachev's circle of advisers, Primakov revitalized and mobilized IMEMO in ways even more far-reaching than those of Yakovlev, and he swayed the general secretary's beliefs on a fundamental issue: the (peaceful) political economy of contemporary capitalism. Before I discuss how, it is important to say a little

about Primakov himself — his impact on IMEMO, the solution looking for a problem he peddled, his ties to Gorbachev, and the open window he successfully used.

Primakov was appointed head of IMEMO in late 1985.[51] In contrast to Yakovlev, he was no outsider to the institute, having spent seven years in the mid-1970s as one of its deputy directors. Like Yakovlev, however, Primakov had intellectual and academic credentials; he was elected a full member of the Academy of Sciences in 1979. His scholarly work — mainly on the Middle East and the developing world — was respected and had often stretched the limits of official Soviet dogma.[52]

Under Primakov, IMEMO was more aggressive than ever in defining and promoting its ideas. Two factors were at work here. First, the domestic reforms Gorbachev was implementing were radically changing the environment within which organizations like IMEMO operated. In contrast with 1982, for example, virtually no constraints remained on the institute's behavior. In fact, the open debates fostered by the policy of glasnost rewarded greater organizational assertiveness.

Second, while Primakov was clearly as intent as Yakovlev on mobilizing IMEMO to back up and substantiate the arguments he was presenting to Gorbachev in private, he also seemed willing to countenance a redefinition of the institute's mission. He mobilized researchers to move beyond issues that fit IMEMO's embedded ideology and took steps to legitimate the study of security issues. Indeed, Primakov's early years at the institute saw the creation of several new departments, most important, a Department of Disarmament and International Security.

His impact was seen in other ways as well. For one, *Memo* became even bolder than it had been in 1983–85. New rubrics were introduced; articles by prominent foreigners were published; there was even a reader survey that could be torn out and mailed back to the institute. In addition, Primakov continued the two rubrics begun by Yakovlev that had often carried advocacy articles.

The sense one gets from these various changes was that Primakov was determined to revitalize the institute. Deputy directors and senior researchers alike describe Primakov's influence on IMEMO in just such terms. They praise the more open and democratic atmosphere he established. Moreover, in a move whose symbolism is impossible to ignore, Primakov appointed German Diligenskiy editor-in-chief of *Memo*.[53]

Diligenskiy had a reputation as a radical within IMEMO — he was respected for his research creativity and fierce independent streak. Of even greater importance was the fact that he had lost his position at IMEMO during the 1982

KGB-party investigation. Thus, an outcast, formerly labeled a dissident, was now overseeing IMEMO's most important publication.

Primakov the policy entrepreneur appears to have had several factors working in his favor. First, he was an assertive organizational leader who knew the institute well. Whereas Yakovlev had been content to take a hands-off approach to its research agenda, Primakov was a much "tougher" leader with a strong sense of what he wanted done. Second, like Yakovlev, Primakov combined scholarship with political skills. This allowed him speedily to take advantage of emerging policy windows.[54]

Third, Primakov had good ties to Yakovlev and hence to Gorbachev. Indeed, it was Yakovlev who personally recommended to Gorbachev that Primakov succeed him at IMEMO. Several interviewees went so far as to describe Primakov and Yakovlev as a team, working to advance foreign policy reform throughout Primakov's years at IMEMO.[55]

Finally, Primakov's entrepreneurship, like Yakovlev's, benefited from the Soviet organizational context in which he operated. This observation might surprise some readers. After all, during the years of Primakov's tenure at IMEMO (1985–88), a clear evolution occurred in state-society relations as the policy of glasnost took hold. The Soviet state was becoming less autonomous. But this process varied according to the issue area, and it was much less rapid in the foreign and national-security policy arenas.[56] This relatively insulated policy environment allowed Primakov to exert considerable influence on IMEMO.

During the first full year of his tenure at IMEMO, Primakov published a series of articles. They served two purposes: promoting the new foreign policy paradigm being articulated by Gorbachev and other top leaders; and advancing certain ideas that further refined it. These "new" ideas, it should be added, were consistent with IMEMO's own long-standing beliefs and interests.

Major articles by Primakov appeared in *Pravda* one month before the Party Congress in 1986 and again a week after its close. More important than the timing was their content. In these articles, Primakov delineated all the basic principles of what would eventually become the new political thinking. The content and high visibility of the articles confirm what is known from other sources: by early 1986, Primakov had become a close adviser to Gorbachev.[57]

One idea that Primakov the entrepreneur was motivated to advance was the need for a drastic revision in Soviet beliefs about capitalist political economy—both its internal (economic) and external (foreign policy) components. Several factors helped create and open his policy window. Most important was the presence (as had been the case for Yakovlev several years earlier) of political leaders willing to listen to new ideas. The problem available for

exploitation was the lack of credibility of the CPSU's two most recent authoritative statements on capitalism.

Both Gorbachev's report (which was innovative on a host of other foreign policy issues) to the 27th Party Congress and the new edition of the Third Party Program adopted at that same meeting were out of touch with a variety of signals coming from the USSR's international environment. These included the capitalist West's continuing success at adapting to the scientific-technical revolution and the fact that the "Reagan revolution" in America had served — contrary to Soviet predictions — as a stimulus for economic growth. These incongruities were clearly appreciated by Primakov.[58]

Here, again, one sees the critical role played by the international environment. Primakov the entrepreneur had a window precisely because these international variables allowed him — in the Soviet domestic political milieu — to promote his solution looking for a problem. Put another way, international factors were clearly affecting domestic politics. They did so, however, not in any predetermined, rationalistic way; rather, they acted as a trigger, stimulating a process of change.

The point Primakov repeatedly made about capitalism was that despite a variety of problems, capitalist systems were still capable of significant economic growth. The new institute leader almost sounded like a convert with his talk of venture capital and the micro-electronic revolution. He was clearly impressed by how successfully the capitalist West had adapted to the scientific-technical revolution.[59]

On the particular question of militarism and its relation to capitalism, Primakov attacked the notion that capitalism "organically cannot exist without militarism" — pointing to the nonmilitarized politics and economies of Japan and Western European countries. He then argued that even large and militarily powerful capitalist states could reverse the militarization of their polities. This, in turn, would reduce the influence of the most reactionary elements over foreign policy decisions.

Primakov mentioned no particular country, but it was quite clear that his reference was to such countries as the United States, Great Britain, and Germany. It was necessary, he argued, "to raise the question of the possible reversibility of the militarization of the economy, even in those capitalist countries where it has attained serious development." The logic was clear: if countries like the United States could outgrow militarism, they could come to adopt a less aggressive foreign policy posture.[60]

As it turned out, IMEMO needed little prodding by Primakov to address the political economy of capitalism. Revisionist views on the topic had been an important part of the institute's ideology of international affairs since at least

the mid-1960s. In mid-1986, however, institute advocacy on the question increased significantly with the introduction of a series of articles in *Memo* on the theory of state-monopoly capitalism and the organization of a conference to examine the Soviet framework for interpreting capitalist foreign policy behavior.[61]

The articles on state-monopoly capitalism addressed the internal, economic component of capitalist political economy. As an indication of the extent to which this focus coincided with the institute's ideology, the series became one of the most extensive ever published in *Memo* on a single topic.[62]

The analyses were heavily empirical. Their starting point was the fact that many of the processes occurring in contemporary capitalist economies (privatization and deregulation, for example) found no reflection in the Soviet theory of state-monopoly capitalism. The article summarizing the entire series was radical. It attacked the notion of nationalization and — resurrecting an institute viewpoint from the late 1960s — argued that the state was not a tool of the ruling class but an independent arbitrator of various interests.[63]

The institute also quickly responded to Primakov's call for a reevaluation of Soviet beliefs on capitalist foreign policy behavior. The issue raised by institute scholars was whether militarism and the aggressive policy it produced were inherent in the capitalist socioeconomic system. The analysis was at first extremely cautious, in part because the concept of militarism was central to Lenin's theory of imperialism, the ideological framework for interpreting capitalist foreign policy behavior. In one case, a deputy director of the institute hinted that militarism might not be a permanent feature of capitalism, cautiously describing his comments as "points for discussion."[64]

By the early spring of 1987, Primakov and other institute scholars had clearly identified the barrier to any truly radical revision of the framework for explaining capitalist foreign policy behavior. This was the claim of Leninist theory that aggression and militarism were inherent in the capitalist socioeconomic system. In March, IMEMO took on precisely this issue, in a bold and visible way. The institute helped organize a conference on "Contemporary Features of the General Crisis of Capitalism," whose proceedings were reported extensively in four different issues of *Memo* through 1987. One of the key agenda topics was the relation of militarism to capitalism.[65]

The overall tone of the conference was set by the opening speeches of Primakov and Petr Fedoseyev (a vice president of the Academy of Sciences). Fedoseyev asked directly to what degree militarism was inherent in contemporary capitalist society. He provided no answer, but urged "serious, comprehensive research" into the matter. Primakov went much farther, declaring that key aspects of Lenin's 1917 essay on imperialism were no longer applicable.[66]

Many IMEMO analysts (as well as conference participants from several other academic organizations) addressed the relation of capitalism to militarism. The bottom line of this advocacy was as simple as it was revolutionary in the Soviet context. Capitalism had an internal vitality that would allow it to maintain more than adequate levels of economic growth for the foreseeable future, and its external behavior posed no threat to the USSR.[67]

These conclusions were simply the logical extension of core beliefs on the nature of capitalism developed at IMEMO over many years. It thus comes as no surprise that institute analysts were so ready to advocate their views on such issues. Indeed, in response to Primakov's comments, several participants offered detailed and empirical justifications of why capitalism could, in effect, outgrow militarism.

There is a striking correlation between this IMEMO-Primakov analysis and the commentary about the nature of capitalism that Gorbachev first used in November 1987. Primakov had mobilized the institute on a topic that was consistent with its own ideology and then presented these arguments to a puzzling and skeptical Gorbachev.[68] This combination of organizational ideology and entrepreneurial access to top leaders created a powerful counterweight to the orthodox beliefs about capitalism that were still being articulated by groups like the Soviet military.[69]

Indeed, by November 1987 Gorbachev was talking about capitalism in a manner that signaled yet another important change in his preferences and, more generally, a paradigm shift in the normative context of Soviet international behavior. In a major speech given on the seventieth anniversary of the Bolshevik revolution, Gorbachev raised a series of "difficult questions" about capitalism. These included whether external factors could constrain its aggressive nature; its relation to militarism; and whether capitalist countries could develop an equitable relationship with the developing world.[70]

Gorbachev's answers showed the influence on his thinking of the non-class interpretative framework of the new policy paradigm. He argued, for example, that imperialism's aggression would be restrained not by the power of the world socialist community but by the "new level of interdependence and integralness" of the world.[71] More important, Gorbachev suggested that developments in the domestic political economy of capitalism were reducing the danger of militarism. Like many analysts at IMEMO, he pointed to the postwar economic miracles of Japan, West Germany, and Italy as examples of a capitalism that had thrived without a militarization of the economy. Employing this same non-class framework, Gorbachev even suggested that the main capitalist power — the United States — could outgrow militarism. In other words, militarism and external aggression, which Lenin had seen as permanent features of capitalism, were in fact transitory phenomena.[72]

As had been the case with other elements of the new foreign policy paradigm, the political leadership exploited its centralized powers to diffuse this new framework for interpreting capitalist foreign policy behavior. Articles addressing the new relation of capitalism to militarism quickly began to appear in the central press. Moreover, Gorbachev himself again raised the issue in his speech to the February 1988 Central Committee plenum.[73]

More generally, throughout 1987 Gorbachev and his political allies continued to exploit the powers of the Soviet state to diffuse and consolidate the central elements of this new liberal foreign policy framework. The key role was played by Yakovlev, who by June 1987 had become a full member of the Politburo. His responsibilities included formal oversight of science and propaganda; informally, he also played a major role in foreign policy. In a series of speeches, Yakovlev urged Soviet social scientists to avoid ideological dogma (that is, the old interpretative framework) in their research on the contemporary world and instead to employ the concepts and categories of the new paradigm.[74]

One speech more than any other made it clear that Yakovlev, with the backing of Gorbachev and his allies, sought to mobilize support for the new thinking. Addressing the Social Sciences Section of the Presidium of the USSR Academy of Sciences in April 1987, Yakovlev tore down one dogma after another relating to domestic and foreign policy — for example, on the nature of contradictions in the contemporary world and on the allowable forms of property ownership under socialism. It was no accident that various portions of this speech were reprinted in *Kommunist, Pravda,* and *Vestnik Akademii Nauk SSSR* (the main journal of the Academy of Sciences).

In the speech, Yakovlev touched on several issues of foreign and security policy. He bitterly attacked the old framework for interpreting international politics, noting that the "objective laws of socialism were often conceived outside the context of world development." More specifically, he called on Soviet scientists-internationalists — a reference to analysts at organizations like IMEMO — to elaborate further and give operational meaning to central elements of the new foreign policy paradigm.[75]

What mobilizing effect did Yakovlev's speech have? Tat'yana Zaslavskaya, a leading social scientist and Gorbachev adviser, has referred to it as "a revolutionary lecture" that undercut old dogmas and cleared the way for new ideas. According to the Yakovlev aide who helped draft the address, it was indeed designed to mobilize the academic community.[76]

The leadership, in other words, wanted these specialists to disseminate and elaborate core aspects of the new foreign policy framework. Numerous analysts were given space in the central media to respond to the new thinking. Not surprisingly, their elaboration of the basic categories (interdependence, global

problems, mutual security, universal values, and the like) of the new approach in foreign policy was sharper and more forceful than in 1986. At the same time, a number of top elites continued to promote various elements of the new political thinking.[77]

It should be noted that, as of late 1987, there was little public top-level disagreement over the new approach to foreign policy. Yegor Ligachev, who would later harshly attack central elements of the new paradigm, did not speak out on issues of foreign policy. During a wide-ranging interview in December 1987, for example, he never brought up foreign policy and seemed content to leave such matters to Gorbachev.[78]

Moreover, even in the privacy of the Politburo, there were evidently few debates at this point over the new ideas on foreign policy. The elite conflict that did erupt in these early years of Gorbachev's tenure as general secretary was primarily over domestic issues. Indeed, all seven Central Committee plenums held during 1985–87 addressed various domestic socioeconomic questions; none dealt with foreign affairs.[79] This relative absence of political conflict allowed ideas — the new foreign policy paradigm — to exert greater influence on preferences and policy than would be the case in later years.[80]

In sum, there is solid evidence that by early 1988 radically new ideas on international politics had made it to the top in the Soviet Union, shaping the beliefs and preferences of key leaders. New ideas on the structure of the international system and capitalist political economy had triumphed over Leninist dogma and those powerful political actors with an interest in maintaining the old worldview. This victory, however, had not been inevitable. It resulted from the efforts of skillful policy entrepreneurs who had a mobilizable organizational ideology at their disposal, as well as access to reformist political leaders.

The broader structure of the Soviet state gave these leaders, in turn, access to a broad range of mechanisms for disseminating the new ideas. The autonomous and authoritarian Soviet state, which for so many years had blocked the diffusion of ideas "from below," eventually became the vehicle for their political empowerment. The centralized nature of the Soviet foreign policy process had allowed Gorbachev and his allies to reach out and around conservative actors with a stake in the existing dogma. This, indeed, is an irony of state strength — the strong state feeding, as it where, on itself.

While this case study provides clear evidence that new ideas on international politics had reached the top levels of the Soviet political system, more needs to be said about how I explain this process. To this point, my analysis has largely been correlational. The issues IMEMO actively promoted during Yakovlev's tenure (1983–85) and the early part of Primakov's institute leadership (1985–

87) correlate well with the three central elements of the new foreign policy paradigm articulated by Gorbachev and other elites. They include a revised understanding of the international system (interdependence, global problems); a new goal structure for foreign policy (priority of non-class over class interests); and a new understanding of capitalism. But, of course, a correlation is not the same thing as a causal explanation.

My consideration of alternative explanations in chapter 1 and use of interview data, however, allow me to move substantially beyond a statement of correlation. Most important, Yakovlev and others interviewed confirm that both he and Primakov acted as conduits for new ideas to a Gorbachev involved in a wide-ranging information search.[81]

This transmission process worked in several ways. First, formal reports were prepared at IMEMO on a range of foreign policy issues and brought to Gorbachev's attention. Indeed, immediately upon his arrival at IMEMO, Yakovlev formed a group of ten to fifteen institute scholars to prepare such reports for Gorbachev. These addressed ideological issues (such as the correlation of class and non-class values in foreign policy) and military-political questions, and they were often deemed so sensitive that Yakovlev personally handed them to Gorbachev.[82]

Second, many less formal, personal memos were prepared for Gorbachev at IMEMO. According to Yakovlev, the fundamental revisions to ideology that eventually became key elements of the new foreign policy paradigm were deemed too sensitive for formal reports and were instead raised in such memos. Third, by early 1985 the foreign policy sections of most of Gorbachev's speeches were being written by researchers at IMEMO. Finally, personal contacts were also key. In particular, after he left IMEMO, Yakovlev would often call Primakov or other researchers at the institute, seeking reports or advice.[83]

Ideas and International Security

On questions of international security (the balance of conventional forces, evaluations of strategic stability, nuclear doctrine and strategy, and the like), a new relation between ideas and the political process would, at least for IMEMO, be more difficult to establish than in other issue areas. This difficulty certainly did not arise from a lack of interest among the political leadership in civilian analyses of security. Beginning in mid-1986, Gorbachev and his allies in the leadership had explicitly and publicly stated that they wanted studies of this type.[84]

Moreover, there were several security issues that could be defined as major problems for the USSR at this point (most prominently, the NATO missile

deployments). In other words, a policy window was open in this issue area as well.

Instead, IMEMO's difficulty in entering the security policy process arose from several other variables at the political and, especially, organizational levels. It is clear that through 1986 the institute had been unable to gain access to important political leaders for the discussion of security issues; this contrasted notably with IMEMO's success regarding other policy areas. The leadership at this point was in fact relying on another group of Soviet specialists for advice and information on security topics.[85]

Even if they had had the necessary access, however, the researchers at IMEMO were poorly equipped to use it. Practical applications of security policy did not fit in with the institute's sense of mission, and as a result they occupied only a minor place in its ideology of international affairs. This alone suggests that any attempt to expand IMEMO's conceptual repertoire or analytic expertise to security matters might prove to be difficult.

During the period of mobilization under Yakovlev, IMEMO aggressively promoted its views on several topics but did not engage in advocacy on several others. Specific questions of international security (military strategy or arms-control verification) received little attention, for example.

This is puzzling not only because the announcement of the SDI program and the commencement of the European missile deployments — both in 1983 — should have created exploitable policy windows but because Yakovlev, the entrepreneur with no fixed personal agenda, had by late 1983 created a new disarmament unit within the institute specifically to mobilize IMEMO on security issues.[86] The head of the new section, Aleksey Arbatov, was a capable analyst of strategic issues; by the mid-1980s, he had a solid publications record on military-strategic questions.[87]

At IMEMO, however, Arbatov was hindered by the lack of organizational interest, resources, and expertise on security issues. The institute had a weakly developed scientific-technical culture, as well as a long-standing unwillingness to seek contacts with groups in the USSR and abroad who studied international security.[88]

The strength of the organizational constraints becomes even more apparent in the period under Primakov's leadership, when IMEMO was influential in both promoting and revising Gorbachev's new foreign policy paradigm. Political leaders were now openly calling for academic analyses on security topics, and by 1987 debate was public and heated over two major issues: the overall size of the Soviet force posture ("reasonable sufficiency") and whether the armed forces should be restructured on more defensive principles ("defensive defense").[89]

To aid IMEMO's participation in this debate, Primakov took two steps. First, in 1986 he upgraded the institute's security-studies section to the full-fledged Department of Disarmament and International Security, keeping Aleksey Arbatov as its head. This placed security studies — for the first time — on a par with other issue areas on IMEMO's research agenda.

Second, beginning in mid-1987, Primakov himself began to publish and speak on such security issues as sufficiency. In this attempt to mobilize IMEMO and redefine its sense of mission, Primakov achieved something of a breakthrough. In the sixteen years covered by this book, he was the first IMEMO director to publicly address specific security issues.[90]

In spite of Primakov's efforts and the skills of Arbatov, IMEMO on the whole remained an uninfluential player in the security debates. Arbatov himself appears to have been an entrepreneur who was motivated to act by open policy windows. Several factors should have worked in favor of his entrepreneurial success: significant expertise on strategic issues; connections to important actors in the process (his father, Georgiy Arbatov, as well as Primakov); extant problems for which he could offer solutions; and politicians in power who were open to new ideas. Yet he failed to convert these entrepreneurial resources into influence, even with the clear backing of his boss, Primakov.[91]

A key factor behind this failure was that Arbatov, in bringing strategic-affairs expertise to IMEMO, challenged the institute's understanding of its interests — an understanding shaped by its ideology of international politics. Military issues were addressed at the institute, but usually from a broader political and economic perspective. They were not typically analyzed from a military-technical point of view, where the focus might be military factors affecting strategic stability or technical aspects of arms-control verification. It was precisely this latter approach, however, that was Arbatov's analytic strength.[92]

The mismatch between organizational ideology and individual approach at IMEMO explains why Arbatov was unable to find a ready cadre of strategic analysts within the institute, as well as why his entrepreneurship was openly and actively resisted by a series of institute scholars. The basic charge they leveled against Arbatov was that he was leading IMEMO away from what it did best. The wide coverage of this dispute in the institute's journal suggests the strong feelings it generated. In sum, Arbatov was in no sense a free agent. He was acting within an organizational context and history — one that hindered his ability to bring new strategic-affairs ideas to IMEMO and the broader political process.[93]

Do we need this analysis of the organizational structure and ideology within IMEMO to explain its inability to assume a major role in the security-policy

process? Many Western scholars have pointed out that IMEMO, like all Soviet civilian research institutes, suffered from the military's monopoly of national-security expertise and information during the Brezhnev era. This handicap is significant, but by itself it is insufficient to account for IMEMO's failure. If the military's monopoly on security expertise was the main factor at work here, one would expect other academy units — especially the other main international affairs unit, ISKAN — to be similarly affected. However, this was not the case. Throughout the latter half of the 1980s, ISKAN consistently proved itself a more knowledgeable and influential participant in the Soviet security debates than IMEMO. The USA Institute, like IMEMO, had a talented researcher motivated by the USSR's changing international environment to assume the role of policy entrepreneur on security matters. This individual, Andrey Kokoshin, was given a powerful assist by a more facilitating organizational environment than Arbatov had at IMEMO.[94]

The comparison between Arbatov at IMEMO and Kokoshin at ISKAN, as well as the record of Yakovlev, Primakov, and IMEMO's success and starkly different behavior in other issue areas, confirm that although individual entrepreneurs and their ideas do indeed play critical roles in making revolutions, they often do so in organizational settings that can constrain or magnify their ability "to affect the flow of history."[95]

Ideas, the Soviet State, and Foreign Policy Behavior

My analysis to this point has examined the empowerment of a particular set of ideas under Gorbachev — ideas that reshaped the preferences and beliefs of key leaders. The next step is to explore whether these ideas affected actual foreign policy behavior. Both theoretical logic and empirical evidence suggest that they did.

My theoretical argument was outlined in Part I and can briefly be summarized here. We would expect that in states that lack intermediate associations (political parties, organized interest group lobbies, and the like) linking government and society, elite decision makers would play an enhanced role in shaping outcomes. Such associations were clearly missing in the USSR under Brezhnev (and earlier leaders), and this was still the case during the early years of the Gorbachev era. While it is true that by 1988 a large number of informal groups had appeared, most were cultural and civic associations that were not particularly engaged in the political process. Moreover, very few concerned themselves with foreign or national security policy.[96]

Empirically, there is abundant evidence that the preferences and beliefs of top elites — the general secretary and, under Gorbachev, the Soviet president —

played a crucial role in bringing about policy change. This seems to have been especially true in foreign and security policy, and remained the case through the early years of Gorbachev's tenure. Interview data and other sources confirm the common wisdom that Gorbachev himself was essential in bringing about fundamental foreign policy change. To start with, he was a forceful public agenda setter, and he used this skill both to diffuse the new policy paradigm and to mobilize others to address it in more detail.[97]

Moreover, in private as well as public settings, Gorbachev communicated his commitment to the new foreign policy ideas. At Politburo meetings, sessions of the Presidential Council, and other top-level gatherings, he insisted that such ideas and the interpretative framework they formed should have real policy consequences. Before the late 1985 Geneva Summit meeting, for example, and later in a "secret speech" at the Soviet Foreign Ministry in May 1986, Gorbachev forcefully asserted to top policymakers that new ideas should inform actual policy. As one member of Gorbachev's inner circle has argued, fundamental change in the authoritarian Soviet political system could occur only with the active encouragement and support of the top leader.[98]

If Gorbachev and his associates did play such an important role, can one take the next step and argue that their actions were informed by the new foreign policy paradigm? Recall that a foreign policy paradigm is an interpretative framework of ideas and norms that specifies the nature of the problems decision makers face, the goals of policy, and the sorts of instruments that should be used to attain them. In other words, it is a set of ideas that gives decision makers a road map for interpreting international politics and defining national interests, as well as a sense for the proper instruments to use in promoting those interests.[99]

In key respects, the liberal set of foreign policy ideas articulated by the Gorbachev leadership does fit this definition of a policy paradigm. It specified a new framework for interpreting international politics (interdependence, globalization, and a benign capitalist adversary) and a goal structure for Soviet policy (promoting universal values and mutual security). These new goals, in turn, legitimized new policy instruments like arms control and international organizations. State interests, as well, were debated and reinterpreted. Old notions of economic autarky and unilateral security were replaced by a new set of interests — stressing integration with the economic and security structures of the industrialized West — that were congruent with the normative bases of the new paradigm.[100]

The question then remains: Did the adoption of this paradigm lead to new patterns of Soviet international behavior? The record suggests that it did; policy began to change in fundamental ways in late 1985. A new, more positive

approach toward nuclear and, eventually, conventional arms control (premised on the need for mutual security) was accompanied by a dramatic reorientation of foreign economic policy (premised on the need for greater Soviet integration into the institutions and processes of an interdependent world economy); and both were followed by the decision to let Eastern Europe go (premised on a fundamentally revised notion of the capitalist threat). Yakovlev, the central architect of the Gorbachev-era reforms, forcefully argues that a change of interpretative context — a new policy paradigm — was a fundamental and necessary prerequisite for these radical shifts in interests and behavior.[101]

It is absurd to attribute changes of such magnitude and import to internal politics or to explain them as a rational, self-interested response to external stimuli. On the latter, William Wohlforth has offered an intelligent defense of realism's ability to explain the end of the Cold War, with his emphasis — similar to my own — on the critical importance of the international environment in promoting radical Soviet policy change. However, we differ over the degree of intentionality in any such response. My argument places much greater stress on the contingencies and uncertainties in this process and on how these created openings for ideas to exert a causal influence. Moreover, by emphasizing the importance of perceptions and introducing other domestic-level variables, it is ultimately not clear whether Wohlforth's analysis is consistent with the theoretical core of realism.[102]

In this chapter, I focused on the early years of the Gorbachev era, exploring the process through which a new foreign policy paradigm was adopted, as well as initial attempts at diffusing and consolidating it. I argued that the broader institutional structure of the Soviet state allowed elites to circumvent extant (and strong) domestic actors who had a stake in the old paradigm, as these elites sought to promote the new one.

Indeed, in executing this end-around strategy, Gorbachev and his allies used a number of traditional mechanisms of Soviet politics. These included centrally guided press campaigns to promote the new thinking in its formative years, a clear effort to mobilize the Soviet academic community in support of it, and the use of appointment powers to place supporters of the new approach in key Party and state positions (Dobrynin as International Department head, Shevardnadze as Foreign Minister, Yakovlev and Primakov as key foreign policy advisers — to name just a few).

During these years, this strategy worked. The new political thinking had a far-reaching impact on Soviet international behavior, and it did much to insure that the Cold War came to an unexpected and peaceful end. By 1990–91, and

especially in the post-Soviet period, however, such a strategy became increasingly problematic, as the institutional logic behind it began to change. In the centralized Soviet state, with numerous resources and controls at their disposal, Gorbachev and his allies had few incentives to institutionalize the new approach to foreign affairs. Yet institutionalization is necessary if policy change and the ideas informing it are to endure and remain influential after its initial sponsor(s) leave office.

The process of institutionalization takes place in two ways. In the near term, it occurs through organizations, as new groups are created or existing agencies revamped. While changing an existing organization is difficult, it is possible, and it often occurs through a combination of enlightened leadership, changes in hiring and promotion practices, and the inculcation of a new organizational ethos or ideology. Over the longer term, institutionalization denotes a process whereby earlier changes influence the terms of political debate and the normative/legal context of policymaking.[103]

In Gorbachev's USSR, the Foreign Ministry under Shevardnadze was the most likely target for a near-term strategy of institutionalization. Yet there is little evidence that Gorbachev or Shevardnadze attempted to translate the latter's personal authority as an advocate of the new thinking into an enduring institutional ethos. Shevardnadze did not carry out the sort of personnel or structural reforms at the Ministry that would have made it a forceful advocate of the new foreign policy paradigm. This lack of a bureaucratic home within the state meant that the new thinking fared poorly as time progressed.[104]

Not surprisingly, then, once the centralized institutions of the Soviet state and the personal advocates of radical change in foreign policy were swept aside in December 1991, the new thinking became only one of several competing foreign policy strategies for the new Russia. As I argue in chapter 6, this shift away from a liberal foreign policy demonstrates how institutional change can radically alter the context of policymaking—and the role of ideas—in transition states such as post-Soviet Russia.

6

A Post–Cold War Cold Peace?
Ideas and Institutions in the New Russia

I tell Yeltsin and I tell you, a prime minister must have elementary power, not just ideas. — Arkady Volsky

I voted for [Russian Prime Minister] Chernomyrdin with both hands. . . . I'm sure Gaidar is clever, but theory must be correlated with practice. — A local industrial manager in Russia

These sentiments, while addressing the domestic political scene in post-Soviet Russia, find striking parallels in the foreign policy arena, where many feel that ideas and theory have also moved ahead of practice and power.[1] Indeed, the set of liberal ideas that informed Soviet foreign policy under Gorbachev has come under withering attack from a number of quarters. This chapter examines these changes, the causal influence of ideas in the process, and how institutional change has fundamentally altered the role of ideas in shaping the international political behavior of post-Soviet Russia.

While employing the same explanatory framework, my analysis is different from that used for the Brezhnev and Gorbachev periods. Most important, it is not complete; there are no clear outcomes described and explained. Indeed, with so much in flux, I instead offer preliminary assessments of several patterns evident in the foreign policy of post-Soviet Russia, and discuss their implications for theory and policy. In addition, my focus is not simply academic units like IMEMO. Befitting the broadened nature of policymaking in contemporary Russia, the analysis itself is broader in scope.

Post-Soviet Russia

The Soviet–post-Soviet transition has produced a change in political institutions, one of my key explanatory variables, thus allowing me to test more rigorously the argument linking ideas and international politics. In particular, Russian institutions have become less autonomous and centralized. According to my theory, therefore, I would expect there to be three important shifts in the causal pathways linking ideas and policy. First, in this newly decentralized environment, it should be easier for foreign policy ideas to reach key elites; however, their eventual implementation and consolidation should be less certain. Second, individual policy entrepreneurs should find that their comparative advantage diminishes relative to their position in a more centralized state. Finally, politics should matter more in the making of foreign policy, as top elites become less insulated from various societal pressures and other parts of the state apparatus.

Evidence from post-Soviet Russia supports these predictions. For one, it is clear that an array of foreign policy ideas has been reaching key elites, including President Yeltsin. Indeed, Yeltsin's own thinking on international politics has come to resemble an unusual and perhaps incompatible mixture of neoliberal institutionalism and realism. The former, with its focus on cooperation and the use of international institutions to mitigate the effects of anarchy, informs many of Yeltsin's policies on relations with the industrialized West.

The latter, with its stress on a threatening security environment and potential use of military instruments, has increasingly come to dominate Russian policy and elite commentary regarding the former Soviet republics. Although such a combination of liberal and realist principles may be of interest to theorists, it is highly questionable that it can form the basis for a coherent Russian policy.[2]

In addition, there is clear evidence that policy entrepreneurs are less influential than they were in the authoritarian Soviet state, where elites were relatively insulated from broader societal and bureaucratic forces. The problem for such individuals in post-Soviet Russia is that they find themselves competing with a growing number of organizations and social forces for the attention of key decision makers.[3]

The behavior of former Russian Foreign Minister Andrey Kozyrev is a case in point. In 1991–93, he was a man with a solution — that is, an entrepreneur. When a policy window was created by the breakup of the USSR, Kozyrev was motivated to advance a set of neoliberal ideas he had long held. In particular, he argued that post-Soviet Russia could best protect its state interests by

closely aligning itself with the institutions and policies of the industrialized democracies. Throughout the first half of 1992, he aggressively promoted these beliefs and clearly influenced Yeltsin's thinking and preferences.

Beginning in the summer of 1992, however, other entrepreneurs and organizations began an open competition with Kozyrev over the definition of state interests. Their policy window was created by a new feature of Russia's international political environment: the independence of the former Soviet republics and Russia's increasingly troubled relations with them. Pointing to this threatening environment, these entrepreneurs argued for a definition of state interests that paid greater attention to traditional geopolitics.

Both Yeltsin's post-1992 commentary as well as the official statement of Russian national interests — the revised "Foreign Policy Concept" released in early 1993 — reflected the influence of ideas from these various sources. Thus, in post-Soviet Russia the difficulty faced by promoters of ideas is not access to the top, as it was in the USSR; rather, it is insuring that their ideas, once they reach elites, have a lasting influence on policy. The adoption of new foreign policy ideas, in other words, is not particularly difficult; their eventual implementation and consolidation, however, is more problematic. From the perspective of the institutional argument developed in this book, this is precisely what one would expect.[4]

Finally, the importance of politics and coalition building has increased as the autonomy of the Russian state has decreased. Indeed, it is not simply a competition among differing ideas that explains the mixture of liberal and realist principles in more recent elite commentary and Russian foreign policy. In addition, Yeltsin is engaged in a complicated coalition-building process as he seeks support for his government and its policies. This process has mandated that he make concessions to the views of other influential actors like the Supreme Soviet (until its dissolution in 1993), the Russian military, and, beginning in the mid-1990s, nationalist political groupings — all of whom have expressed much more conservative opinions on a range of foreign policy issues. My point here is not that ideas no longer matter; rather, I argue that they will have less direct influence on elite preferences and state policy than formerly. As one government minister put it: "Political realities force Yeltsin to do some things that are not always explainable or easily accepted."[5]

With this overview in hand, I turn to the details of the Russian case, beginning with the uncertainty felt by decision makers and the policy windows this created for entrepreneurs. I next consider institutional change — its effects on foreign policymaking and on the role played by ideas. These changes are illuminated by the debate over Russian state interests that took place from

1991 to 1993. Finally, I examine how a failure of political leadership by the Yeltsin government further politicized the foreign policy process and weakened the capacity of the Russian state in this critical area.

In the concluding section, I ask whether my emphasis on ideas and institutions as determinants of Russian behavior is misplaced. Perhaps Russia's more assertive foreign policy can be inferred — in the best neorealist tradition — from its new international political position.

Whither the Russian State?

In the wake of the USSR's collapse, the Russian Federation found itself in a strikingly new international environment. There is abundant evidence that decision makers were aware of this fact and felt themselves to be in new and uncertain surroundings. Thus, on the demand side, a critical condition — cognitive uncertainty — was in place for Russian policymakers to consider new ideas as they redefined preferences and state interests.

Indeed, uncertainty and crisis were prominent themes in speeches, personal conversations, and newspaper articles of the early post-Soviet years. Policymakers like President Yeltsin and Foreign Minister Kozyrev talked of a fundamentally new international environment surrounding Russia. It was an international context defined by the lack of a superpower enemy, a militarily strong and independent Ukraine, and Russian ethnic minority populations in many of the countries that had been a part of the USSR (the "near abroad" to Russians).[6]

The sense of uncertainty was manifested in other ways as well. The Foreign Ministry, for example, spent much of 1992–93 drafting a "concept" for Russian foreign policy that was intended to give general guidelines for addressing this new and turbulent international environment. Early in 1992, top scholars at IMEMO even thought it necessary to hold a press conference, at which they discussed the contemporary international challenges facing post-Soviet Russia.[7]

Throughout 1992–93, government officials often expressed bewilderment at how to acquire and analyze information on a significant new foreign policy problem: independent Ukraine. Indeed, when one high-ranking Foreign Ministry official was asked how Russia obtained good intelligence on Ukraine, he shrugged and declared, "We, too, have CNN."[8]

Two significant changes in the nature of Russian political institutions occurred in the post-Soviet period. First, access to foreign policy decision makers increased. Indeed, a complaint one heard in the Moscow policy community

was that too many people and lobbies had access to such policymakers as
Yeltsin and Kozyrev and their staffs. Personal ties, then, were still key; however, there were many more connections possible.

This state of affairs angered some of those who had been privileged by their
access under the Soviet system. Georgiy Arbatov, a man with direct ties to top
decision makers under Brezhnev as well as Gorbachev, complained of the
confusion resulting from this enhanced access. But younger researchers at
Moscow think tanks — who had not been privileged under the old system —
marveled at the access they had to policymakers. Of course, access does not au-
tomatically translate into influence. Indeed, although the former has increased,
the direct influence of individual academics on policy has decreased as their
proposals compete with many others in a more decentralized environment.[9]

Second, the foreign policy process became less centralized. This was seen
most dramatically in the significant role the Supreme Soviet created for itself
during 1992–93. It regularly demanded reports from Kozyrev on various
issues, sent out fact-finding missions (to Serbia, among other places), and
attempted to subject the defense and foreign ministers to parliamentary confir-
mation. Of course, this assertiveness by the Supreme Soviet on questions of
foreign policy was just one manifestation of a much larger debate over the
division of powers between the executive and legislative branches.[10]

These broader institutional changes made the coordination of foreign policymaking much more difficult. Yeltsin and Kozyrev bemoaned this fact, and
the Russian press carried a number of articles on the topic. Russian policymaking, it would appear, was becoming more like that found in America,
where there are multiple access points to the process, and power is dispersed.[11]

Such a comparison may have been valid in late 1992, but events since then
paint a somewhat different picture. Indeed, a trend toward partial recentralization was evident throughout 1993–94. In the first months after the collapse of the USSR, Yeltsin, Gennadiy Burbulis (Yeltsin's closest adviser at that
point), and Kozyrev had argued in favor of decentralization, with the Foreign
Ministry playing a much greater role than before in the formulation and implementation of Russian policy. Given the Soviet historical context — where
virtually all foreign policy decision making was centralized in the Central
Committee and, later, presidential apparatus — such a move would have signaled an important change.[12]

Over the course of 1993–94, however, this trend was moderated and partly
reversed. The first change came in November 1992, when Yeltsin decreed that
the Foreign Ministry coordinate the work of all governmental ministries in the
sphere of foreign policy. This was less a victory for the Ministry in its battle to

play a more prominent role in policymaking than a recognition on Yeltsin's part that his government was speaking with too many voices on key foreign policy issues.[13]

There were further signs of recentralization. In particular, Yeltsin sought more direct, personal control over foreign policy by vesting the newly created Russian Security Council with the coordinating role previously accorded to the Foreign Ministry. The Security Council, which has grown in size to include a number of interdepartmental committees that coordinate various aspects of foreign and domestic policy, is part of the presidential apparatus and under Yeltsin's direct supervision.[14] In addition, the violent dissolution of the Supreme Soviet, its replacement by a considerably weakened legislature, and the promulgation and adoption of a new, executive-centered constitution all pointed to a clear desire for a more centralized policy process.

These years thus reveal a somewhat contradictory picture of Russian institutional development. The pattern of decentralization-recentralization I have described suggests how difficult it is to change historically constructed institutions. But if we compare these years with the Soviet era, it is clear that the Russian state comprises a considerably less powerful set of institutions and practices than its authoritarian predecessor. Its coercive abilities have declined, it is less centralized, and policymaking elites are more susceptible to pressure from a broad range of societal forces (powerful energy and agricultural lobbies, say) and other parts of the state apparatus. Although such trends are more evident in the domestic socioeconomic realm, the analysis here suggests similar movements at work in the foreign policy sphere.[15]

These broader institutional changes have deeply affected the bureaucratic politics of Russian foreign policymaking. While such processes were at work throughout the Soviet era and, especially, in the post-Stalin period, their influence on policy was limited by the central control exercised by key decision-making elites. This has now changed in a dramatic way.[16]

Of special importance is the death of one particular organization: the CPSU and its associated apparatus. Its deeply embedded ideology, which emphasized class conflict and a zero-sum view of international politics, has lost the bureaucratic platform that so greatly enhanced its influence on policy. Indeed, former CPSU officials, current policymakers, and scholars are unanimous in stressing the pivotal importance of this fact; all feel that a broad ideational constraint on policymaking has been lifted.[17]

The removal of this constraint along with the weakening of central control has clearly motivated the surviving bureaucratic players to seek an enhanced role in foreign policymaking. As was the case in the Soviet era, two of the key

players are the Ministry of Foreign Affairs and the Defense Ministry. In important ways, both organizations are continuations of their Soviet counterparts; thus, to understand their current behavior a brief look back is necessary.

Historically, the Foreign Ministry was a less insulated organization than the military. This difference arose in part because the Ministry's role dictated that it have a greater amount of international contact in various negotiating forums and embassies than did the Defense Ministry. These contacts increased steadily over the 1970s and 1980s as the USSR sought greater interaction with its international political, security, and economic environments. The degree of insulation had an important bearing on the extent to which ideologies became embedded in each organization.

During the Soviet era, a particular ideology of international affairs had taken root at the Defense Ministry. This organizational ethos appears to have survived the Soviet-Russian transition more or less intact. The Russian Ministry's organizational structure is similar to its Soviet counterpart; it includes the General Staff system that did so much to instill a sense of corporate identity in the military during the Soviet era. In terms of worldview, the Russian Ministry of Defense continues to stress a threatening external security environment and the importance of military instruments (for example, in insuring the safety of Russian minority populations in the former Soviet republics). It has also developed a military doctrine that overlaps significantly with doctrine of the Soviet era.[18]

The situation at the Foreign Ministry is different. Here, the lower degree of insulation created a less ideologically determined organization. This in turn left greater room for leadership; Foreign Minister Kozyrev was able to introduce, in the early post-Soviet years, a number of changes designed to give his Ministry the resources, information, and expertise to participate fully in policymaking. Most important, the Ministry acted to increase its access to new ideas. In a break with past practice, several of Kozyrev's early appointees as deputy foreign ministers came from academic backgrounds. In addition, the Ministry created a Foreign Policy Council. Both the new appointees and the council were purposely designed to bring new ideas into the Ministry.[19]

In addition, Kozyrev invested a great personal stake in articulating for the Ministry and Russia a new, liberal ideology of international politics. He argued that the present international system was fundamentally different from that which existed in either the tsarist or Soviet periods. It is a system where the majority of great powers are united by a common system of values centered on market economics and political pluralism, and where status is defined most importantly by levels of scientific-technical progress and a country's position in world markets. Moreover, growing ties of economic interdepen-

dence have led to a situation where interstate relationships are no longer a zero-sum game. As the Foreign Minister often declared, "the better off my neighbor is, the better off I am." Indeed, Kozyrev's bottom line was that "no developed, democratic, civil society . . . can threaten us."[20]

The Foreign Minister also saw international institutions as playing an important role in world politics. This should come as no surprise since Kozyrev worked for sixteen years (1974–1990) in the Directorate of International Organizations at the Soviet Foreign Ministry. Such institutions, he argued, can have their greatest effect in those regions where countries are not united by shared norms and values. Kozyrev thus stressed the role institutions can play in resolving conflicts within and between the former Soviet republics.[21]

Ideas and Russian State Interests

Let us consider the effect these institutional changes had on the role of ideas in the debate that took place during much of 1991–93 about Russia's state interests. In the immediate wake of the USSR's collapse, Kozyrev's liberal ideas seemed set to play a dominant role in shaping Russia's interests and policies. Inspired by the beliefs embodied in Gorbachev's new thinking, these ideas would have provided a radically different paradigm for interpreting Russia's new international realities.[22]

As of early 1992, the Foreign Ministry (and Kozyrev) had been accorded a new and more important role in the policy process. Key elites had made it clear through their pronouncements and a government-mandated search for a foreign policy concept that they were looking for new ideas to make sense of Russia's new international environment. Moreover, Yeltsin, in his statements on foreign policy, had echoed many of the same themes as Kozyrev. This paradigm reached its greatest influence in June 1992, when Yeltsin forcefully articulated many of its central elements in a speech to the U.S. Congress.[23]

In addition, throughout 1992 the Foreign Ministry was at work on a draft of the foreign policy concept that was heavily influenced by Kozyrev's liberal international vision. The draft, officially entitled "On the Basic Propositions of the Foreign Policy Concept of the Russian Federation," took as its "holy book" the documents and charter of the Organization on Security and Cooperation in Europe (OSCE) and other international institutions. It favored the promotion of Russian interests "in the first place through participation in different international organizations."[24]

This suggests that a new set of beliefs for defining Russian interests was on the verge of being adopted. Unfortunately for Yeltsin, the Foreign Ministry, and Kozyrev, they were about three years too late. That is, the changing nature

of political institutions in post-Soviet Russia—the decrease in state autonomy and partial decentralization of decision making—had drastically reduced the likelihood that this particular set of ideas would have any lasting policy impact.

In fact, beginning in June, the draft concept became a political football—something unthinkable in the former USSR—as other, competing ideas for defining Russian state interests were advanced and debated. The International Affairs Committee of the Supreme Soviet played an important role here. Under the leadership of its strong-willed chair, Yevgeniy Ambartsumov, the committee rejected the Ministry's draft concept and sent it back for reworking.[25]

Making use of the policy window created by Russia's increasingly troubled relations with the former Soviet republics, Ambartsumov played the role of entrepreneur, promoting a different and more conservative set of foreign policy ideas. In particular, he attacked the Foreign Ministry's belief that the rights of Russian minority populations abroad could best be served by reliance on norms and procedures of international institutions. Ambartsumov instead advocated a Russian version of the Monroe Doctrine. Declaring the "entire geopolitical space of the former Union [to be] a sphere of vital interests," he argued that Russia should be given the legal right to defend its ethnic kin throughout the region.[26]

Using his bureaucratic base to block the Foreign Ministry's concept and with access to (less autonomous) top decision makers, Ambartsumov was successful in advancing this set of beliefs. Yeltsin was partially swayed by such thinking; by early 1993, he had incorporated elements of both the Ambartsumov and Kozyrev paradigms into his pronouncements. He spoke more forcefully about protecting Russian minorities in the near abroad and came increasingly to employ geopolitical frameworks in his discussions of Russian policy.[27]

The revised version of the Foreign Ministry's foreign policy concept, completed in late 1992, also reflected this mixed set of beliefs. A concern for utilizing "the technical resources as well as expert advice" of international institutions to define and advance Russian interests was still present, but it now coexisted with a stress on interests as given by geopolitical situation. However, on the issue of protecting Russian minorities in the former Soviet republics, the revised concept maintained the earlier commitment to politico-diplomatic methods and to using the "mechanisms of international organizations."[28]

This brief review suggests the importance of the changing institutional structure to contemporary Russian foreign policymaking. Its partial decentralization has introduced new access points for those wishing to promote particular ideas. As students of public policy could have predicted, this en-

hanced access has led to more static in the process and less coherence in policy goals. Put another way, the politics of policymaking have come to play a much greater role as the Russian state has weakened.[29]

In this fluid and less insulated institutional environment, elites and their policy preferences are susceptible to greater political pressures. Responding to and managing such pressures requires effective leadership — a skill notably lacking in the Yeltsin government. In post-Soviet Russia, political leadership in the foreign policy sphere requires bureaucratic skills to engage in the give-and-take inherent in a more decentralized environment; a commitment to building state capacity so that the government has the instruments needed to implement policy; and articulation of a coherent foreign policy by top elites to mobilize political support. On all three accounts, Yeltsin and his allies have failed.

Former Foreign Minister Kozyrev clearly exemplifies the bureaucratic problem. In Russia's decentralized decision-making arena, bureaucratic leadership means the ability to engage in political give-and-take with other influential competitors (the legislature or Ministry of Defense, for example). On this point, Kozyrev's record during the early post-Soviet years was nothing short of abysmal. Interviewees at the Foreign Ministry praise his vision while simultaneously criticizing his lack of political acuity. He was not political by nature, and all too often he let his emotions get the better of him. In a speech given at the Foreign Ministry in late 1992, Yeltsin hinted at this problem — strongly urging Kozyrev to improve relations with various parts of the government and keep his emotions in check.[30]

The second element of political leadership — a commitment to building state capacity in foreign policy — has also been notably lacking. *Capacity* refers to the administrative and coercive abilities of the state to implement official goals. Such abilities are increased by the existence of career officials who are relatively insulated from ties to dominant socioeconomic interests; a promotion and tenure system based on merit review; and a large and coherent bureaucratic machine.[31]

The development of state capacity is a long-term, historical process, and one cannot fault the Yeltsin government for failing to create it in the relatively brief time since the USSR's collapse. But the Yeltsin team can be criticized for not articulating a coherent plan in this area. Observing the actions of the government, one can only conclude there is no long-term plan; rather, there have been a series of ad hoc measures. During 1992 the emphasis was on building a bureaucratic infrastructure around a reinvigorated and professionalized Foreign Ministry.[32]

Since late 1992, however, a different plan seems to have been at work.

Yeltsin and his close advisers decided that the best strategy for building state capacity was to recentralize foreign policy decision making and strengthen the bureaucratic structures associated with the office of the president. Hence, they created the Security Council and significantly increased the presidential apparatus devoted to foreign affairs.[33]

This lack of direction has hampered the ability of the Russian government to build a cadre of professional foreign policy expertise — a critically important goal, given the highly politicized apparatus bequeathed it by the USSR. Moreover, this confusion alienated members of the Moscow foreign policy establishment who should have been allies of the Yeltsin-Kozyrev team.[34]

The lack of political leadership along these first two dimensions was overshadowed and perhaps caused by the inability of the Yeltsin government to articulate a coherent foreign policy vision for Russia in the post-Soviet, post–Cold War world. Here, the blame must be laid directly at Yeltsin's door. There are both empirical and theoretical reasons for arguing that his role must be central. Empirically, there is the tsarist-Soviet context: tsars and, more recently, CPSU general secretaries have always played a central role in foreign policymaking. Their preferences and beliefs have mattered — a point dramatically demonstrated during the Gorbachev years.

A second reason for according a central role in foreign policy to the person in Yeltsin's position is more theoretically grounded. In Russia today, there is a weak link in its evolving set of institutions — something comparativists call intermediate associations. These are the political parties and interest groups that link government and society. As I argued in earlier chapters, when such links are poorly developed, elite decision makers can play an enhanced role in shaping outcomes.

Some might dispute my assertion, arguing, for example, that Russia contains a growing number of political parties. This is true; however, one must not mistake form for substance. With few exceptions, these "parties" are in reality loose groupings, with little discipline and poorly articulated foreign policy platforms.[35]

Thus, Yeltsin and his foreign policy beliefs should play an important role in policymaking. Does he have a vision? Has he decided what sort of role Russia should play in the post-Soviet world? Early signs to the contrary, the evidence indicates that the answer is "no." Whether one is interviewing policymakers and specialists in Moscow or reviewing Yeltsin's own commentary, the conclusion is inescapable: he is uncertain. His foreign policy vision is defined primarily by negatives: Yeltsin does not want a return to Soviet-era diplomacy, nor will he countenance the forceful, militarized foreign policy of the radical nationalists. Beyond this, however, he is unclear.[36]

This lack of vision had two important political ramifications in the early post-Soviet years. For one, it made it difficult for the government to mobilize support for the moderate-centrist foreign policy it seemingly wanted. Equally important, Yeltsin's lack of conviction made him more susceptible to the political pressures that are a central feature of politics in contemporary Russia.[37]

In late 1993, these pressures increased with the election of a sizable right wing fraction to the new state Duma. Many of these "national patriots" define Russian interests in stark balance-of-power terms and hold a zero-sum view of international politics; they also demand the forcible protection of Russian minorities in the near abroad and reestablishment of the Soviet Union. Vladimir Zhirinovskiy, for example, leader of the misleadingly named Liberal-Democratic Party, has argued that the Russian Federation should pursue a foreign policy similar to that of imperial, tsarist Russia — seeking, among other goals, the restoration of Russian sovereignty over the territory of the former USSR.[38]

Do the ideas of the extremists have any influence on foreign policy? They do indeed, but not by shaping the preferences of elites in the Yeltsin government. Rather, it is Yeltsin's own uncertainty, along with the growing importance of politics and coalition building, that accorded these extremist beliefs a role. Throughout 1993 and most clearly after the defeat of reformist parties in the December elections, politicians in the Yeltsin camp were compelled to pay greater attention to the views of the nationalist right — especially on the question of Russian minorities in the former Soviet republics. Indeed, even such a committed liberal as Kozyrev felt it necessary to moderate his ideology by mixing it with elements of realpolitik. Asked in the spring of 1994 to explain this shift in his views, Kozyrev noted that "as a democrat he felt constrained to take into account public opinion on foreign policy matters."[39]

It is important to ask whether these politicians could become prisoners of their own rhetoric. That is, could a form of "ideological blowback" occur as future elite generations came to believe in the nationalist ideology originally articulated for the instrumental reason of building a viable political coalition? The answer, unfortunately, is that it all depends — in this case, on the nature of the political institutions that emerge in post-Soviet Russia. If the country continues a slow transition to a more pluralist political system, the likelihood of such blowback will be lessened because of the institutional checks and balances and the free exchange of information present in such settings.[40]

To sum up, a qualitatively new set of ideas on international politics failed to take hold and decisively shape elite preferences and state interests primarily because of fundamental changes in the structure of politics in post-Soviet Russia. Leadership failures and a changed international environment also

clearly played a role, but their influence was mediated by this broader institutional context. These changes, along with the weakly institutionalized basis of Gorbachev-era new thinking, combined to work against a continuing liberal foreign policy in contemporary Russia. The strategic partnership with the West first envisioned by Yeltsin and Kozyrev had by the mid-1990s given way to a post–Cold War "cold peace."

I have examined how institutional change shaped the debate over Russia's emerging state interests in the early 1990s in order to sketch the parameters of this debate and examine the role of ideas in it. It is now clear that institutions matter. In post-Soviet Russia, changing institutional structure simultaneously constrained the ability of decision makers to implement their foreign policy preferences while insuring that ideas played a more ambiguous role in shaping those preferences in the first place.

Perhaps, though, my emphasis on ideas and institutions is misplaced. Instead, Russian state interests can be inferred from its position in the international system. This is the neorealist argument, and at first glance it seems to offer important insights on the growing assertiveness evident in recent Russian policy. Structuralists emphasize the impact of anarchy on state behavior — how it leads states to build up their military forces and act assertively in a self-help international system.

As many have noted anarchy does not seem to be an accurate depiction of the present international system. Where states are joined by shared values, economic ties, and international institutions, the effects of anarchy are mitigated — and the structural logic does not obtain. Such a situation currently holds among the industrialized democracies. At the same time, where countries do not share common values or norms, economic linkages are poorly developed, and international organizations are ineffective, the structural logic may be more relevant.[41]

It is precisely the latter situation that describes a critically important aspect of Russia's new international environment: its place among the independent republics of the former Soviet Union. Do the countries of the Commonwealth of Independent States (CIS) share a common commitment to market economics and pluralist democracy? Are they bound by the kinds of economic relations that are typical among the industrial democracies? Is the CIS an effective international institution — one with a strong bureaucratic infrastructure, clear rules, and agreed-upon sanction mechanisms? In all cases, the answer is "no."

This structural context creates powerful incentives for Russia to act more forcefully and fill any incipient power vacuums. Indeed, given the presence of a militarily strong neighbor (Ukraine) and the anarchy and conflict evident else-

where in the CIS (the Trans-Caucasus and Tadzhikistan), it would have been surprising not to see Russia reassert a more dominant role in the former Soviet area: great powers often carve out spheres of influence. One need not know anything about Russia's leaders, changing political institutions, or the differing ideas in play to have predicted such an outcome.

In other respects, however, international structure is proving to be a weak predictor of Russian behavior and policies. Neorealist balance-of-power theory would predict balancing behavior by major competitor states to the United States in the post–Cold War world. Russia, by virtue of its significant military, human, and material resources, remains one such competitor. Yet it seems less concerned with balancing U.S. power and more intent on bandwagoning around certain norms, institutions, and practices shared by the industrialized democracies.[42]

Neorealists commonly distinguish between internal and external balancing behavior. On the former, Russia has shown little interest in rebuilding its armed forces and military-industrial base to levels that would allow it to balance the United States. Externally, Russia has seemed less concerned with balancing German or U.S. power, say, than with bandwagoning around the institutions and norms of the West. Its application for membership in the G-7 grouping of industrial democracies, International Monetary Fund, World Bank, World Trade Organization, and Council of Europe are all indicative of such behavior.[43]

All this suggests that international structure is indeterminate as a predictor of Russian (and other great power) behavior in the post–Cold War world. Decision makers like Kozyrev, Yeltsin, and Ambartsumov are indeed reacting to and seizing upon signals from the external environment as they formulate state interests and policies. Yet the nature of these signals differs depending upon where one looks: to the West, where interdependence and cooperation dominate, or toward the former Soviet republics, where anarchy and conflict are in evidence. The signals are therefore ambiguous, their message to elite decision makers indeterminate.[44]

Thus, international structural explanations must be supplemented — an argument that will come as no surprise to readers of this book. As the account here suggests, ideas do have a role to play, as individuals (Kozyrev and his belief in a neoliberal vision of international politics) and organizations (the Russian Defense Ministry with its deeply embedded Hobbesian worldview) respond to their new structural situations. Put another way, Russia's interests cannot be objectively inferred from its new position in the international political system. International stimuli are indeed affecting the process of interest redefinition, but in a much less mechanistic way than neorealist accounts might suggest.

PART **III**

Ideas, Institutions, and International Change

7

Ideas and Foreign Policy

The end of the Cold War has been accompanied by profound transformations in the domestic political economies of a growing number of countries throughout Eastern Europe, the former USSR, Latin America, and Africa. If nothing else, these transformations should remind us that international relations theory is not well equipped to conceptualize this domestic context and its impact on foreign and security policy. Indeed, some have argued that international-relations theory more generally needs retooling in the post–Cold War era.

By exploring the relation of ideas to international political change, I seek to assist in this effort by demonstrating that theorists of international relations have much to gain by utilizing approaches first developed in such fields as comparative political economy or American politics. I suggest a way to think more systematically about the effect of domestic politics on international politics and about how the two arenas intersect.[1]

I have also tried to develop an explanation of change that takes account of both individual agents and the structural constraints that limit and motivate them. My aim is not to show either the primacy of agents over structure or the reverse. Rather, I have explored how advocates of change and political leaders are constrained and motivated by institutions and international structure. Put another way, I sought to explore the interaction between process and struc-

ture, a type of explanation that has received increasing attention in both the comparative-politics and international-relations fields.[2]

By arguing for an interplay of international stimuli with domestic ideational and institutional variables, I purposely highlighted the diverse sources of change in state behavior. Yet an argument of this sort, as my case studies demonstrate, is prone to overdetermination: any of the main causal variables can independently explain the outcome. It is difficult, in other words, to determine whether the variance in elite foreign policy preferences is best explained as the adoption of new ideas, as a rational, self-interested response to new international circumstances, or, most likely, as some combination of the two.

Ideas, Institutions, and the End of the Cold War

In assessing my argument, it is useful to recall the hypotheses that guided it; we are now in a position to judge how well the empirical data support them.

>•Under conditions of high international uncertainty or foreign policy crisis, decision makers engage in an information search and are thus more receptive to new ideas. Their foreign policy preferences, in other words, are in flux.
>•Conditions of high international uncertainty or foreign policy crisis create policy windows. These windows link the international and domestic environments and motivate advocates of new ideas to promote them.
>•In centralized states, there are fewer pathways by which ideas can reach elites; their initial adoption is thus more difficult. Once adopted, however, such ideas stand a greater chance of being implemented and thus of altering state behavior.
>•In less centralized states, there are a greater number of pathways by which new ideas can reach elites; their initial adoption is thus less problematic. Once adopted, however, such ideas are less likely to be implemented in a way that has a lasting effect on state behavior.
>•Policy entrepreneurs will play a critical role in empowering new ideas in centralized states because many of the other pathways for affecting change are blocked or diminished in importance. In a decentralized state, entrepreneurs will see their comparative advantage diminish as elite insulation decreases.

The historical and contemporary record supports these propositions. In all my cases, individual entrepreneurs seeking to exploit open policy windows were central to the process that empowered new ideas. Their success, however, was dependent on several factors. In particular, changing international circumstances and pressures were key. In the late 1960s, these were of sufficient magnitude to motivate entrepreneurs to promote their solutions; yet they were insufficiently large to force key decision makers into a cognitive information search that would make them open to new ideas.

During the Gorbachev and post-Soviet periods, international stimuli created a number of large policy windows. Under Gorbachev, with key decision makers engaged in a wide-ranging cognitive search, these pressures were successfully exploited by well-positioned entrepreneurs to promote a new normative basis for Soviet foreign behavior.

In the post-Soviet period, entrepreneurs have met with more mixed success, despite policy windows and clear signs of uncertainty in foreign policy beliefs and preferences. To understand why, one must consider the role of (changing) political institutions. As I argued in chapter 1 and as the case studies demonstrate, the likely influence of entrepreneurs as agents of ideas-based change is heightened in states with highly centralized and autonomous policymaking structures. In such states, the job of entrepreneurs will not be easy, but they face less competition from other sources of change, which are present in more pluralist political systems, either interest-based (agricultural lobbies, political parties) or ideas-based (domestic and international NGOs).

In post-Soviet Russia, changing international circumstances motivated entrepreneurs to act. Yet, domestic institutional change meant that these individuals operated in a more competitive and politicized environment, which minimized the influence of any particular set of ideas. Indeed, as I noted in chapter 6, the foreign policy preferences of key decision makers as well as actual Russian behavior have been less coherent (in comparison to the Soviet era), as multiple ideas have been advanced, and political pressures have mounted.

As I argue throughout this book, however, it was not simply individuals and their beliefs who determined the role played by ideas. In particular, ideas that were historically rooted in particular organizations and agencies also played a crucial role — both in hindering and promoting international political change. On the former, ideas about the class nature (in the CPSU apparatus) and zero-sum quality of international politics (in the Ministry of Defense) played a central role in shaping Soviet interests and behavior throughout the post-Stalin years. This is not to deny periods of moderate foreign policy change (the late Khrushchev or early Brezhnev years, for example). Rather, these reforms represented a change in the instruments of Soviet policy, not in the fundamental hierarchy of goals and interests.

Only in the Gorbachev years did goals and interests themselves change. In this case, ideas promoted radical policy shifts, as Gorbachev and his allies reached out and around the deeply embedded beliefs of the Soviet state to a different set of ideas on international politics. Indeed, it is impossible to understand the particular form and content of Gorbachev's liberal foreign policy — and the peaceful end of the Cold War — without a detailed knowledge of the historically constructed ideas embedded in organizations like IMEMO. These ideas mattered because new political elites wanted them to matter, and these

elites controlled a number of policy instruments in the authoritarian Soviet state for turning their desire into reality.

My theory cannot easily account for idiosyncratic factors that promoted successful entrepreneurship and politics. The former defies any systematic attempt at conceptualization: simply put, entrepreneurs with political savvy enjoyed the greatest success in promoting new ideas. Indeed, of the four entrepreneurs discussed (Inozemtsev, Yakovlev, Primakov, and Kozyrev), it was the politically adept Yakovlev and Primakov who were the most successful. Yakovlev, in particular, understood the system he was trying to fight.[3]

A second factor not adequately addressed in my argument is the role of politics. Neglecting political-coalitional factors was analytically and empirically justifiable as long as the broader institutional structure minimized their importance, as my Brezhnev and, especially, early Gorbachev-era case studies demonstrated. But the post-Soviet example suggests the essential limits of a purely institutional argument.[4]

Indeed, the empirical material on contemporary Russia forced me to introduce coalitional factors into my explanation of how elite foreign policy preferences change. Inevitably, because of the book's institutional focus, their introduction was ad hoc in nature. My defense of such "ad hoc-ism" is twofold. First, any theory, by focusing on certain causal factors at the expense of others, misses a part of the story. The crucial test is whether the factors it highlights are causally important. By this criterion, the utility of an institutional argument is supported by all three of my cases, including the post-Soviet one. Second, as argued in chapter 1, my approach should be seen as a supplement to and not a replacement for existing theories, including those that stress the role of coalition politics.[5]

Public Policy, Domestic Politics, and Transnationalism

My analysis contributes to three debates in the policy studies and international relations literatures. On the former, there is a clear need to move beyond the stages model of policymaking developed in the 1970s and 1980s. This book, with its emphasis on the role of chance in the process, has much in common with John Kingdon's alternative to the stages heuristic: the policy-streams approach. It also provides fairly strong empirical support for Kingdon's work. My main amendment to Kingdon would be greater attention to the institutional context in which entrepreneurs operate.[6]

Within international relations, there is a seemingly endless debate over the influence of domestic politics on state behavior, with many arguing that this is still a neglected area of research. Several theorists have sought to fill this

lacuna by applying a variant of coalition theory to explain the domestic political basis of state behavior. Their work offers a sophisticated argument on how interest-based coalitional logrolling affects the foreign policy of states.[7]

Arguments of this sort accord ideas a secondary role. Ideas are instrumentally used by political elites seeking to advance their political position; in themselves, they are an epiphenomenon. The power of interests wins out over ideas. In chapter 1, I noted several problems with this explanation, at least in its stronger forms. Although such arguments should not be dismissed, they need to be recognized for what they are: a form of domestic-level realism, which claims that politics concerns only power, interests, and coalition making.[8]

Yet politics does not just concern power. Political leaders are more than empty vessels; they are not simply waiting to respond rationally to the next set of international or domestic stimuli. As Hugh Heclo reminds us: "Politics finds its sources not only in power but also in uncertainty — men collectively wondering what to do. Finding feasible courses of action includes, but is more than, locating which way the vectors of political pressure are pushing. Governments not only 'power' . . . they also puzzle." As I have suggested throughout this book, there are certain times when policy windows open and politicians puzzle as well as power. During these periods, it is worth exploring how ideas, and the institutions that channel them, can reshape interests and ultimately the exercise of state power in the international arena.[9]

Finally, the 1990s have seen a new round of debate on how international institutions and transnational actors influence state behavior. This research shares several insights with the analysis presented here — for example, a commitment to exploring the intersection of domestic and international politics and a recognition that ideas can play an important role in world politics.[10] Many would argue that these analyses mark an important advance over earlier research on international institutions and regimes, which typically black boxed states and their decision-making processes in the interest of theoretical parsimony.[11]

In spite of its greater attention to domestic political process, the more recent work remains underspecified at the domestic level. In particular, it suffers from not developing theories of domestic politics to explain why the influence of transnationally generated ideas varies across countries. Indeed, much of this body of work adopts a narrow view of domestic politics as essentially a game of elites, who change policy as their preferences are reshaped by new ideas. Although this may hold in some countries, in others domestic politics is a more complicated process involving interest groups, social and legal norms, party politics, and coalition building.[12]

One way to think more systematically about the connections between ideas

and domestic politics is to develop an institutional approach, something I seek to do in this book. In highly centralized polities like the former USSR, policy changed once the preferences of key decision-making elites were influenced by new ideas, either transnationally generated or home grown. Regardless of whether an institutional approach is the most appropriate, the basic point remains. Advocates of the new transnationalism need to develop theories of domestic politics if we are to gain a more complete understanding of the conditions under which ideas are causally important.[13]

Ideas and Political Change

Nearly all recent work in the ideas literature argues that uncertainty, failure, or crisis — by delegitimizing existing policies, organizations, and beliefs — creates greater room for ideas as determinants of change. Most important, their existence can motivate key decision-making elites to engage in an information search that makes them more receptive to new ideas. At the level of politics and institutions, uncertainty and failure can weaken powerful actors who have a stake in existing policies and beliefs.[14]

While few analysts frame their discussions in terms of policy windows, the concept is implicit when failure and crisis are invoked as mechanisms that open up politics. Explicit use of the concept, with its focus on policy entrepreneurs, would help bring the individual back in to the study of ideas-based policy change. Indeed, for a literature that should be biased in favor of individual agents and their ideas, there is surprisingly little systematic attention to agency. This has led to a situation where researchers "continue to be vague on how ideas and norms specifically influence international relations," and where little is known of the "processes and mechanisms through which ideas come to influence state policies and practices." In rectifying this problem, the ideas literature might benefit from the work of those who have systematically explored the causal mechanisms that open up politics.[15]

A second constant of the ideas-policy relation is that ideas often play a dual role in the process of change, having both a cognitive and a political impact. In a cognitive sense, they provide elites with new understandings of state interests and allow them to learn. As Heclo would put it, they help decision makers puzzle better. Yet, ideas can have an equally important political impact. New ideas, in other words, not only help policymakers learn, they also assist them in resolving political problems. As one analyst puts it: "Ideas do change minds, but it is their practical value in solving political dilemmas which gives them a force in history."[16]

This simply restates a central dilemma for the ideas literature: which comes first, ideas or interests? Are ideas mere tools of convenience, with political elites instrumentally seizing upon them to legitimate a policy change made for interest-based reasons? Or are changes in preferences and interests caused by changes in ideas, with elites adopting new ideas as they puzzle and learn?

Should one of these roles — the political or cognitive — be stressed over the other? If the goal is to develop parsimonious, generalizable theories, then perhaps the answer is "yes."[17] But to capture the complexity of change and the role of ideas within it, one is better off accepting the messy world of policymaking for what it is: a place where ideas have both cognitive and political impact. Instead of positing an ideas-interests dichotomy, scholars should explore how ideational and rationalist accounts can supplement each other.[18]

As for differences in the ideas-behavior relation, one factor that clearly varies cross-nationally is the process through which new ideas reach key elites. In the (centralized and autonomous) Soviet state, I argued that policy entrepreneurs were an essential link in the mechanism bringing new ideas to politics. Kathryn Sikkink and Emanuel Adler, in their studies on the role of ideas in the (strong) Brazilian state, argue in a similar fashion that particular organizational leaders (Sikkink) or well-placed individuals (Adler's "weathermakers" and "subversive elites") played key roles in empowering new ideas.[19]

Margaret Weir, in her study of employment policy in the (decentralized) American state, sees a complex set of factors determining whether government agencies implement policies based on new ideas. The ideas themselves come from a wide array of actors with access to the policy process — including Congress and professional associations. Walter Salant, in examining the spread of Keynesian economic ideas to the United States during the 1930s and 1940s, comes to similar conclusions. In particular, he argues that a key factor in the quick adoption of Keynesian ideas was the openness of American policymaking structures. Many "strategic places in the government," he notes, came to be occupied by academics with a strong grounding in Keynesian doctrines.[20]

Peter Hall argues that in Great Britain (somewhat more autonomous and centralized than America) key state leaders and the media played important roles in empowering new ideas on macroeconomic policymaking under Margaret Thatcher. Likewise, I suggested that in (partially decentralized) post-Soviet Russia key policymakers are still playing major roles in the battle of ideas over defining state interests.[21]

As the parenthetical comments suggest, cross-national variation in political institutions may be key in explaining the variance in pathways. In highly centralized and autonomous states like the former USSR, as well as in less

centralized but still strong states like Brazil, enlightened political leadership and policy entrepreneurs played key roles in bringing new ideas to politics. In these states, other pathways were essentially blocked.[22]

At the opposite end of the institutional spectrum are such states as America where policymaking is decentralized and fragmented. The political process is relatively open and, consequently there are many avenues by which new ideas can reach key decision makers. Weir's study confirms that in the United States, the problem is not so much getting new ideas to policymakers; rather, it is developing coherent, long-term policies based on those ideas.[23]

It is thus evident that crisis, uncertainty, and failure play key roles in the process through which new ideas are empowered. It also matters whether an idea is timely. That is, the likelihood of an idea's adoption is enhanced by the extent that it offers both cognitive support (learning about puzzles) and political assistance (resolving problems) to key policymakers. In addition, evidence drawn from a variety of national settings indicates that political institutions are a key variable mediating the role ideas play in shaping policy outcomes.

Finally, work on ideas and policy change would benefit from a greater cross-national, comparative focus. Much of the literature advances multicausal explanations on the role ideas play, yet it does so in the context of single-country studies; use of the comparative method would reduce the problems of over-determination in the analysis.[24]

My comments here point to both the strengths and weaknesses of current ideas-based research. This body of work has shown without a doubt that ideas are causally important; they explain empirical anomalies left unresolved by structural or interest-based theories. Indeed, some of the most interesting research suggests that ideas have a role to play even if one assumes rational, interest-maximizing behavior on the part of agents.[25] Yet, like any young research program, the work on ideas has left several issues unresolved. Indeed, the literature reviewed above overwhelmingly concentrates on the ideas-policy relation within the domestic political economy of various countries. I should therefore like to make a few points specifically on the relation of ideas to international political change.[26]

First, this type of research suffers from conceptual confusion. The words *idea, ideology,* and *norm* are sometimes used interchangeably, even though the analyst implies different concepts by them. Ideas are beliefs held by individuals. Norms and ideology, in contrast, are historically constructed and often embedded in organizational structures or other shared collectivities; they are thus less susceptible to change. Ideas, ideology, and norms, as defined here, are certainly relevant to research on the nonstructural sources of state behavior. To minimize conceptual confusion and thus clarify the logic of their argu-

ments, theorists in foreign policy ideas might benefit from considering recent work on international norms, which explicitly addresses these deeper normative bases of state behavior.[27]

Second, future work on ideas and foreign policy should broaden its focus beyond elites. Stressing their role is understandable, for it is ultimately elite preferences that must change for policy and behavior to change. Yet at the same time, elites do not exist in ideational vacuums. Certain ideas they adopt may not resonate with understandings held by the broader public or with national discourses. In spite of this, much of the ideas literature portrays society as a passive actor in the process of ideas-based change.[28]

This may indeed be the case in certain countries (the authoritarian USSR, say). In other contexts, however, social norms and discourses may matter more in any process of ideational change. This is another area where research on ideas and that on norms could benefit from intellectual exchange; the former could explore the role of elite beliefs and mechanisms of change, while the latter probed the social discourses and norms that structure the political contest.[29]

Third, there is a need for greater efforts at theory building. A primary reason for the lack of theorizing is the intellectual heritage of much of the work on ideas and policy change. Many of the scholars working in this area draw upon insights of historical institutionalism; their preferred method involves richly detailed, comparative case studies where there is little emphasis on the testing of specific propositions. Not surprisingly, their hypotheses are generally inductively derived.[30]

As I argued in chapter 1, however, the generation and testing of specific hypotheses that relate ideas to foreign policy should contribute to middle-range theory building. This type of theory, although rich in explanatory detail, typically presents multicausal explanations that are overdetermined, with the outcome of interest predicted by any of several independent variables.

Careful use of the comparative method and greater attention to research design can minimize this problem. For example, a design where the issue area is constant but the national setting varies could make an important contribution to a better understanding of the role of ideas. Indeed, such a design is precisely the sort needed to explore the generalizability of the framework elaborated in this book.

Single-country studies, where the role of ideas is compared across policy areas or over time (longitudinally), can also make several contributions. Those in the first category would contribute to a long-running debate over the role of issue area in foreign-policy analysis. Such studies could also help resolve some intriguing empirical puzzles in the case of the former Soviet Union. For

example, why did new ideas have such a far-reaching impact on elite foreign policy preferences in Gorbachev's USSR, but little effect on leadership thinking about the domestic economy? Longitudinal designs, especially if they employ Alexander George's focused-comparison case study method, can better control for the relative importance of new ideas in cases that are complex and detailed.[31]

Finally, in developing theories that link ideas and foreign policy, it is important not to devalue the international context. It is all too easy when exploring the domestic aspects of state behavior to forget about the international environment in which all nations operate. We must not artificially separate the two spheres but explore how they interact. This exercise inevitably makes our theories less parsimonious and our lives as scholars more difficult, but such interaction captures the essence of the world we should be attempting to understand and model.[32]

Appendix: Schedule of Interviews

Unless otherwise noted, all interviews were conducted in Moscow.

IMEMO, Russian Academy of Sciences

Sergey E. Blagovolin, head, Department of Strategic Analysis, and president, Institute for National Security and Strategic Studies, July 20, 1992

Oleg N. Bykov, deputy director and head, Department of International Political Relations, May 7, 1992

German Diligenskiy, head, Department of Social and Domestic-Political Problems of Western Countries, and editor-in-chief of *Memo,* July 16, 1992

Kamo Gadzhiev, chief, Sector for Analysis of Western Political Science, Department of Social and Political Problems of Capitalist Countries, May 6, 1992

Igor Ye. Gur'yev, deputy director, May 6, 1992

Andrey Karabashkin, scientific secretary, May 1992

Nikolay A. Kosolapov, deputy head, Department of International Political Relations, May 6, 1992; May 8, 1992; July 13, 1992

Ruslan Kumakhov, research fellow, Department of West European Studies, May 1991 (Pittsburgh, Pa.); November 1991; May 1992

Vladimir G. Leschke, deputy director, May 8, 1992

Margarita Maksimova, senior researcher, May 6, 1992

Aleksandr Naumenkov, research fellow, Department of West European Studies, November 1991; May 1992

Elgiz Pozdnyakov, chief, Sector for International Relations Theory, Department of International Political Relations, November 1991

Vladimir Razmerov, senior researcher, Department of International Political Relations, July 17, 1992

Aleksandr Savelyev, vice president, Institute for National Security and Strategic Studies, May 6, 1992

Nodari A. Simonia, deputy director, March 1994 (Washington, D.C.)

Valeriy A. Slavinskiy, deputy editor-in-chief of *Memo,* July 16, 1992

Dmitriy Tomashevskiy, senior researcher, Department of International Political Relations, July 17, 1992

Lyudmila Zonova, senior research fellow, November 1991; May 1992

ISKAN, Russian Academy of Sciences

Georgiy Arbatov, director, May 7, 1992

Vladimir Benevolenskiy, scientific secretary, November 1991; July 17, 1992

Anatoliy Porokhovskiy, deputy director, November 1991

Russian Foreign Ministry

Yuriy Dubinin, Department for Relations with CIS, July 14, 1992

Aleksandr Katushev, counselor, Department for Relations with CIS, May 12, 1992; July 15, 1992; July 20, 1992

Vladimir B. Kudryavtsev, third secretary, Department of Analysis and Planning, April 29, 1992; July 21, 1992

Yevgeniy Kutouvoy, deputy head, Department of Analysis and Planning, April 29, 1992

Vladimir Kuzmin, deputy head, Department of Analysis and Planning, July 21, 1992

Aleksandr A. Lebedev, third secretary, Department of USA and Canada, April 29, 1992

Boris Marchuk, Department of USA and Canada, April 29, 1992

Nikolay Smirnov, deputy head, Department of USA and Canada, April 29, 1992

Viktor Smolin, first deputy head, Department of Analysis and Planning, May 7, 1992

Yevgeniy Voronin, head, Division for Contacts with Foreign Scientific/Research Centers, Department of Analysis and Planning, May 5, 1992; July 21, 1992

General

Yuriy E. Fedorov, chair, Faculty of Political Science, Moscow State Institute of International Relations, April 29, 1992; April 30, 1992; May 5, 1992

Aleksandr Yakovlev, vice president for research, Gorbachev Foundation, July 21, 1992

Notes

Preface

1. This is especially true of researchers in the subfield of international political economy. See W. Rand Smith, "International Economy and State Strategies: Recent Work in Comparative Political Economy," *Comparative Politics* 25 (April 1993). Recently, a number of theorists in the foreign and security subfield have also called for explanatory frameworks that integrate levels of analysis. For a review, see Jeff Checkel, "Ideas, Institutions and the Gorbachev Foreign Policy Revolution," *World Politics* 45 (January 1993), 273–75. Representative arguments that favor a mixing of levels are Stephan Haggard, "Structuralism and Its Critics: Recent Progress in International Relations Theory," in Emanuel Adler and Beverly Crawford, Editors, *Progress in Postwar International Relations* (New York: Columbia University Press, 1991); and Andrew Moravcsik, "Integrating International and Domestic Theories of International Bargaining," in Peter Evans et al., Editors, *Double-Edged Diplomacy: International Bargaining and Domestic Politics* (Berkeley, Calif.: University of California Press, 1993). The seminal theoretical treatment of the need to integrate domestic and international sources of state behavior is Robert Putnam, "Diplomacy and Domestic Politics: The Logic of Two-Level Games," *International Organization* 42 (Summer 1988).

2. Timothy McKeown, "The Limitations of 'Structural' Theories of Commercial Policy," *International Organization* 40 (Winter 1986), 56.

3. As Robert Gilpin has argued, "eclecticism may not be the route to theoretical precision, but sometimes it is the only route available." Gilpin, *The Political Economy of International Relations* (Princeton, N.J.: Princeton University Press, 1987), p. 25. On the

need to build bridges between comparative politics and international relations, also see Harald Mueller and Thomas Risse-Kappen, "From the Outside In and from the Inside Out: International Relations, Domestic Politics and Foreign Policy," in David Skidmore and Valerie Hudson, Editors, *The Limits of State Autonomy: Societal Groups and Foreign Policy Formulation* (Boulder, Colo.: Westview Press, 1993).

4. In the field of international relations, a persistent advocate of middle-range theory has been Alexander George. See Alexander George and Richard Smoke, *Deterrence in American Foreign Policy: Theory and Practice* (New York: Columbia University Press, 1974), Appendix; and Alexander George, *Bridging the Gap: Theory and Practice in Foreign Policy* (Washington, D.C.: United States Institute of Peace Press, 1993), chapter 9 and "Summary and Conclusions."

5. On the area-studies approach, see Jack Snyder, "Richness, Rigor and Relevance in the Study of Soviet Foreign Policy," *International Security* 9 (Winter 1984/85); and idem, "Science and Sovietology: Bridging the Methods Gap in Soviet Foreign Policy Studies," *World Politics* 40 (January 1988). Examples of work on Soviet policy written from an area-studies perspective include Allen Lynch, *The Soviet Study of International Relations* (New York: Cambridge University Press, 1987); and Michael Sodaro, *Moscow, Germany and the West: From Khrushchev to Gorbachev* (Ithaca, N.Y.: Cornell University Press, 1990).

6. See Sodaro, *Moscow, Germany and the West,* pp. 12–19, and the sources cited therein. An exception to this generalization is the work of Matthew Evangelista. See Evangelista, *Innovation and the Arms Race: How the United States and the Soviet Union Develop New Military Technologies* (Ithaca, N.Y.: Cornell University Press, 1988), especially Part I.

7. See Daniel Deudney and G. John Ikenberry, "The International Sources of Soviet Change," *International Security* 16 (Winter 1991/92); Jack Snyder, *Myths of Empire: Domestic Politics and International Ambition* (Ithaca, N.Y.: Cornell University Press, 1991), chapter 6; and Sarah Mendelson, "Internal Battles and External Wars: Politics, Learning and the Soviet Withdrawal from Afghanistan," *World Politics* 45 (April 1993), for example.

8. On the drawbacks of parsimony and the trade-off between it and explanatory richness, see Haggard, "Structuralism and Its Critics," pp. 417–18; and Peter Hall, *Governing the Economy: The Politics of State Intervention in Britain and France* (New York: Oxford University Press, 1986), pp. 259–60.

Chapter 1: Ideas and Policy Change

1. Examples from international political economy include John Odell, *US International Monetary Policy: Markets, Power and Ideas as Sources of Change* (Princeton, N.J.: Princeton University Press, 1982); Peter Haas, *Saving the Mediterranean: The Politics of International Environmental Cooperation* (New York: Columbia University Press, 1990); and Judith Goldstein, *Ideas, Interests and American Trade Policy* (Ithaca, N.Y.: Cornell University Press, 1993). In the foreign and security subfield, see Jeff Checkel, "Ideas, Institutions and the Gorbachev Foreign Policy Revolution," *World Politics* 45 (January 1993); Judith Goldstein and Robert Keohane, Editors, *Ideas and Foreign Pol-*

icy: Beliefs, Institutions and Political Change (Ithaca, N.Y.: Cornell University Press, 1993); and Edward Rhodes, "Do Bureaucratic Politics Matter? Some Disconfirming Findings from the Case of the US Navy," *World Politics* 47 (October 1994). In the comparative political economy literature, see Emanuel Adler, *The Power of Ideology: The Quest for Technological Autonomy in Argentina and Brazil* (Berkeley: University of California Press, 1987); Peter Hall, Editor, *The Political Power of Economic Ideas: Keynesianism Across Nations* (Princeton, N.J.: Princeton University Press, 1989); and Kathryn Sikkink, *Ideas and Institutions: Developmentalism in Brazil and Argentina* (Ithaca, N.Y.: Cornell University Press, 1991). In the literature on American political economy, see Margaret Weir, *Politics and Jobs: The Boundaries of Employment Policy in the United States* (Princeton, N.J.: Princeton University Press, 1992).

2. On the ideas-individuals connection, see Odell, *US International Monetary Policy.* For institutional approaches, see Sikkink, *Ideas and Institutions,* chapters 1 and 7, for example.

3. On the historical-institutionalist approach, see Kathleen Thelen and Sven Steinmo, "Historical Institutionalism in Comparative Politics," in Frank Longstreth et al., Editors, *Structuring Politics: Historical Institutionalism in Comparative Analysis* (New York: Cambridge University Press, 1992). Important examples of this work include Peter Hall, *Governing the Economy: The Politics of State Intervention in Britain and France* (New York: Oxford University Press, 1986); Stephan Haggard, *Pathways from the Periphery: The Politics of Growth in the Newly Industrializing Countries* (Ithaca, N.Y.: Cornell University Press, 1990); and Victoria Hattam, "Institutions and Political Change: Working-Class Formation in England and the United States, 1820–1896," *Politics & Society* 20 (June 1992). On the new institutionalism more generally and its application in the international-relations and comparative-politics literatures, see James Caporaso, "International Relations Theory and Multilateralism: The Search for Foundations," *International Organization* 46 (Summer 1992), 620–32; and Ellen Immergut, *Health Politics: Interests and Institutions in Western Europe* (New York: Cambridge University Press, 1992), pp. 18–29.

4. See, especially, Sikkink, *Ideas and Institutions;* Peter Hall, "The Movement from Keynesianism to Monetarism: Institutional Analysis in British Economic Policy," in Longstreth et al., Editors, *Structuring Politics;* and Goldstein, *Ideas, Interests and American Trade Policy.*

5. See Thelen and Steinmo, "Historical Institutionalism in Comparative Politics," pp. 13–26; and Hall, "The Movement from Keynesianism to Monetarism," pp. 90, 106–09.

6. On consensual knowledge, see Peter Haas, "Introduction: Epistemic Communities and International Policy Coordination," *International Organization* 46 (Winter 1992), 3; and Robert Rothstein, "Consensual Knowledge and International Collaboration: Some Lessons from the Commodity Negotiations," *International Organization* 38 (Autumn 1984), 736–40. On the epistemic approach more generally, see Peter Haas, "Do Regimes Matter? Epistemic Communities and Mediterranean Pollution Control," *International Organization* 43 (Summer 1989); idem, *Saving the Mediterranean;* Ernst Haas, *When Knowledge Is Power: Three Models of Change in International Organizations* (Berkeley: University of California Press, 1990), chapters 1–2; Emanuel Adler, "The Emergence of Cooperation: National Epistemic Communities and the International Evo-

lution of the Idea of Nuclear Arms Control," *International Organization* 46 (Winter 1992); and Sarah Mendelson, "Internal Battles and External Wars: Politics, Learning and the Soviet Withdrawal from Afghanistan," *World Politics* 45 (April 1993).

7. Haas, "Introduction: Epistemic Communities and International Policy Coordination," pp. 1–35.

8. Helen Milner has also noted the lack of attention to domestic politics in the epistemic literature. See Milner, "International Theories of Cooperation Among Nations: Strengths and Weaknesses (Review Article)," *World Politics* 44 (April 1992), 479, 488–95.

9. See Haas, "Do Regimes Matter?"; idem, *Saving the Mediterranean*; and, more recently, idem, "Introduction: Epistemic Communities and International Policy Coordination," pp. 33–34.

10. See, especially, Adler, "The Emergence of Cooperation," pp. 133–40. Also see Mendelson, "Internal Battles and External Wars."

11. In Checkel, "Ideas, Institutions and the Gorbachev Foreign Policy Revolution," pp. 273–76, I review the growing body of international-relations literature employing such middle-range approaches. For the need to develop similar approaches in the comparative-politics field, see Thelen and Steinmo, "Historical Institutionalism in Comparative Politics," pp. 10–13, 26–28.

12. For definitions similar to mine, see Odell, *US International Monetary Policy,* p. 63; Hall, "The Movement from Keynesianism to Monetarism," pp. 91–92; and Goldstein and Keohane, Editors, *Ideas and Foreign Policy,* pp. 13–17. The term *policy paradigm* is taken from Hall.

13. See G. John Ikenberry, "Conclusion: An Institutional Approach to American Foreign Economic Policy," in Ikenberry et al., Editors, *The State and American Foreign Economic Policy* (Ithaca, N.Y.: Cornell University Press, 1988), pp. 226–29; Robert Keohane, "International Institutions: Two Approaches," *International Studies Quarterly* 32 (December 1988), 382–86; and Hall, "The Movement from Keynesianism to Monetarism," pp. 96–97.

14. Likewise, the constructivist literature in international relations, despite a radically different epistemology and ontology from earlier structural theories, often fails to explicate processes and mechanisms of change. See Peter Katzenstein, "Norms and National Security: Germany and Japan at the End of the Cold War," paper presented at University of Pittsburgh Colloquium on International Relations Theory, January 1995. For critiques of structural approaches in international relations and comparative politics, see Stephan Haggard, "Structuralism and Its Critics: Recent Progress in International Relations Theory," in Emanuel Adler and Beverly Crawford, Editors, *Progress in Postwar International Relations* (New York: Columbia University Press, 1991); and Thelen and Steinmo, "Historical Institutionalism in Comparative Politics."

15. See Graham Allison, *Essence of Decision: Explaining the Cuban Missile Crisis* (Boston: Little, Brown, 1971).

16. Several authors working within the historical-institutionalist literature also explore this middle ground. See Sikkink, *Ideas and Institutions*; Weir, *Politics and Jobs,* pp. 17–18, and passim; and Hall, "The Movement from Keynesianism to Monetarism."

17. In the former Soviet field, one important exception to this generalization is Mat-

thew Evangelista, *Innovation and the Arms Race: How the US and Soviet Union Develop New Military Technologies* (Ithaca, N.Y.: Cornell University Press, 1988).

18. For earlier explorations of the role played by institutional structure, see Helen Milner, *Resisting Protectionism: Global Industries and the Politics of International Trade* (Princeton, N.J.: Princeton University Press, 1988), pp. 274–88; Thomas Risse-Kappen, "Public Opinion, Domestic Structure and Foreign Policy in Liberal Democracies," *World Politics* 43 (July 1991), 484–88; and Evelyn Davidheiser, "Strong States, Weak States: The Role of the State in Revolution," *Comparative Politics* 24 (July 1992), 463–65. On the relation between the pathways available to carriers of ideas and state structures, also see Desmond King, "The Establishment of Work-Welfare Programs in the United States and Britain: Politics, Ideas and Institutions," in Longstreth et al., Editors, *Structuring Politics,* pp. 219–20.

19. On these points, also see Sikkink, *Ideas and Institutions,* pp. 2, 196; Weir, *Politics and Jobs,* pp. 19–22; and Hall, "The Movement from Keynesianism to Monetarism," p. 98.

20. See Sikkink, *Ideas and Institutions,* pp. 248–51; and Weir, *Politics and Jobs,* passim. Historical institutionalists are sensitive to the charge that their enterprise is more one of storytelling than theory building. For a discussion and rebuttal, see Thelen and Steinmo, "Historical Institutionalism in Comparative Politics," pp. 12–13.

21. Peter Gourevitch, *Politics in Hard Times: Comparative Responses to International Economic Crises* (Ithaca, N.Y.: Cornell University Press, 1986). Also see Stephan Haggard, *Pathways from the Periphery.* There is a tension between structure (social forces with interests determined by position in the international political economy; state institutions) and agency in Gourevitch's work. He gives considerably more explanatory weight to the former, yet particular agents — politicians in a position to exercise leadership — are often key in explaining outcomes. See pp. 83, 236, 240.

22. Katzenstein, "International Relations and Domestic Structures: Foreign Economic Policies of Advanced Industrial States," *International Organization* 30 (Winter 1976); and idem, Editor, *Between Power and Plenty: Foreign Economic Policies of Advanced Industrial States* (Madison: University of Wisconsin Press, 1978).

23. On this last point, also see Matthew Evangelista, "Issue-Area and Foreign Policy Revisited," *International Organization* 43 (Winter 1989); Risse-Kappen, "Public Opinion, Domestic Structure and Foreign Policy in Liberal Democracies"; Aaron Friedberg, "Why Didn't the United States Become a Garrison State?" *International Security* 16 (Spring 1992); and Peter Katzenstein and Nobuo Okawara, "Japan's National Security: Structures, Norms and Policies," *International Security* 17 (Spring 1993).

24. Among others, see Kenneth Waltz, *Theory of International Politics* (Menlo Park, Calif.: Addison-Wesley, 1979); David Lake, *Power, Protection and Free Trade: International Sources of US Commercial Strategy, 1887–1939* (Ithaca, N.Y.: Cornell University Press, 1988); and Christopher Layne, "The Unipolar Illusion: Why New Great Powers Will Rise," *International Security* 17 (Spring 1993).

25. See Gourevitch, *Politics in Hard Times,* pp. 81–83 and passim; and Haggard, *Pathways from the Periphery,* pp. 46–47.

26. See, especially, Gourevitch, *Politics in Hard Times*; Ikenberry et al., Editors, *The State and American Foreign Economic Policy,* pp. 233–36; and John Keeler, "Opening

the Window for Reform: Mandates, Crises and Extraordinary Policymaking," *Comparative Political Studies* 25 (January 1993). Much of the theoretical basis for the argument linking crises, uncertainty, and preference change derives from decision making and organizational theory. See James Moltz, "Divergent Learning and the Failed Politics of Soviet Economic Reform," *World Politics* 45 (January 1993), 301–09, for example.

27. See Odell, *US International Monetary Policy*; Kathryn Sikkink, "Human Rights, Principled Issue-Networks and Sovereignty in Latin America," *International Organization* 47 (Summer 1993); Thomas Risse-Kappen, "Ideas Do Not Float Freely: Transnational Coalitions, Domestic Structures and the End of the Cold War," *International Organization* 48 (Spring 1994); and idem, *Bringing Transnational Relations Back In: Non-State Actors, Domestic Structures and International Institutions* (Cambridge: Cambridge University Press, 1995), chapter 1.

28. On this, also see Matthew Evangelista, "The Paradox of State Strength: Transnational Relations, Domestic Structures and Security Policy in Russia and the Soviet Union," *International Organization* 49 (Winter 1995), 1–7.

29. For an example of the descriptive emphasis, see Paula King and Nancy Roberts, "Policy Entrepreneurs: Their Activity Structure and Function in the Policy Process," *Journal of Public Administration Research and Theory* 1 (April 1991). Criticizing the lack of theory development are Mark Schneider and Paul Teske, "Toward a Theory of the Political Entrepreneur: Evidence from Local Government," *American Political Science Review* 86 (September 1992); and Frank Baumgartner and Bryan Jones, *Agendas and Instability in American Politics* (Chicago: University of Chicago Press, 1993), p. 48.

30. Schneider and Teske, "Toward a Theory of the Political Entrepreneur," p. 737.

31. On entrepreneurial resources, see John Kingdon, *Agendas, Alternatives and Public Policy* (Boston: Little, Brown, 1984); and Jack Walker, "The Diffusion of Knowledge, Policy Communities and Agenda Setting," in John Tropman, Robert Lind, and Milan Dluhy, Editors, *New Strategic Perspectives on Social Policy* (New York: Pergamon, 1981). In the literature on ideas and politics, several researchers ascribe a key role to ideas carried by individuals but do not cast the analysis in terms of policy entrepreneurship. See Odell, *US International Monetary Policy*, chapter 2; and Judith Goldstein, "Ideas, Institutions and American Trade Policy," *International Organization* 42 (Winter 1988).

32. Kingdon, *Agendas, Alternatives and Public Policy*, pp. 89–94. Also useful are Michael Cohen, James March, and Johan Olsen, "A Garbage Can Model of Organizational Choice," *Administrative Science Quarterly* 17 (March 1972); and King and Roberts, "Policy Entrepreneurs."

33. On entrepreneurship in foreign policymaking, also see Matthew Evangelista, "Sources of Moderation in Soviet Security Policy," in Philip Tetlock et al., Editors, *Behavior, Society, and Nuclear War*, vol. 2 (New York: Oxford University Press, 1991).

34. Gourevitch, *Politics in Hard Times*; and Keeler, "Opening the Window for Reform."

35. I define organizations as hierarchical, functionally specialized entities. See Charles Perrow, *Complex Organizations: A Critical Essay*, 3d ed. (New York: Random House, 1986), chapter 5.

36. See Anthony Downs, *Inside Bureaucracy* (Boston: Little, Brown, 1967), chapters 6 and 12; James Thompson, *Organizations in Action: Social Science Bases of Administra-*

tive Theory (New York: McGraw-Hill, 1967); and Pasquale Gagliardi, "The Creation and Change of Organizational Cultures: A Conceptual Framework," *Organization Studies* 7 (1986).

37. For definitions similar to mine, see Sikkink, *Ideas and Institutions,* chapters 1, 7; and Jack Snyder, *The Ideology of the Offensive: Military Decision Making and the Disasters of 1914* (Ithaca, N.Y.: Cornell University Press, 1984), pp. 30–31. Recent work by organization theorists on "behavioral frames" parallels in important ways my discussion here. See Lynn Eden, "Constructing Deconstruction: Development of Organizational Knowledge in Nuclear Targeting," seminar, Massachusetts Institute of Technology, November 3, 1993.

38. On the British Treasury, see Margaret Weir, "Ideas and Politics: The Acceptance of Keynesianism in Britain and the United States," in Hall, Editor, *Political Power of Economic Ideas.* This understanding of the process of interest definition stands in marked contrast to the dominant orthodoxy in international political economy and international relations that sees interests as rationally, materially determined. For influential works stressing the material nature of interests (at the level of the state or units within it), see Gourevitch, *Politics in Hard Times;* Milner, *Resisting Protectionism;* and Waltz, *Theory of International Politics.*

39. Sikkink, *Ideas and Institutions,* p. 250.

40. For an excellent application of this scientific method and its benefits for theory development, see John Owen, "How Liberalism Produces Democratic Peace," *International Security* 19 (Fall 1994).

41. Students of public policy are beginning to make similar arguments. See Paul Sabatier, "Political Science and Public Policy," *PS: Political Science and Politics* 24 (June 1991), for example.

42. Robert Jervis, *Perception and Misperception in International Politics* (Princeton, N.J.: Princeton University Press, 1976).

43. Making clear the differences between constructivist and ideas-based approaches is Alexander Wendt, "Anarchy Is What States Make of It: The Social Construction of Power Politics," *International Organization* 46 (Spring 1992). John Jacobsen, "Much Ado About Ideas: The Cognitive Factor in Economic Policy," *World Politics* 47 (January 1995), highlights the role of "interest" in much of the ideas literature.

44. Waltz, *Theory of International Politics,* is the clearest statement of the neorealist argument. For critiques, see, among many others, Haggard, "Structuralism and Its Critics." There have been few efforts to explain Soviet behavior from a neorealist perspective. For one attempt, see Raymond Taras and Marshal Zeringue, "Grand Strategy in a Post-Bipolar World: Interpreting the Final Soviet Response," *Review of International Studies* 18 (October 1992). Using a process-oriented classical realism reminiscent of Morgenthau to explain Soviet behavior is William Wohlforth, "Realism and the End of the Cold War," *International Security* 19 (Winter 1994/95). Wohlforth's argument is plausible, yet his stress on the importance of perceptions and his introduction of other domestic-level causal variables makes it ultimately unclear whether his account is consistent with the theoretical core of realism.

45. See Daniel Deudney and G. John Ikenberry, "Soviet Reform and the End of the Cold War: Explaining Large-Scale Historical Change," *Review of International Studies*

17 (July 1991), 226–44; and idem, "The International Sources of Soviet Change," *International Security* 16 (Winter 1991/92), where the authors list no fewer than eight international sources for the changes in Soviet foreign behavior under Gorbachev.

46. See Timothy McKeown, "The Foreign Policy of a Declining Power," *International Organization* 45 (Spring 1991), 259–61, 276–78. Even quite sophisticated realist theories exhibit these weaknesses. See G. John Ikenberry, David Lake, and Michael Mastanduno, "Toward a Realist Theory of State Action," *International Studies Quarterly* 33 (December 1989); and Wohlforth, "Realism and the End of the Cold War," for example.

47. This leadership explanation was implicit in many of Jerry Hough's interpretations of the Gorbachev era. See Hough, *Russia and the West: Gorbachev and the Politics of Reform* (New York: Simon and Schuster, 1988). On Brezhnev, see Georgiy Arbatov, *Zatyanuvsheesya vyzdorovleniye: Svidetel'stvo sovremennika* (Moscow: Mezhdunarodnye otnosheniya, 1991), pp. 282–96; and Fedor Burlatskiy, *Khrushchev and the First Russian Spring* (New York: Charles Scribner's Sons, 1991), chapter 11. Burlatskiy was an adviser to Brezhnev in the mid-1960s; Arbatov had a much closer and sustained relationship to the former general secretary, having advised him from the late 1960s to the early 1980s.

48. Mendelson, "Internal Battles and External Wars." This fact was also confirmed during interviews with Georgiy Arbatov, Sergey Blagovolin, and Aleksandr Yakovlev.

49. See Eduard Shevardnadze, *Moy vybor: v zashchitu demokratii i svobody* (Moscow: Novosti, 1991), pp. 62–63; and Mikhail Gorbachev, *Zhivoye tvorchestvo naroda* (Moscow: Politizdat, 1984). Georgiy Arbatov and Aleksandr Yakovlev, in separate interviews with the author, confirmed this interpretation.

50. On this last point, also see Mendelson, "Internal Battles and External Wars," passim. Evangelista, "Sources of Moderation in Soviet Security Policy," provides an excellent overview and critique of learning theories.

51. Coalition-building theories of this sort have received considerable attention in both the comparative-politics and international-relations literatures in recent years. See, especially, Gourevitch, *Politics in Hard Times*; Haggard, *Pathways from the Periphery*; and Jack Snyder, *Myths of Empire: Domestic Politics and International Ambition* (Ithaca, N.Y.: Cornell University Press, 1991). Sikkink, *Ideas and Institutions,* pp. 15–19, offers an important rebuttal to such "political" explanations.

52. This ambiguity is evident throughout the Gourevitch and Snyder books. See Gourevitch, *Politics in Hard Times,* pp. 43, 45, 55, 94, 102, 114–16, 159, 216–17; and Snyder, *Myths of Empire,* pp. 44, 67, 98, 241, 314.

53. See the symposium "Toward Better Theories of the Policy Process," *PS: Political Science and Politics* 24 (June 1991).

54. Also see Peter Hall, "Policy Paradigms, Social Learning and the State: The Case of Economic Policymaking in Britain," *Comparative Politics* 25 (April 1993), 283–87; and Carol Weiss, "Policy Research: Data, Ideas, or Arguments?" in Peter Wagner et al., Editors, *Social Sciences and Modern States: National Experiences and Theoretical Crossroads* (New York: Cambridge University Press, 1991), p. 318.

55. This has been an important finding of work on agenda setting. See Nelson Polsby, "Policy Initiation in the American Political System," in I. Horowitz, Editor, *The Use and Abuse of Social Science: Behavioral Research and Policymaking* (New Brunswick, N.J.:

Transaction Books, 1975); Kingdon, *Agendas, Alternatives and Public Policy*; and Walker, "The Diffusion of Knowledge, Policy Communities and Agenda Setting." A more balanced understanding of the power of vested interests versus other causal variables also emerges from recent historical-institutionalist work on American political economy. See Weir, *Politics and Jobs*.

56. See, for example, Michel Tatu, *Power in the Kremlin: From Khrushchev to Kosygin* (New York: Viking Press, 1969); Harry Gelman, *The Brezhnev Politburo and the Decline of Detente* (Ithaca, N.Y.: Cornell University Press, 1984); and Bruce Parrott, "Soviet National Security under Gorbachev," *Problems of Communism* 37 (November–December 1988). A more theoretically sophisticated analysis of Politburo politics is Richard Anderson, "Why Competitive Politics Inhibits Learning in Soviet Foreign Policy," in George Breslauer and Philip Tetlock, Editors, *Learning in US and Soviet Foreign Policy* (Boulder, Colo.: Westview, 1991).

57. Exceptions include Thane Gustafson, *Reform in Soviet Politics: Lessons of Recent Policies on Land and Water* (New York: Cambridge University Press, 1981); and Peter Solomon, *Soviet Criminologists and Criminal Policy: Specialists in Policymaking* (New York: Columbia University Press, 1978).

58. Gourevitch, *Politics in Hard Times*, p. 68; and Snyder, *Myths of Empire*, chapters 1, 6, 8.

59. The quote comes from Snyder, *Myths of Empire*, p. 214.

60. I thank an anonymous reviewer for helping to clarify my thinking on these points.

61. Many interviewees requested anonymity and I have respected their wishes. Thus, the interview data referenced in the endnotes do not always include names and dates. See the appendix for the interview schedule.

62. For an example of how process tracing can help validate a complex thesis, see John Duffield, "International Regimes and Alliance Behavior: Explaining NATO Conventional Force Levels," *International Organization* 46 (Autumn 1992).

63. On focused comparisons, see Alexander George, "Case Studies and Theory Development: The Method of Structured, Focused Comparison," in Paul Lauren, Editor, *Diplomacy: New Approaches in History, Theory and Policy* (New York: Free Press, 1979).

Chapter 2: Policymaking in an Authoritarian State

1. See William Zimmerman, *Soviet Perspectives on International Relations, 1956–67* (Princeton, N.J.: Princeton University Press, 1969); Robert Tucker, *The Soviet Political Mind: Stalinism and Post-Stalin Change* (New York: Norton, 1971), chapter 10; and Allen Lynch, *The Soviet Study of International Relations* (New York: Cambridge University Press, 1987), chapter 3. On the Academy and the role of scientific knowledge more generally in Soviet society, see Loren Graham, *The Soviet Academy of Sciences and the Communist Party* (Princeton, N.J.: Princeton University Press, 1967); and idem, *Science in Russia and the Soviet Union: A Short History* (New York: Cambridge University Press, 1993), parts II–III.

2. On the Brezhnev period, see Thane Gustafson, *Reform in Soviet Politics: Lessons of Recent Policies on Land and Water* (New York: Cambridge University Press, 1981).

The power of political elites to control specialist access to policymaking was still in evidence through the first three years of the Gorbachev era. See Jeff Checkel, "Ideas, Institutions and the Gorbachev Foreign Policy Revolution," *World Politics* 45 (January 1993); and Sarah Mendelson, "Internal Battles and External Wars: Politics, Learning and the Soviet Withdrawal from Afghanistan," *World Politics* 45 (April 1993).

3. On permeability, see Evelyn Davidheiser, "Strong States, Weak States: The Role of the State in Revolution," *Comparative Politics* 24 (July 1992), 465. For analyses depicting the centralized nature of Soviet foreign policymaking, see Elizabeth Teague, "The Foreign Departments of the Central Committee of the CPSU," Radio Liberty *Research Bulletin,* Supplement (October 27, 1980); and Thomas Wolfe, *The SALT Experience* (Cambridge, Mass.: Ballinger Press, 1979). On the nature of Soviet institutions, also see the outstanding work of Matthew Evangelista, *Innovation and the Arms Race: How the US and the Soviet Union Develop New Military Technologies* (Ithaca, N.Y.: Cornell University Press, 1988), passim; and idem, "Issue Area and Foreign Policy Revisited," *International Organization* 43 (Winter 1989), 151–55.

4. As noted in chapter 1, how ideologies become embedded in organizations is a key question that the literature on ideas and politics needs to address. In the Soviet field, this issue received little serious analytic attention. Many discussions of ideology were highly stylized ("ideology as a guide to action"; "ideology as a conceptual filter"), descriptive in nature, and focused on the individual or group level. Scholars have begun to address questions of Soviet ideology in a more rigorous fashion. Even here, however, the importance of an ideas-institutions nexus for empowering particular sets of ideas is not adequately addressed. See Jack Snyder, *Myths of Empire: Domestic Politics and International Ambition* (Ithaca, N.Y.: Cornell University Press, 1991), chapter 6; and James Richter, "Perpetuating the Cold War: Domestic Sources of International Patterns of Behavior," *Political Science Quarterly* 107 (Summer 1992).

5. On the Ministry's role, see Condoleezza Rice, "The Party, the Military and Decision Authority in the Soviet Union," *World Politics* 40 (October 1987). My depiction of the military's ideology of international politics derives from a reading of numerous Ministry publications from the early and mid-1980s, as well as published interviews with many top Ministry and General Staff officers. Military organizations in general tend toward the realist worldview described here. See John Lepingwell, "Soviet Civil-Military Relations and the August Coup," *World Politics* 44 (July 1992), 547–48.

6. On the International Department's role in policymaking, see Mark Kramer, "The Role of the CPSU International Department in Soviet Foreign Relations and National Security," *Soviet Studies* 42 (July 1990). My characterization of Suslov, Ponomarev, and the department's ideology draws on Kramer, as well as on interviews with two former high-ranking officials in the department; an interview with Aleksandr Yakovlev (who observed Ponomarev's behavior at a number of Politburo meetings they both attended); and Roy Medvedev and Dmitriy Ermakov, *'Seryy kardinal': M. A. Suslov — Politicheskiy portret* (Moscow: Respublika, 1992).

7. See chapters 3–5, below.

8. The argument here — that reform in foreign policy was essentially a top-down process — broadly accords with Evangelista's analysis of weapons innovation in the former USSR. See Evangelista, *Innovation and the Arms Race.*

9. This last point, as I discuss in chapter 6, is critical for understanding the differing nature of the contemporary Russian debate over state interests — and why, in particular, an opportunity was lost to consolidate a fundamentally new ideology of international politics under the Yeltsin leadership.

10. The quotes comes from John Odell, "Understanding International Trade Policies: An Emerging Synthesis," *World Politics* 43 (October 1990), 153. Previous studies of the role played by academic specialists in the Soviet policy process failed to consider the organizational and broader institutional contexts elaborated here. See Zimmerman, *Soviet Perspectives on International Relations, 1956–67*; Elizabeth Valkenier, *The Soviet Union and the Third World: An Economic Bind* (New York: Praeger, 1983); Jerry Hough, *The Struggle for the Third World: Soviet Debates and American Options* (Washington, D.C.: Brookings Institution, 1986); Lynch, *The Soviet Study of International Relations*; and Stephen Shenfield, *The Nuclear Predicament: Explorations in Soviet Ideology* (New York: Routledge and Kegan Paul, 1987).

11. On the institutes, see Barbara Dash, *A Defector Reports: The Institute of the USA and Canada* (Falls Church, Va.: Delphic Associates, 1982); Oded Eran, *Mezhdunarodniki: An Assessment of Professional Expertise in the Making of Soviet Foreign Policy* (Tel Aviv: Turtledove Publishing, 1979); and Yuriy Polsky, *Soviet Research Institutes and the Formation of Foreign Policy: The Institute of the World Economy and International Relations* (Falls Church, Va.: Delphic Associates, 1987).

12. The differing nature of ISKAN's formal mandate is best seen in the unsigned lead editorial published in the first issue of its journal, *SShA*. See "K chitatelyam," *SShA* No. 1 (January 1970). Information on the plans comes from interviews with three current and former academic secretaries at IMEMO and ISKAN, one of whose primary responsibilities was to make sure that institute research agendas addressed the issues raised in such documents. The plans themselves were formulated at the Presidium of the Academy of Sciences — often in close collaboration with personnel in relevant departments of the CPSU Central Committee.

13. See Peter Gourevitch, *Politics in Hard Times: Comparative Responses to International Economic Crises* (Ithaca, N.Y.: Cornell University Press, 1986), pp. 81–83 and passim; and Stephan Haggard, *Pathways from the Periphery: The Politics of Growth in Newly Industrializing Countries* (Ithaca, N.Y.: Cornell University Press, 1990), pp. 46–47.

14. On the Brezhnev period, see Bruce Parrott, *Politics and Technology in the Soviet Union* (Cambridge, Mass.: MIT Press, 1983), chapters 5–6; and, for the Gorbachev years, Stephen Meyer, "The Sources and Prospects of Gorbachev's New Political Thinking on Security," *International Security* 13 (Fall 1988). For more general arguments on the importance of political leadership in fostering policy change in the USSR, see George Breslauer, *Khrushchev and Brezhnev as Leaders: Building Authority in Soviet Politics* (Boston: Allen and Unwin, 1982); and Valerie Bunce, *Do New Leaders Make a Difference? Executive Succession and Public Policy Under Capitalism and Socialism* (Princeton, N.J.: Princeton University Press, 1981).

15. Useful reviews of Soviet policy in this period include John Newhouse, *Cold Dawn: The Story of SALT* (New York: Holt, Rinehart, and Winston, 1973); Parrott, *Politics and Technology in the Soviet Union*, chapters 5–6; Samuel Payne, *The Soviet Union and*

SALT (Cambridge, Mass.: MIT Press, 1980); Marshall Shulman, "SALT and the Soviet Union," in John Rhinelander and Mason Willrich, Editors, *SALT: The Moscow Agreements and Beyond* (New York: Free Press, 1974); Peter Volten, *Brezhnev's Peace Program: A Study of Soviet Domestic Political Process and Power* (Boulder, Colo.: Westview, 1982); and Thomas Wolfe, *Soviet Power and Europe, 1945–70* (Baltimore: Johns Hopkins University Press, 1970).

16. See Breslauer, *Khrushchev and Brezhnev as Leaders,* chapters 8–11; Wolfe, *Soviet Power and Europe,* chapters 11–15; and Valkenier, *The Soviet Union and the Third World,* pp. 11–22.

17. One can point to numerous cases of Khrushchev's "improvised" style of policymaking. In 1958, for example, he announced a set of educational policy reforms without first seeking Politburo approval. One of the charges later leveled at Khrushchev — "voluntarism" — reflected the elites' discomfort at his approach to policymaking.

18. Leonid Brezhnev, *Ob osnovnykh voprosakh ekonomicheskoy politiki KPSS na sovremennom etape. Rechi i doklady, Tom I* (Moscow: Politizdat, 1975), pp. 420–21 (a speech given at a December 1969 Central Committee Plenum), is representative of elite commentary on this topic. Also see Breslauer, *Khrushchev and Brezhnev as Leaders,* pp. 169–71.

19. Parrott, *Politics and Technology in the Soviet Union,* chapters 5–6.

20. On the process and foreign-policy changes associated with the Gorbachev era, see Jeff Checkel, "Gorbachev's 'New Political Thinking' and the Formation of Soviet Foreign Policy," Radio Liberty *Research Bulletin* No. 429/88 (September 23, 1988); idem, "Ideas, Institutions and the Gorbachev Foreign Policy Revolution"; Walter Clemens, *Can Russia Change? The USSR Confronts Global Interdependence* (Boston: Unwin Hyman, 1990); Robert Legvold, "The Revolution in Soviet Foreign Policy," *Foreign Affairs* 68 (America and the World 1988/89); Allen Lynch, *Gorbachev's International Outlook: Intellectual Origins and Political Consequences* (New York: Institute for East-West Security Studies, 1989); Mendelson, "Internal Battles and External Wars"; Meyer, "The Sources and Prospects of Gorbachev's New Political Thinking on Security"; and John Van Oudenaren, *The Role of Shevardnadze and the Ministry of Foreign Affairs in the Making of Soviet Defense and Arms Control Policy* (Santa Monica, Calif.: Rand Corporation, 1990).

21. On the distinction between general beliefs and strategic prescriptions, see George Breslauer, "Ideology and Learning in Soviet Third World Policy (A Review Essay)," *World Politics* 31 (April 1987), 430–31.

22. On the debate, see Ernst Kux, "Contradictions in Soviet Socialism," *Problems of Communism* 33 (November–December 1984). Also see Yuriy Andropov, "Ucheniye Karla Marksa i nekotorye voprosy sotsialisticheskogo stroitel'stva v SSSR," *Kommunist* No. 3 (February 1983), 13, 20–22. For an overview of the economic debates of the Andropov and Chernenko years, see Ed Hewett, *Reforming the Soviet Economy: Equality versus Efficiency* (Washington, D.C.: Brookings Institution, 1988), chapter 6.

23. See Philip Hanson, "The Novosibirsk Report: Comment," *Survey* 28 (Spring 1984); and Bohdan Nahaylo, "Interview with Tatyana Zaslavskaya," Radio Liberty *Research Bulletin* No. 365/87 (September 15, 1987), 12, 14–18.

24. The meeting was held on June 11, 1985. For details, see Mikhail Gorbachev, *M. S. Gorbachev. Izbrannye rechi i stat'i, Tom 2* (Moscow: Politizdat, 1987), pp. 251–78;

Boris Rumer, "Realities of Gorbachev's Economic Program," *Problems of Communism* 35 (May–June 1986), 24–26; and Hewett, *Reforming the Soviet Economy*, pp. 307–09.

25. See Bruce Parrott, "Soviet National Security Under Gorbachev," *Problems of Communism* 37 (November–December 1988); and Harry Gelman, *The Brezhnev Politburo and the Decline of Detente* (Ithaca, N.Y.: Cornell University Press, 1984), chapter 4. For evidence on the fragmenting elite consensus, see Valkenier, *The Soviet Union and the Third World*, pp. 52–59; David Albright, "The USSR and the Third World in the 1980s," *Problems of Communism* 38 (March–June 1989), 55–59; and Leonid Brezhnev, "Rech' tovarishcha L. I. Brezhneva na soveshchanii voyenachal'nikov v Kremle," *Kommunist* No. 16 (November 1982), a speech to a special meeting of military leaders in October 1982.

26. The roots of this uneasy coexistence extended back to the 20th CPSU Party Congress in 1956, where the leadership had called for a revitalization of the social sciences, including those connected to the international arena.

27. See Mikhail Gorbachev, *Zhivoye tvorchestvo naroda* (Moscow: Politizdat, 1984), pp. 38–40; idem, "Vystupleniye M. S. Gorbacheva v Britanskom parlamente," *Pravda*, December 19, 1984, p. 4; Aleksandr Yakovlev, "Istoki ugrozy i obshchestvennoye mneniye," *Memo* No. 3 (March 1985), 11; and Yakovlev's comments in "Kruglyy stol *Memo*: Bor'ba za novyy mezhdunarodnyy ekonomicheskiy poryadok — itogi desyatiletiya," *Memo* No. 7 (July 1984), 101.

28. See Mikhail Gorbachev, "Otvety M. S. Gorbacheva na voprosy gazety 'Yumanite'," *Pravda*, February 8, 1986, p. 1; Oleg Peresypkin, "Obsuzhdayem tezisy TsK KPSS: Nauku — na sluzhbu politike," *Pravda*, June 24, 1988, p. 5; and Vladimir Lapygin, "Glasnost' i gosudarstvennaya bezopasnost'," *Izvestiya*, June 26, 1989, p. 2.

29. See Mikhail Gorbachev, "Politicheskiy doklad Tsentral'nogo Komiteta KPSS XXVII s'ezdu Kommunisticheskoy Partii Sovetskogo Soyuza," in *XXVII s'ezd Kommunisticheskoy Partii Sovetskogo Soyuza: Stenograficheskiy otchet, Tom I* (Moscow: Politizdat, 1986), pp. 24–25, 39–41; Georgiy Shakhnazarov, "Internatsionalizatsiya — istoki, soderzheniye, stupeni razvitiya," *Memo* No. 5 (May 1986); and M. Bunkina and N. Petrov, "Vsemirnoye khozyaystvo — ekonomicheskiy fundament mirnogo sosushchestvovaniya," *Memo* No. 9 (September 1986).

30. Seweryn Bialer, "Danger in Moscow," *New York Review of Books*, February 16, 1984.

Chapter 3: Entrepreneurs Looking for a Window

1. See the various sources listed in chapter 2.

2. On what has been called the power of nondecision making, see Peter Bachrach and Morton Baratz, "Decisions and Non-Decisions: An Analytic Framework," *American Political Science Review* 57 (September 1963).

3. For details on the early history of IMEMO, see Jerry Hough, "The Evolution of the Soviet World View," *World Politics* 32 (July 1980), 512–13; Yuriy Polsky, *Soviet Research Institutes and the Formation of Foreign Policy: The Institute of the World Economy and International Relations* (Falls Church, Va.: Delphic Associates, 1987), pp. 1–10; and Georgiy Arbatov, *Zatyanuvsheyesya vyzdorovleniye (1953–1985 gg.):*

Svidetel'stvo sovremennika (Moscow: Mezhdunarodnye otnosheniya, 1991), chapter 3. On Varga, see, especially, Yevgeniy Varga, *Izmeneniya v ekonomike kapitalizma v itoge vtoroy mirovoy voyny* (Moscow: Gospolizdat, 1946); and William Wohlforth, *The Elusive Balance: Power and Perceptions During the Cold War* (Ithaca, N.Y.: Cornell University Press, 1993), pp. 76–88. On Arzumanyan and the priority he gave to the study of the domestic and international political economy of capitalism, see "Yubiley uchenogo-kommunista," *Memo* No. 3 (March 1964); "Na uchenom sovete IMEMO: Pamyati Akademika Anushavana Agafonovicha Arzumanyana," *Memo* No. 5 (May 1984); and Andrey Gromyko et al., Editors, *Diplomaticheskiy slovar', Tom I* (Moscow: Nauka, 1984), p. 95.

4. This listing is based on an analysis of the contents of the institute's journal, *Memo*, and interviews with several researchers whose tenure at IMEMO extends back to the early 1960s. Also see William Zimmerman, *Soviet Perspectives on International Relations, 1956–67* (Princeton, N.J.: Princeton University Press, 1969); Hough, "The Evolution in the Soviet World View"; Blair Ruble and Mark Teeter, Editors, *A Scholar's Guide to Humanities and Social Sciences in the Soviet Union: The Academy of Sciences of the USSR and the Academies of Sciences of the Union Republics* (Armonk, N.Y.: M. E. Sharpe, 1985), pp. 69–71.

5. For the book-publication data, see N. Kuchinskiy, "Anotatsii—Nauchnye trudy Instituta mirovoy ekonomiki i mezhdunarodnykh otnosheniy AN SSSR v 1966 godu," *Memo* No. 1 (January 1967); and idem, "Anotatsii—Nauchnye trudy Instituta mirovoy ekonomiki i mezhdunarodnykh otnosheniy AN SSSR v 1967 godu," *Memo* No. 2 (February 1968). Hough, "The Evolution in the Soviet World View," pp. 513, 527, addresses the training and background of IMEMO researchers. On organizational structure, see Polsky, *Soviet Research Institutes and the Formation of Foreign Policy*, p. 30.

6. Here and below, my information on Inozemtsev derives from the following: interviews with Dr. Margarita Maksimova, senior researcher at IMEMO and widow of Inozemtsev, and with Inozemtsev's former personal assistant at the institute; Gromyko et al., Editors, *Diplomaticheskiy slovar', Tom I*, p. 400; "Akademik Nikolay Nikolayevich Inozemtsev" (Obituary), *Memo* No. 9 (September 1982); Yevgeniy Primakov, "Uchenyy, rukovoditel', chelovek (k 70-letiyu Akademika N. N. Inozemtseva)," *Memo* No. 4 (April 1991); and Oleg Bykov, "Sovremennye problemy mirovoy ekonomiki i mezhdunarodnykh otnosheniyy (k 70-letiyu N. N. Inozemtseva)," *Memo* No. 6 (June 1991). For representative examples of Inozemtsev's emphasis on questions of political economy and theoretical aspects of international relations, see Nikolay Inozemtsev, "Oktyabr', mezhdunarodnye otnosheniya i sotsial'nyy progress chelovechestva," *Memo* No. 11 (November 1967); and idem, "XXVI s'ezd KPSS i nashi zadachi," *Memo* No. 3 (March 1981).

7. On the importance of foreign-policy process, see the theses prepared under Inozemtsev's guidance, in IMEMO Akademii Nauk SSSR, "Ucheniye V. I. Lenina ob imperializme i sovremennost': K 50-letiyu vykhoda v svet raboty 'Imperializm, kak vysshaya stadiya kapitalizma,'" *Memo* No. 5 (May 1967), 16–17. Also see Inozemtsev's comments in "Problemy teorii mezhdunarodnykh otnosheniy (Kruglyy stol *Memo*)," *Memo* No. 9 (September 1969), 89–90.

8. See Inozemtsev's remarks in "Yubileynoye zasedaniye uchenogo soveta IMEMO, posvyashchennoye 50-letiyu Velikoy oktyabr'skoy sotsialisticheskoy revolyutsii," *Memo*

No. 1 (January 1968), 122; Nikolay Inozemtsev, "Marks i sovremennyy kapitalizm," *Memo* No. 6 (June 1968), 4–6; and idem, "Osobennosti sovremennogo imperializma i ego osnovnye protivorechiya," *Memo* No. 5 (May 1970).

9. On the changing nature of international politics, see Inozemtsev, "Oktyabr', mezhdunarodnye otnosheniya i sotsial'nyy progress chelovechestva"; and idem, "Osobennosti sovremennogo imperializma i ego osnovnye protivorechiya," p. 24.

10. On the relation between leadership tenure and ideological legacies, also see Kathryn Sikkink, *Ideas and Institutions: Developmentalism in Brazil and Argentina* (Ithaca, N.Y.: Cornell University Press, 1991), p. 250.

11. The impact of leadership is also seen in how the academy's two leading international-affairs units — IMEMO and the USA Institute — have evolved in quite different ways over the past twenty-five years, despite operating under the same set of broader constraints. See Jeff Checkel, "Organizational Behavior, Social Scientists and Soviet Foreign Policymaking" (Ph.D. diss., Massachusetts Institute of Technology, 1991). The Arzumanyan story is related by Georgiy Arbatov in *Zatyanuvsheyesya vyzdorovleniye,* p. 72. On the *nomenklatura* status of the IMEMO directorship, see the comments by Aleksandr Yakovlev in "Na uchenom sovete IMEMO: Pamyati Akademika Anushavana Agafonovicha Arzumanyana," p. 133.

12. See Zimmerman, *Soviet Perspectives on International Relations,* pp. 61–70; United States Arms Control and Disarmament Agency, *Arms Control and Disarmament Agreements: Texts and Histories of Negotiations* (Washington, D.C.: U.S. Government Printing Office, 1982), pp. 83–86; and U.S. Department of State, *Documents on Disarmament* (Washington, D.C.: U.S. Government Printing Office, 1965), pp. 7–9.

13. On the points made in this and the preceding paragraph, see L. Moskvin, "Tvorcheskiy marksizm-leninizm i vneshnyaya politika SSSR," *Memo* No. 3 (March 1964), 12; S. Bogatov, "Peregovory po razoruzheniyu i yadernye problemy," *Memo* No. 9 (September 1966); and Vladimir Aboltin, Editor, *SSSR, SShA i razoruzheniye* (Moscow: Nauka, 1967) — especially the introduction and chapter 2.

14. Compare, for example, Brezhnev's changing analysis of East-West security in the following: Leonid Brezhnev, *Leninskim kursom: Rechi i stat'i, Tom I* (Moscow: Politizdat, 1970), pp. 27–28 (a speech delivered in the Kremlin on November 6, 1964); and p. 231 (a speech at a Central Committee plenum on September 29, 1965). Also see Brezhnev, "Otchetnyy doklad Tsentral'nogo Komiteta KPSS XXIII s'ezdu Kommunisticheskoy Partii Sovetskogo Soyuza," in *XXIII s'ezd Kommunisticheskoy Partii Sovetskogo Soyuza: Stenograficheskiy otchet, Tom I* (Moscow: Politizdat, 1966), pp. 46–47, a speech to the 23rd Party Congress in March 1966; and idem, "Pyat'desyat let velikikh pobed sotsializma," *Kommunist* No. 16 (November 1967), 39–40, a Kremlin speech on the fiftieth anniversary of the October Revolution. In *Kommunist,* compare "Mirnoye sosushchestvovaniye v deystvii," *Kommunist* No. 10 (July 1964), 4; "Vneshnyaya politika i sovremennyy mir," *Kommunist* No. 3 (February 1965), 13; and "Sovetskaya vneshnyaya politika i obshchestvennyy progress," *Kommunist* No. 12 (August 1965), 11. These were all published as unsigned — and hence authoritative — lead editorials.

15. Within the state, it was the Ministry of Defense that played the dominant role in national-security policymaking during these years. See Thomas Wolfe, *The SALT Experience* (Cambridge, Mass.: Ballinger Press, 1979), pp. 62–64, 73–74.

16. See "K chitatelyam," *SShA* No. 1 (January 1970), 5. For details on ISKAN, see Checkel, "Organizational Behavior, Social Scientists and Soviet Foreign Policymaking," chapter 6.

17. The discussion that follows confirms and extends Zimmerman's study on the writings of Soviet foreign-policy specialists. See Zimmerman, *Soviet Perspectives on International Relations, 1956–67*. While Zimmerman's analysis is primarily descriptive, mine is more explanatory. That is, I seek to explain the predominance of certain ideas in this research and to show how, in IMEMO's case, these embedded ideas affected its behavior in the later policy debates over SALT and detente.

18. Iosif Lemin, "Vneshnyaya politika SShA: Dvizhushchiye sily i tendentsii," *Memo* No. 6 (June 1965), 25–26; and Lemin's comments in "Yubileynoye zasedaniye uchenogo soveta IMEMO, posvyashchennoye 50-letiyu Velikoy oktyabr'skoy sotsialisticheskoy revolyutsii," p. 129. Lemin, who died in 1968 at the age of seventy-one, had an affiliation with IMEMO that stretched back to 1933. During the mid-1960s, he headed its unit responsible for analyzing the domestic and foreign policy of the United States. Details on Lemin's career can be found in "Iosif Mikhaylovich Lemin" (Obituary), *Memo* No. 7 (July 1968).

19. V. Androsov, "Rol' pravitel'stva SShA v otnosheniyakh mezhdu trudom i kapitalom," *Memo* No. 5 (May 1964); and V. Larin, "Amerikanskiye uchenye o nasushchnoy probleme sovremennosti," *Memo* No. 5 (May 1964).

20. On militarization, see Lemin, "Vneshnyaya politika SShA: Dvizhushchiye sily i tendentsii"; and V. Tivanov, "Zapadnogermanskiy sotsiolog o problemakh sokhraneniya mira," *Memo* No. 11 (November 1966). On the dangers of economic reductionism, see Iosif Lemin, "Velikaya oktyabr'skaya sotsialisticheskaya revolyutsiya i mirovaya politika," *Memo* No. 6 (June 1967), 8; and D. Mel'nikov, "Novaya epokha v mezhdunarodnykh otnosheniyakh," *Memo* No. 11 (November 1965), 8–9. Lenin's theory of imperialism is reductionist because it locates the causal factors driving capitalist foreign policy at the national as opposed to the international level.

21. See Inozemtsev's commentary in "Yubileynoye zasedaniye uchenogo soveta IMEMO, posvyashchennoye 50-letiyu Velikoy oktyabr'skoy sotsialisticheskoy revolyutsii," p. 122; his analysis in G. A. Ponomarev, "Evropeyskaya bezopasnost' i otnosheniya gosudarstv dvukh sistem: Mezhdunarodnaya nauchnaya konferentsiya, sostoyavshayasya v Moskve 23–25 aprelya 1968 g.," *Memo* No. 7 (July 1968), 104–06; and Inozemtsev, "Marks i sovremennyy kapitalizm," pp. 4–6, 8–9. The attack on Stalin appears in the first source.

22. Galkin, "Suzhdeniye sotsiologa: Pravyashchaya elita sovremennogo kapitalizma," *Memo* No. 3 (March 1969), passim. Also see Vladimir Shamberg, "Vnutripoliticheskiye dilemmy pravitel'stva Niksona," *Memo* No. 7 (July 1969). For a similar Western discussion of the policy cycle, see Herbert Simon, "Political Research: The Decision-Making Framework," in David Easton, Editor, *Varieties of Political Theory* (Englewood Cliffs, N.J.: Prentice-Hall, 1966).

23. For leadership statements on the nature of capitalism, see Brezhnev, "Otchetnyy doklad Tsentral'nogo Komiteta KPSS XXIII s'ezdu Kommunisticheskoy Partii Sovetskogo Soyuza," pp. 24–28; and idem, "Pyat'desyat let velikikh pobed sotsializma," p. 25.

Even Brezhnev's more moderate statements on capitalism show a considerable divergence between elite beliefs and the ideas advanced by IMEMO. See Brezhnev, *Leninskim kursom: Rechi i stat'i, Tom II* (Moscow: Politizdat, 1970), p. 413, a speech to a June 1969 international communist meeting.

24. Zimmerman, *Soviet Perspectives on International Relations, 1956–67*, chapters 2–4, provides evidence that the institute's interest in this particular idea extended back at least to the late 1950s.

25. See V. Israelyan, "Kapital'noye issledovaniye mirovoy politiki," *Memo* No. 10 (October 1964); T. Vladimirov, "Politika KPSS i sovremennyy mir," *Memo* No. 5 (May 1966); and the commentary in "Mezhdunarodnaya konferentsiya marksistov: K 50-letiyu vykhoda v svet knigi V. I. Lenina 'Imperializm, kak vysshaya stadiya kapitalizma,'" *Memo* No. 6 (June 1967), 71–73. For the editorial, see "Aktual'nye zadachi izucheniya problem mirovogo razvitiya," *Memo* No. 11 (November 1966), 15.

26. Yuriy Zhilin, "Faktor vremeni v yadernyy vek," *Kommunist* No. 11 (July 1986), 120–22. For earlier discussions at IMEMO of the chance factor in international politics and accidental-nuclear-war scenarios, see Inozemtsev, "Oktyabr', mezhdunarodnye otnosheniya i sotsial'nyy progress chelovechesvta," p. 21 and passim; and S. Bogatov, "Peregovory po razoruzheniyu i yadernye problemy," *Memo* No. 9 (September 1966).

27. Inozemtsev, "Oktyabr', mezhdunarodnye otnosheniya i sotsial'nyy progress chelovechestva," pp. 13–14; and Gennadiy Gerasimov, "Teoriya igr i mezhdunarodnye otnosheniya," *Memo* No. 7 (July 1966): the quote comes from p. 105. Gerasimov, who during the Gorbachev years worked at the Foreign Ministry, used a discussion of Western writing on game theory to address the zero sum, non–zero sum issue.

28. Inozemtsev in "Mezhdunarodnaya konferentsiya marksistov," p. 62; and Inozemtsev, "Oktyabr', mezhdunarodnye otnosheniya i sotsial'nyy progress chelovechestva," p. 15 and passim. On "objective" processes more generally, see Ivan Frolov, Editor, *Filosofskiy slovar'* (Moscow: Politizdat, 1986), p. 337.

29. Yu. Sheynin, "Nauchno-tekhnicheskaya revolyutsiya i nekotorye problemy sovremennosti," *Memo* No. 2 (February 1968), 4–7. Also see Iosif Lemin, "Ekonomika i vneshnyaya politika imperializma," *Memo* No. 10 (October 1968), 20. On the similarities between these ideas and Gorbachev-era elite commentary, see chapter 5, below.

30. Allen Lynch, *The Soviet Study of International Relations* (New York: Cambridge University Press, 1987), pp. 43–48, provides a useful introduction to the roundtable.

31. See the commentaries by Gantman, Inozemtsev, Kondakov, Pechenev, Petrovskaya, Razmerov, and Yermolenko as well as the editorial summary in "Problemy teorii mezhdunarodnykh otnosheniy (Kruglyy stol *Memo*)," *Memo* Nos. 9 and 11 (September and November 1969). Also see Aleksey Nikonov, "Sovremennaya revolyutsiya v voyennom dele i nauka o mezhdunarodnykh otnosheniyakh," *Memo* No. 2 (February 1969), 5.

32. On Tomashevskiy, see "Problemy teorii mezhdunarodnykh otnosheniy (Kruglyy stol *Memo*)," *Memo* No. 9 (September 1969), 94–95. Concerning the inadequacy of zero-sum approaches, see Petrovskaya and Yermolenko in *Memo* No. 11 (November 1969), 94–95, and 89, respectively.

33. Aside from the earlier primary source citations, useful descriptions of elite beliefs on international politics covering the period of interest here include Stephen Shenfield,

The Nuclear Predicament: Explorations in Soviet Ideology (New York: Routledge and Kegan Paul, 1987), passim; and Margot Light, *The Soviet Theory of International Relations* (New York: St. Martin's Press, 1988), chapters 2–3, 8–9.

34. Mel'nikov, "Novaya epokha v mezhdunarodnykh otnosheniyakh," p. 9. Also see "Aktual'nye zadachi izucheniya problem mirovogo razvitiya," p. 15.

35. "Aktual'nye zadachi izucheniya problem mirovogo razvitiya," pp. 15–17. On the importance of studying socialist-capitalist political interactions, also see the comments by A. G. Mileykovskiy, an IMEMO section head, in "Mezhdunarodnaya konferentsiya marksistov," pp. 71–72.

36. Brezhnev, *Leninskim kursom: Rechi i stat'i, Tom I*, p. 228. Also see Brezhnev, "Otchetnyy doklad Tsentral'nogo Komiteta KPSS XXIII s'ezdu Kommunisticheskoy Partii Sovetskogo Soyuza," pp. 38–47, where the general secretary explicitly links any improvement in bilateral relations to the cessation of U.S. aggression in Vietnam.

37. See Iosif Lemin's comments in "Mezhdunarodnaya konferentsiya marksistov: K 50-letiyu vykhoda v svet knigi V. I. Lenina 'Imperializm, kak vysshaya stadiya kapitalizma,'" *Memo* No. 7 (July 1967), 70–71. Also see Lemin, "Velikaya oktyabr'skaya sotsialisticheskaya revolyutsiya i mirovaya politika," pp. 7–13; and V. Zevin, "V. I. Lenin o vneshney politike Sovetskogo gosudarstva (po novym dokumentam)," *Memo* No. 4 (April 1966), 23.

38. The bold analyst was Sheynin, "Nauchno-tekhnicheskaya revolyutsiya i nekotorye problemy sovremennosti," pp. 11–13. Also see Lemin in "Yubileynoye zasedaniye uchenogo soveta IMEMO, posvyashchennoye 50-letiyu Velikoy oktyabr'skoy sotsialisticheskoy revolyutsii," p. 129; and Gennadiy Gerasimov, "O nekotorykh burzhuaznykh 'kontseptsiyakh' mezhdunarodnykh otnosheniy," *Memo* No. 8 (August 1968), 17–18. For Inozemtsev's commentary, see G. Ponomarev, "Evropeyskaya bezopasnost' i otnosheniya gosudarstv dvukh sistem," *Memo* No. 8 (August 1968), 81; and ibid., *Memo* No. 7 (July 1968), 104.

39. Inozemtsev in "Problemy teorii mezhdunarodnykh otnosheniy (Kruglyy stol *Memo*)," *Memo* No. 9 (September 1969), 89–92. Inozemtsev's contribution is entitled "Pressing [*aktual'nye*] Tasks of Theoretical Research."

40. See, for example, Nikonov, "Sovremennaya revolyutsiya v voyennom dele i nauka o mezhdunarodnykh otnosheniyakh," pp. 5, 12–14; the editorial summary in "Problemy teorii mezhdunarodnykh otnosheniy (Kruglyy stol *Memo*)," *Memo* No. 11 (November 1969), 97–98; and the analysis by M. S. Voslenskiy in IMEMO Akademii nauk SSSR, *Sovremennye problemy razoruzheniya* (Moscow: Mysl', 1970), pp. 303–04.

41. On elite calls for scientific policymaking in the aftermath of Khrushchev's dismissal, see chapter 2. In August 1967 the Central Committee issued a decree on the social sciences, a part of which addressed the need for better and more timely analyses of foreign-policy issues from various institutions within the Academy of Sciences. It did not argue for a change in the nature of foreign policymaking; rather, IMEMO researchers made this point. See "Postanovleniye TsK KPSS: O merakh po dal'neyshemu razvitiyu obshchestvennykh nauk i povysheniyu ikh roli v kommunisticheskom stroitel'stve," *Kommunist* No. 13 (September 1967).

42. Margaret Weir, in her study of American employment policy, clearly implies that the answer is "No." See Weir, *Politics and Jobs: The Boundaries of Employment Policy in*

the United States (Princeton, N.J.: Princeton University Press, 1992). In his study of British macroeconomic policymaking, Peter Hall, however, answers with a conditional "Yes." See Hall, "Policy Paradigms, Social Learning and the State," *Comparative Politics* 25 (April 1993). Similar to the argument advanced here, Hall suggests that under certain conditions — marked by crisis and policy failure — broad concepts and ideas can bring about radical change.

43. See chapter 2; and Jack Snyder, "The Gorbachev Revolution: A Waning of Soviet Expansionism?" *International Security* 12 (Winter 1987–88). On the general point that ideas should matter most in highly centralized, authoritarian polities, also see the comments by Stephen Krasner in the "Roundtable on Ideas and Foreign Policy," Annual Convention of the American Political Science Association, Washington, D.C., September 1993.

44. The worsening state of Soviet-American relations during the mid-1960s and Varga's abortive attempt to advance a complex image of capitalism were two such disincentives. For good discussions of the ideas-interests relation, see Sikkink, *Ideas and Institutions,* chapter 7; and John Jacobsen, "Much Ado About Ideas: The Cognitive Factor in Economic Policy," *World Politics* 47 (January 1995).

45. My analysis here is limited to the views of Brezhnev and Kosygin — the two most dominant Politburo figures in the half-dozen years after Khrushchev's dismissal.

46. See Leonid Brezhnev, *Ob osnovnykh voprosakh ekonomicheskoy politiki KPSS na sovremennom etape. Rechi i doklady, Tom I* (Moscow: Politizdat, 1975), pp. 244–50 (speech at September 1967 Central Committee Plenum), 371–76 (address to December 1968 Central Committee Plenum); and idem, "Vernost' ideyam Lenina, delu kommunizma — zalog vsekh nashikh pobed," *Pravda,* December 29, 1968, pp. 1–2 at p. 2. For Kosygin's commentary, see Bruce Parrott, *Politics and Technology in the Soviet Union* (Cambridge, Mass.: MIT Press, 1983), chapter 5.

47. George Breslauer, *Khrushchev and Brezhnev as Leaders: Building Authority in Soviet Politics* (Boston: Allen and Unwin, 1982), pp. 140–44; and Parrott, *Politics and Technology in the Soviet Union,* pp. 182–85.

48. Brezhnev, *Ob osnovnykh voprosakh ekonomicheskoy politiki KPSS na sovremennom etape,* pp. 244–50 (speech at September 1967 Plenum of the Central Committee). Also see B. Vladimirov, "Polveka ekonomicheskogo sorevnovaniya dvukh sistem," *Kommunist* No. 1 (January 1968), 43–45. In *Kommunist vooruzhennykh sil* (hereafter *Kvs*), see, among others, V. Dutov, "Berezhlivost' — cherta kommunisticheskaya," *Kvs* No. 13 (July 1968); and M. Cherednichenko, "Ekonomika i voyenno-tekhnicheskaya politika," *Kvs* No. 15 (August 1968).

49. Raymond Garthoff, "BMD and East-West Relations," in Ashton Carter and David Schwartz, Editors, *Ballistic Missile Defense* (Washington, D.C.: Brookings Institution, 1984), pp. 295–300; and John Lepingwell, "Organizational and Bureaucratic Politics in Soviet Defense Decisionmaking: A Case Study of the Soviet Air Defense Forces" (Ph.D. diss., Massachusetts Institute of Technology, 1988), pp. 139–47.

50. On the lack of change in elite preferences and state interests, also see Franklyn Griffiths, "The Sources of American Conduct: Soviet Perspectives and Their Policy Implications," *International Security* 9 (Fall 1984); idem, "Attempted Learning: Soviet Policy Toward the United States in the Brezhnev Era," in George Breslauer and Philip Tet-

lock, Editors, *Learning in US and Soviet Foreign Policy* (Boulder, Colo.: Westview Press, 1991); and Wohlforth, *The Elusive Balance,* chapter 7.

51. The following draws on interviews with Margarita Maksimova and a former personal assistant to Nikolay Inozemtsev; Arbatov, *Zatyanuvsheyesya vyzdorovleniye,* chapters 3, 5–7, 9 (an especially valuable source given Arbatov's position as one of Brezhnev's closest and longest-serving advisers); Roy Medvedev, *Lichnost' i epokha: Politicheskiy portret L. I. Brezhneva* (Moscow: Novosti, 1991), pp. 101–93; and Fedor Burlatskiy, *Khrushchev and the First Russian Spring: The Era of Khrushchev Through the Eyes of His Advisor* (New York: Charles Scribner's Sons, 1991), chapter 11.

52. Arbatov mentions, for example, Brezhnev's fear of being misled by Sergey Trapeznikov, the conservative head of the C.C.'s Science and Education Department.

53. Arbatov, *Zatyanuvsheyesya vyzdorovleniye,* pp. 169–70.

54. My characterization of Inozemtsev draws on interviews with several deputy directors at IMEMO, as well as with Inozemtsev's personal assistant. Also see Georgiy Arbatov, *The System: An Insider's Life in Soviet Politics* (New York: Times Books, 1992), pp. 75–76.

55. Another example is a conference on the Leninist theory of imperialism that Inozemtsev helped organize in late 1969. See "Leninskaya teoriya imperializma i revolyutsionnye sily sovremennosti," *Memo* No. 3 (March 1970).

56. Arbatov, *Zatyanuvsheyesya vyzdorovleniye,* chapters 6–7. In *Kommunist,* see B. Shabad, "Ideologiya militarizma i agressii," *Kommunist* No. 15 (October 1969), among others.

57. These social scientists were thus striving for the same partial freedom from ideological dogma that many of the physical sciences in the USSR had enjoyed for years.

58. See A. Galkin, "Suzhdeniye sotsiologa: Nekotorye istoki sotsial'no-politicheskogo krizisa v kapitalisticheskikh stranakh (stat'ya vtoraya)," *Memo* No. 2 (February 1970); and "Nauchnaya zhizn': Tvorcheskoye naslediye Yevgeniy Vargi," *Memo* No. 1 (January 1970).

59. See I. Aleshina and T. Timoshik, "Ekonomicheskaya rol' burzhuaznogo gosudarstva," *Memo* No. 11 (November 1970). For Varga's depiction of the capitalist state, see Varga, *Izmeneniya v ekonomike kapitalizma v itoge vtoroy mirovoy voyny,* chapters 1, 15.

60. G. Rudenko, "O prisposoblenii imperializma k novym istoricheskim usloviyam," *Memo* No. 11 (November 1970). On law-governed processes, see the entry "Razvitiye" in Frolov, Editor, *Filosofskiy slovar',* pp. 400–401.

61. See N. Solodovnik, "Mezhdu 'globalizmom' i 'regionalizmom' (O nekotorykh tendentsiyakh v voyennoy politike SShA)," *Memo* No. 1 (January 1970); and Yevgeniy Bugrov, "Razdum'ya Gansa Morgentau i ego sovety belomu domu," *Memo* No. 1 (January 1970).

62. See Rachik Faramazyan, "Sovremennost' i militarizm," *Memo* No. 6 (June 1971), quote on pp. 36–37.

63. Inozemtsev, "Osobennosti sovremennogo imperializma i ego osnovnye protivorechiya"; quotes on p. 17 and pp. 7–8, respectively.

64. See Inozemtsev's comments in "Nauchnaya zhizn': Tvorcheskoye naslediye Yevgeniy Vargi," pp. 123–25; and Nikolay Inozemtsev, "Sovremennye SShA i sovetskaya amerikanistika," *SShA* No. 1 (January 1970), 9–12.

65. Interviews with two deputy directors of the institute. My comments here have broader theoretical implications for recent work in international relations, particularly that on transnational politics. See chapter 7.

66. See, especially, V. Shestov, "Morskiye glubiny i mirovaya politika," *Memo* No. 3 (March 1970); idem, "Razoruzheniye—ideal sotsializma," *Memo* No. 10 (October 1971) (published as a lead article); Aleksandr Kalyadin, "Ogranicheniye yadernykh voor-uzheniy i mezhdunarodnaya bezopasnost'," *Memo* No. 4 (April 1968); idem, "Problema razoruzheniya i kontseptsiya 'ustrasheniya' (Obzor amerikanskoy literatury)," *Memo* No. 11 (November 1971), 135; and Vladimir Aboltin, "Engel's i aktual'nye problemy bor'by protiv militarizma," *Memo* No. 11 (November 1970), 60–66. Kalyadin was a senior researcher in the institute's Department of International Relations; Aboltin, a scholar long affiliated with IMEMO, had been one of its deputy directors since 1962.

67. Inozemtsev, "Osobennosti sovremennogo imperializma i ego osnovnye protivo-rechiya," p. 24. This was published as a lead article in *Memo*.

68. On the former, see *Sovremennye problemy razoruzheniya,* chapters 15, 3, 7, and 9, respectively. On the latter, see, for example, Vladimir Gantam and Dmitriy Tomashev-skiy, "Mir v god Leninskogo yubileya (Tekushchiye problemy mirovoy politiki)," *Memo* No. 4 (April 1970), 89–91.

69. See Sergey Fedorenko and V. Kulish, "Po povodu diskussii v SShA o strategicheskikh vooruzheniyakh," *Memo* No. 3 (March 1970); V. Vaneyev, "Nesbalansirovannyy balans," *Memo* No. 3 (March 1970); Sergey Fedorenko, "Nashi kommentarii: Byudzhet agressii i gonki vooruzheniy," *Memo* No. 7 (July 1971); Aleksandr Kalyadin and V. Vaneyev, "Issledovaniye problem gonki vooruzheniy i razoruzheniya," *Memo* No. 5 (May 1971); and Kalyadin, "Problema razoruzheniya i kontseptsiya 'ustrasheniya' (Obzor amerikanskoy literatury)." Source material included *Time, Newsweek,* the *New York Times,* the *Congressional Record,* monographs by the Stockholm International Peace Research Institute and the U.S. Arms Control and Disarmament Agency, and articles by American civilian defense analysts (George Rathjens and Herbert York, for example).

70. On factual errors, see Fedorenko and Kulish, "Po povodu diskussii v SShA o strategicheskikh vooruzheniyakh," p. 43, where the authors provide a seriously flawed description of MIRV technology by confusing it with maneuvering reentry vehicles (so-called MARVs). Of the analysts cited here, Fedorenko was a physical scientist by training, while Kulish and Vaneyev were retired military officers.

71. See Jeff Checkel, "An Analysis of Soviet Military Writing on United States Re-entry Vehicle Technology, 1965–1983," Research Report 86–3, Soviet Security Studies Work-ing Group (Cambridge, Mass.: MIT Center for International Studies, 1986), pp. 4–13.

72. For evidence that key Soviet political elites and civilian negotiators involved in the SALT process were profoundly ignorant of a whole range of strategic concepts, see John Newhouse, *Cold Dawn: The Story of SALT* (New York: Holt, Rinehart, and Winston, 1973); and Arbatov, *Zatyanuvsheyesya vyzdorovleniye,* pp. 193–94. On Mil'shteyn, see "Amerikanskiye voyennye doktriny: Preyemstvennost' i modifikatsiya," *Memo* No. 8 (August 1971). Mil'shteyn's footnotes are a mixture of U.S. newspapers, weekly news magazines, and government documents (for example, the *Department of State Bulletin*).

73. My reconstruction of this case was hindered by an inability to interview key partici-pants in it: Inozemtsev was dead, and Nikonov was too old to speak to me. I have instead

relied on the recollections of a number of institute researchers who were aware of the events at the time.

74. Nikonov, "Sovremennaya revolyutsiya v voyennom dele i nauka o mezhdunarodnykh otnosheniyakh."

75. See David Holloway, *The Soviet Union and the Arms Race* (New Haven: Yale University Press, 1983), pp. 30–31. Nikonov clearly understood that he was picking a turf battle with the military — arguing, for example, that it was increasingly problematic for strategy to be elaborated "only by military specialists." See "Sovremennaya revolyutsiya v voyennom dele i nauka o mezhdunarodnykh otnosheniyakh," p. 14.

76. On the new section, see Wolfe, *The SALT Experience,* p. 67. Before the establishment of this section, IMEMO for many years had operated a small Sector for Problems of Disarmament. See Vladimir Aboltin, Editor, *Molodye natsional'nye gosudarstva i razoruzheniye* (Moscow: Nauka, 1967), p. 4. According to Wolfe, the sector was disbanded in 1968.

77. Information in this section draws on interviews with three members of the Department of International Relations, as well as Polsky, *Soviet Research Institutes and the Formation of Foreign Policy,* pp. 28–39.

78. See, for example, Inozemtsev's comments in "Nauchnaya zhizn': Tvorcheskoye naslediye Yevegeniy Vargi," pp. 124–25; and Inozemtsev, "Sovremennye SShA i sovetskaya amerikanistika." An interview with Inozemtsev's long-time personal assistant was also of great help. Beyond Inozemtsev's comments, there were other examples of the relatively low priority IMEMO attached to security studies during these years. See especially "Vnimaniyu uchastnikov teoreticheskikh seminarov sistemy partiynoy ucheby," *Memo* No. 6 (June 1971), 3 — a listing of key subjects the institute planned to study during the early 1970s.

79. See chapters 4–5, below.

80. For a sampling of ISKAN's research on strategic affairs during these years, see M. V. Belousov, "Tekhnicheskiye aspekty sistemy 'Seyfgard'," *SShA* No. 5 (May 1970); Valentin Larionov, "Strategicheskiye debaty," *SShA* No. 3 (March 1970); idem, "Transformatsiya kontseptsii 'strategicheskoy dostatochnosti'," *SShA* No. 11 (November 1971); and Genrikh Trofimenko, "Nekotorye aspekty voyenno-politicheskoy strategii SShA," *SShA* No. 10 (October 1970). Georgiy Arbatov, founding director of ISKAN, has recalled its "pioneering efforts" in the late 1960s to create a new category of Soviet specialist — a civilian expert on military-strategic issues. See Arbatov, *The System,* p. 174. For further details, see Checkel, "Organizational Behavior, Social Scientists and Soviet Foreign Policymaking," chapter 6.

81. Work that highlights this understudied dimension of change in Soviet security policy includes Emanuel Adler, "The Emergence of Cooperation: National Epistemic Communities and the International Evolution of the Idea of Nuclear Arms Control," *International Organization* 46 (Winter 1992); and, especially, Matthew Evangelista's work in progress "Taming the Bear: Transnational Relations and the Demise of the Soviet Threat." It is important to emphasize, however, that at least through the late 1960s Soviet participants in such conferences as Pugwash were more likely to be physical scientists (affiliated with technical divisions of the Academy of Sciences) than social scientists. During

the SALT policy debates, for example, only three social scientists were members of the Soviet Pugwash Committee, which was dominated by physical scientists who occupied twelve of its fifteen positions. See *Sovremennye problemy razoruzheniya*, p. 300.

82. For a frank admission of this fact, see Vadim Zagladin, "Obsuzhdayem tezisy TsK KPSS: Kursom razuma i gumanizma," *Pravda*, June 13, 1988, p. 6. Zagladin was for many years a high-ranking official in the C.C.'s International Department.

83. Zimmerman, *Soviet Perspectives on International Relations*, p. 104.

84. See, respectively, Brezhnev, *Leninskim kursom, Tom II*, p. 413; and idem, *Leninskim kursom: Rechi i stat'i, Tom III* (Moscow: Politizdat, 1972), pp. 389–90. Also see Brezhnev, "Otchetnyy doklad Tsentral'nogo Komiteta KPSS XXIV s'ezdu Kommunisticheskoy Partii Sovetskogo Soyuza," *Kommunist* No. 5 (March 1971), 4–25.

85. Brezhnev, *Ob osnovnykh voprosakh ekonomicheskoy politiki KPSS na sovremennom etape*, pp. 417–19. Also see note 46, above. For similar views on capitalism as articulated by Brezhnev's fellow Politburo member Aleksey Kosygin, see Parrott, *Politics and Technology in the Soviet Union*, pp. 232–34.

86. See Arbatov, *Zatyanuvsheyesya vyzdorovleniye*, pp. 169–70; and idem, *The System*, pp. 130–34.

87. On the plenum, see Parrott, *Politics and Technology in the Soviet Union*, pp. 251–52. A review of the information reports for C.C. plenums held between the mid-1960s and early 1980s indicates that it was rare for a candidate member to address the committee.

88. The 24th Party Congress of March–April 1971 was the setting for key personnel changes that established Brezhnev as the dominant player within the Politburo. See Breslauer, *Khrushchev and Brezhnev as Leaders*, p. 194.

89. "Obozrevatel'," "Vazhnaya problema," *Pravda*, March 7, 1970, p. 4; and V. Viktorov, "Nekotorye itogi i perspektivy: K peregovoram ob ogranichenii strategicheskikh vooruzheniy," *Pravda*, July 7, 1971, pp. 4–5. The authoritative nature of the former is indicated by its nameless author (Observer); "Viktorov" was in fact a pseudonym for a mid-ranking official at the Foreign Ministry. See Garthoff, "BMD and East-West Relations," p. 307. Other articles in *Pravda* followed the same pattern. Compare, for example, Tomas Kolesnichenko, "Mezhdunarodnoye obozreniye: Dva mira, dve politiki," *Pravda*, January 26, 1969, pp. 1, 4; B. Strel'nikov, "Yadernyy kot v meshke," *Pravda*, June 10, 1969, p. 5; and Gennadiy Vasil'yev, "Kolonka kommentatora: Polozhitel'nyy shag," *Pravda*, December 24, 1969, p. 5.

90. I return to this issue in chapter 6, showing how changes in the institutional structure of post-Soviet Russia have increased the salience of politics and thus diminished the causal role of ideas.

91. The importance of this fractionation will become apparent when the Gorbachev case is considered in chapter 5.

92. See, respectively, "Politika mira i druzhby mezhdu narodami," *Kommunist* No. 11 (July 1969), 21–22; and Shabad, "Ideologiya militarizma i agressii." The title of the latter article, "Ideology of Militarism and Aggression," is indicative of the conservative ideas it contained.

93. See, for example, Suslov's article in *Kommunist*, No. 15 (October 1969), and

Shelepin's commentary in *Trud,* December 11, 1971, and March 21, 1972 — all as reported in Parrott, *Politics and Technology in the Soviet Union,* pp. 235–36, 254–55.

94. The latter goal still clearly obtained in the late 1960s. See I. Grudinin, "Kachestvennaya i kolichestvennaya opredelennost' voysk," *Kommunist vooruzhennykh sil* No. 11 (June 1968), 17, 21–22; and Valentin Larionov, "Politicheskaya storona sovetskoy voyennoy doktriny," *Kommunist vooruzhennykh sil* No. 22 (November 1968), 14. Also see Georgiy Sturua, "Sovetsko-amerikanskiye otnosheniya na novom etape," *Memo* No. 9 (September 1988), pp. 29–30.

95. Ye. Rybkin, "Kritika burzhuaznykh kontseptsiy voyny i mira," *Kommunist vooruzhennykh sil* No. 18 (September 1968), 90.

96. See A. Petrov, "Zloveshchiy soyuz mecha i dollara," *Kommunist vooruzhennykh sil* No. 17 (September 1969), 82, 84, for example.

97. Andrey Grechko, "V. I. Lenin i stroitel'stvo sovetskikh vooruzhennykh sil," *Kommunist* No. 3 (February 1969); and Aleksey Yepishev, "Leninizm — osnova vospitaniya Sovetskikh voinov," *Kommunist* No. 6 (April 1969), quote on p. 68. There are many other examples of military analyses that reinforced this message from top leaders. See Peredovaya, "Velikaya pobeda Sovetskogo naroda," *Kommunist vooruzhennykh sil* No. 8 (April 1968); and V. Shelyag, "V. I. Lenin i Sovetskiye vooruzhennye sily," *Kommunist* No. 3 (February 1968). *Peredovaya* were unsigned — and hence authoritative — lead editorials.

98. See Anatoliy Gromyko, "American Theoreticians Between 'Total War' and Peace," *Military Thought* No. 4 (April 1969). Gromyko, the son of Foreign Minister Andrey Gromyko, was head of a sector at ISKAN.

99. These are Thomas Kuhn's terms. The connection between them and the role of policy ideas is elaborated in Hall, "Policy Paradigms, Social Learning and the State." See Arbatov, *The System,* pp. 169–72, 189, for vivid descriptions of the staying power of the old paradigm.

100. As Inozemtsev's colleague Georgiy Arbatov has put it: Inozemtsev was "sometimes . . . too cautious in his positions, especially while dealing with the country's leaders." Arbatov, *The System,* pp. 75–76.

101. Arbatov, *Zatyanuvsheyesya vyzdorovleniye,* pp. 170–73, quote on p. 173.

Chapter 4: Windows Opening?

1. Bruce Parrott, "Soviet National Security Under Gorbachev," *Problems of Communism* 37 (November–December 1988), 2.

2. Brezhnev, "Otchetnyy doklad Tsentral'nogo Komiteta KPSS XXVI s'ezdu Kommunisticheskoy Partii Sovetskogo Soyuza i ocherednye zadachi partii v oblasti vnutrenney i vneshney politiki," *Kommunist* No. 4 (March 1981), 10–13, 21. Robert Legvold, "The 26th Party Congress and Soviet Foreign Policy," in Seweryn Bialer and Thane Gustafson, Editors, *Russia at the Crossroads: The 26th Congress of the CPSU* (London: George Allen and Unwin, 1982), provides useful background on this speech and Soviet policy more generally in the early 1980s.

3. Brezhnev, "Otchetnyy doklad," pp. 16–25. On the principle, see Andrey Gromyko et al., Editors, *Diplomaticheskiy slovar', Tom II* (Moscow: Nauka, 1985), p. 440; and

David Holloway, *The Soviet Union and the Arms Race* (New Haven: Yale University Press, 1983), p. 75.

4. The "storm clouds" quote comes in the opening moments of Brezhnev's report. "Otchetnyy doklad," p. 4.

5. Parrott, "Soviet National Security Under Gorbachev," p. 2. For other elite commentary, see the following official editorials: "V bor'be za budushchee chelovechestva," *Kommunist* No. 14 (September 1981); and "Posledovatel'naya i chestnaya politika mira," *Kommunist* No. 8 (May 1982). Also see Mikhail Suslov, "Vysokoye prizvaniye i otvetstvennost'," *Kommunist* No. 16 (November 1981), 5–6; and Andrey Gromyko, "Radi mira na zemle," *Kommunist* No. 18 (December 1982). On the Brezhnev elite's adherence to the Leninist policy paradigm, also see Coit Blacker, *Hostage to Revolution: Gorbachev and Soviet Security Policy, 1985–1991* (New York: Council on Foreign Relations Press, 1993), chapter 1.

6. For a plausible kremlinological interpretation of elite maneuvering during Brezhnev's last year, see Harry Gelman, *The Brezhnev Politburo and the Decline of Detente* (Ithaca, N.Y.: Cornell University Press, 1984), pp. 181–85. Also see Walter Clemens, *Can Russia Change? The USSR Confronts Global Interdependence* (Boston: Unwin Hyman, 1990), pp. 132–35.

7. For example, the three Central Committee plenums held during Andropov's tenure as general secretary were all devoted to questions of domestic socioeconomic policy. In addition, Andropov's only major theoretical pronouncement during this period dealt with questions of domestic policy. See Andropov, "Ucheniye Karla Marksa i nekotorye voprosy sotsialisticheskogo stroitel'stva v SSSR," *Kommunist* No. 3 (February 1983).

8. The various proposals are catalogued in Yuriy Andropov, "Otvety Yu. V. Andropova na voprosy gazety 'Pravda'," *Kommunist* No. 16 (November 1983).

9. See, among many others, "Vernost' leninskomu vneshnepoliticheskomu kursu," *Kommunist* No. 3 (February 1983); and Andrey Gromyko, "V. I. Lenin i vneshnyaya politika sovetskogo gosudarstva," *Kommunist* No. 6 (April 1983). The class struggle quote comes from the Gromyko article.

10. Chernenko took the lead in arguing for a normalization of U.S.-Soviet relations. See Konstantin Chernenko, "Rech' tovarishcha K. U. Chernenko na vstreche s izbiratelyami," *Kommunist* No. 4 (March 1984), 10–13; and idem, "Sozdavat' atmosferu doveriya v mire," *Kommunist* No. 11 (July 1984), 21.

11. "Aktual'nye voprosy analiza kapitalizma," *Kommunist* No. 8 (May 1984), pp. 11–12.

12. See "Deklaratsiya stran-chlenov Soveta ekonomicheskoy vzaimopomoshchi 'Sokhraneniye mira i mezhdunarodnoye ekonomicheskoye sotrudnichestvo,'" *Kommunist* No. 9 (June 1984), 31; and "Kommunisty i problemy sovremennosti," *Kommunist* No. 15 (October 1984). The Chernenko quote comes from p. 100 of the latter source.

13. For example, the Institute of Philosophy had paid some attention to the study of global problems. See "Chelovek i sreda ego obitaniya," *Voprosy filosofii*, Nos. 1–4 (January–April 1973); and Viktor Los', "Issledovaniya v oblasti global'nykh problem: itogi i perspektivy," *Voprosy filosofii* No. 12 (December 1983). Los' provides an extensive review of Soviet research on global problems in the 1970s and early 1980s. For useful Western overviews, see Walter Clemens, *The USSR and Global Interdependence: Alter-*

native Futures (Washington, D.C.: American Enterprise Institute, 1978); idem, *Can Russia Change?* chapters 5–6; and Allen Lynch, *The Soviet Study of International Relations* (New York: Cambridge University Press, 1987), chapters 4–7.

14. The council was jointly founded by the USSR Academy of Sciences, the State Committee on Science and Technology and the Soviet Committee in Defense of Peace, and it received financial support from the Soviet Peace Fund. See Nikolay Inozemtsev, Editor, *Mir i razoruzheniye: Nauchnye issledovaniya, 1980* (Moscow: Nauka, 1980), p. 5. It was probably the successor to the academy's Commission on the Scientific Problems of Disarmament, which had been established in 1963.

15. The Central Committee's International Information Department had been established in 1978 for precisely this reason. It is telling that the first deputy head of this department, N. N. Chetverikov, sat on the council's governing body. See Petr Fedoseyev, Editor, *Mir i razoruzheniye: Nauchnye issledovaniya, 1984* (Moscow: Nauka, 1984), pp. 245–46.

16. On Frolov, see Loren Graham, "Ivan Timofeevich Frolov: New Editor of *Kommunist,*" *Sovset' News* 2 (May 15, 1986); and idem, *Science, Philosophy, and Human Behavior in the Soviet Union* (New York: Columbia University Press, 1987), pp. 20–21, 153–55. On the council's study of global problems, see Viktor Los', "Nauchnaya zhizn': Global'nye problemy sovremennoy epokhi," *Memo* No. 4 (April 1981); and Elizabeth Valkenier, *The Soviet Union and the Third World: An Economic Bind* (New York: Praeger, 1983), pp. 62–63.

17. On the greater interest in the second council, see Los', "Nauchnaya zhizn': Global'nye problemy sovremennoy epokhi"; and V. Vaulin, "Nauchnaya zhizn': Global'nye problemy nauchno-tekhnicheskoy revolyutsii," *Memo* No. 11 (November 1981). In June 1983 IMEMO and the second council jointly sponsored a symposium on global problems. See *Memo* No. 4 (April 1983), p. 129.

18. For example, the only organizational link for the Council on the Philosophical and Social Problems of Science and Technology was to the Presidium of the Academy of Sciences (an academic body). In contrast, the first council had statutory links to the Soviet Committee in Defense of Peace and the Soviet Peace Fund (both propagandistic organizations), as well as to the academy's Presidium.

19. Unless otherwise noted, information in this section draws on interviews with Margarita Maksimova, with Inozemtsev's former personal assistant at the institute, with Georgiy Arbatov, with Aleksandr Yakovlev, and with four deputy directors and three department heads at IMEMO.

20. See Yuriy Polsky, *Soviet Research Institutes and the Formation of Foreign Policy: The Institute of the World Economy and International Relations* (Falls Church, Va.: Delphic Associates, 1987), pp. 28–39; "Nauchnaya zhizn': Vysokaya otsenka," *Memo* No. 9 (September 1981); and Petr Fedoseyev and B. Koval', "Nauchnaya zhizn': V sektsii obshchestvennykh nauk prezidiuma Akademii Nauk SSSR," *Memo* No. 4 (April 1983). The quote comes from "Nauchnaya zhizn'," which is a report of remarks by Petr Fedoseyev (a vice president of the academy).

21. The percentages for articles were compiled from the annual index in the December issue of *Memo*. See *Memo* No. 12 (December 1981), 149–57. On the book publication data, see S. Kapranov, "Novye knigi Instituta mirovoy ekonomiki i mezhdunarodnykh otnosheniy AN SSSR," *Memo* No. 4 (April 1981); and chapter 3.

22. See "Nauchnaya zhizn': Chestvovaniye yubilyara," *Memo* No. 4 (April 1981); V. Vaulin, "Nauchnaya zhizn': Vsesoyuznaya shkola molodykh uchenykh i spetsialistov," *Memo* No. 4 (April 1981); and "Nauchnaya zhizn': Mirovoy kapitalisticheskiy rynok i sovremennye mezhdunarodnye ekonomicheskiye otnosheniya," *Memo* No. 1 (January 1982).

23. See A. Ognev, "Nauchnaya zhizn': O deyatel'nosti spetsializirovannykh sovetov pri IMEMO AN SSSR," *Memo* No. 6 (June 1981); idem, *Memo* No. 5 (May 1982); idem, *Memo* No. 7 (July 1983); and idem, *Memo* No. 5 (May 1984).

24. The following is based on interviews with Georgiy Arbatov, Aleksandr Yakovlev, and three deputy directors of IMEMO. Also see Georgiy Arbatov, *Zatyanuvsheyesya vyzdorovleniye: Svidetel'stvo sovremennika* (Moscow: Mezhdunarodnye otnosheniya, 1991), chapter 8.

25. On Inozemtsev's death, see "Akademik Nikolay Nikolayevich Inozemtsev," *Memo* No. 9 (September 1982). The close friend was Georgiy Arbatov; my information here is based on an interview with him. Also see Arbatov, *Zatyanuvsheyesya vyzdorovleniye*, pp. 273–74.

26. Arbatov and Bovin were present when Brezhnev called Grishin and demanded that the attacks on IMEMO be halted. Grishin denied that any investigation was occurring. After Brezhnev hung up, Arbatov declared that a Politburo member had just lied to the CPSU general secretary. In response, Brezhnev "only grinned." Arbatov, *Zatyanuvsheyesya vyzdorovleniye*, pp. 276–77.

27. See chapter 2.

28. For details, see Jeff Checkel, "Organizational Behavior, Social Scientists and Soviet Foreign Policymaking" (Ph.D. diss., Massachusetts Institute of Technology, 1991), chapter 8.

29. In reconstructing the content of this ideology, interviews were also essential. See note 19, above.

30. See Inozemtsev's remarks in *Mir i razoruzheniye: Nauchnye issledovaniya, 1980*, pp. 11–12, 16.

31. The speech was later reprinted as a lead article in the institute's journal. See Nikolay Inozemtsev, "XXVI s'ezd KPSS i nashi zadachi," *Memo* No. 3 (March 1981).

32. Inozemtsev, "XXVI s'ezd KPSS i nashi zadachi," pp. 17, 21. Interview (for Maksimova). Also see Maksimova's comments in Vaulin, "Nauchnaya zhizn': Global'nye problemy nauchno-tekhnicheskoy revolyutsii," pp. 133–34. Aside from her research position at IMEMO, Maksimova was also deputy head of the section on global problems of the Scientific Council on the Philosophical and Social Problems of Science and Technology.

33. Inozemtsev, "XXVI s'ezd KPSS i nashi zadachi," p. 18. The graduate degree categories to which Inozemtsev referred were under the control of the Higher Attestation Commission attached to the USSR Council of Ministers. On a science of international relations, see chapter 3.

34. See Yevgeniy Primakov, "Uchenyy, rukovoditel', chelovek (k 70-letiyu akademika N. N. Inozemtseva)," *Memo* No. 4 (April 1991); and Oleg Bykov, "Sovremennye problemy mirovoy ekonomiki i mezhdunarodnykh otnosheniy," *Memo* No. 6 (June 1991). Primakov had served as a deputy director of IMEMO for seven years in the 1970s and returned to become its director for several years in the mid-1980s. Bykov was a long-

time head of IMEMO's Department of International Relations and an institute deputy director.

35. Primakov, "Uchenyy, rukovoditel', chelovek," pp. 109, 107.

36. See chapter 1.

37. For the institute monograph, see Nikolay Inozemtsev, Editor, *Global Problems of Our Age* (Moscow: Progress Publishers, 1984), a translation of the 1981 Russian version. On Maksimova, see her article "Global'nye problemy mirovogo razvitiya," *Memo* No. 1 (January 1981). Also see Ivan Ivanov, "Perestroyka mezhdunarodnykh otnosheniy i global'nye problemy," *Memo* No. 2 (February 1981). Ivanov was a deputy director of IMEMO.

38. Maksimova in Vaulin, "Nauchnaya zhizn': Global'nye problemy nauchno-tekhni-cheskoy revolyutsii," pp. 133–34. Vaulin's report was published in the "scientific life" section of *Memo*. As used by Maksimova, a "single world economy" implied a global economic order governed by laws common to *both* capitalism and socialism. Institute scholars advanced similar ideas in other contexts as well. See Oleg Bykov et al., *Aktual'nye problemy razoruzheniya* (Moscow: Nauka, 1978), pp. 12, 165, for example; and "Nauchnaya zhizn': Mirovoy kapitalisticheskiy rynok i sovremennye mezhdunarodnye ekonomicheskiye otnosheniya," passim.

39. On the slight increase in expertise, compare, for example, IMEMO Akademii Nauk SSSR, *Sovremennye problemy razoruzheniya* (Moscow: Mysl', 1970); and Aleksey Nikonov, Editor, *Problemy voyennoy razryadki* (Moscow: Nauka, 1981). One IMEMO researcher, Aleksey Arbatov, stands out in the early 1980s for his sophisticated and informed strategic research. He was exceptional, however, for analyses of this type were not IMEMO's forte. For further detail on IMEMO's study of security issues during these years, see Checkel, "Organizational Behavior, Social Scientists and Soviet Foreign Policymaking," chapter 8; and Tyrus Cobb, "National Security Perspectives of Soviet 'Think Tanks,'" *Problems of Communism* 30 (November–December 1981). On Arbatov, see chapter 5, below.

40. On the military-affairs section, see Polsky, *Soviet Research Institutes and the Formation of Foreign Policy*, pp. 35–36. The Palme Commission, an international body, met between September 1980 and April 1982; the two Soviet participants were both from ISKAN (Georgiy Arbatov and Mikhail Mil'shteyn). The Committee of Soviet Scientists was established in May 1983 and was dominated by physical scientists (twenty-three of twenty-five members). The two social scientists on the committee were from ISKAN (Kokoshin) and the Africa Institute (Anatoliy Gromyko). In September 1983, SIPRI held a conference on "common security." Three Soviets participated: Zhurkin of ISKAN, Zagladin of the Central Committee and a physical scientist (Silin).

41. See Inozemtsev, "XXVI s'ezd KPSS i nashi zadachi," pp. 17–18. Also see his remarks in O. Zaytseva, "Nauchnaya zhizn': V nauchnom sovete po issledovaniyu problem mira i razoruzheniya," *Memo* No. 7 (July 1981), 131–32. Also see Vladimir Razmerov, "Nauchnaya zhizn': Vstrecha ekspertov postoyannoy komissii," *Memo* No. 7 (July 1984).

42. On the official priority given to verification by national technical means, see Brezhnev's comments as reported in *Pravda*, November 3, 1981, p. 1; and Roland Timerbayev, *Kontrol' za ogranicheniyem vooruzheniy i razoruzheniyem* (Moscow: Mezhdunarodnye

otnosheniya, 1983). Timerbayev was a deputy head of the Foreign Ministry's International Organizations Department. For examples of IMEMO researchers' not questioning these ideas and policies, see Oleg Bykov, "Na vtoroy spetsial'noy sessii General'noy Assambley OON po razoruzheniya," *Memo* No. 8 (August 1982); idem, "Razum i otvetstvennost' (Imperativy yadernogo veka)," *Memo* No. 11 (November 1983), 14; and Inozemtsev, "XXVI s'ezd KPSS i nashi zadachi," p. 15.

43. For example, see A. Astaf'yev and Aleksey Nikonov, "Militarizm SShA — ugroza miru," *Memo* No. 3 (March 1982), 8; and Tomilin's comments in "Rol' OON v sovremennom mire i puti povysheniya ee effektivnosti (Kruglyy stol *Memo*)," *Memo* No. 6 (June 1984), 106.

44. On the status of the two institutes during these years, see Cobb, "National Security Perspectives of Soviet 'Think Tanks' "; and Oded Eran, *Mezhdunarodniki: An Assessment of Professional Expertise in the Making of Soviet Foreign Policy* (Tel Aviv: Turtledove Publishing, 1979).

45. See Georgiy Arbatov, "The Main Political Issue," *USA* No. 10 (October 1982), 7 [JPRS 82773]. Also see his remarks in "Discussion at a Session of the Foreign Policy Section of the Academic Council on US Economic, Political and Ideological Problems," *USA* No. 6 (June 1982), 99 [JPRS 81920]; and " 'Common Security': A Program for Disarmament," *USA* No. 9 (September 1982), 79–81 [JPRS 82551]. Arbatov had headed ISKAN since its founding in the late 1960s.

46. On these points, see Cobb, "National Security Perspectives of Soviet 'Think Tanks,' " p. 53; "Discussion at a Session of the Foreign Policy Section of the Academic Council on US Economic, Political and Ideological Problems," *USA* No. 5 (May 1982), 88 [JPRS 81454]; and note 40, above. By late 1983, ISKAN had seven researchers working with various working groups of the Committee of Soviet Scientists (IMEMO had two). See "Dokumenty: Strategicheskiye i mezhdunarodno-politicheskiye posledstviya sozdaniya kosmicheskoy protivoraketnoy sistemy s ispol'zovaniyem oruzhiya napravlennoy peredachi energii," *SShA* No. 11 (November 1985), 112–14. My analysis is consistent with research documenting ISKAN's greater openness to transnationally generated security concepts. See Thomas Risse-Kappen, "Ideas Do Not Float Freely: Transnational Coalitions, Domestic Structures and the End of the Cold War," *International Organization* 48 (Spring 1994).

47. These analysts included Andrey Kokoshin, Aleksandr Konovalov, and Aleksey Vasil'yev. Information on personnel policy comes from interviews with Georgiy Arbatov, a deputy institute director and ISKAN's academic secretary.

48. On these points, see Georgiy Arbatov, *The System: An Insider's Life in Soviet Politics* (New York: Times Books, 1992), p. 174; and S. Aytmatov, "Dangers and Problems of the 'Trident,' " *USA* No. 12 (December 1981) [JPRS 80433], for example.

49. See Radomir Bogdanov et al., Editors, *SShA: Voyenno-strategicheskiye kontseptsii* (Moscow: Nauka, 1980); S. Stashevskiy, "For Peaceful Space," *USA* No. 11 (November 1981) [JPRS 80250]; Andrey Kokoshin, "Debaty v SShA vokrug planov sozdaniya kosmicheskoy protivoraketnoy sistemy," *SShA* No. 11 (November 1983); and Mikhail Mil'shteyn, "Ob evolyutsii voyenno-strategicheskikh kontseptsiy Vashingtona," *SShA* No. 11 (November 1984), among many others. Source material was drawn from the U.S. defense and technical communities and included such publications as *Strategic Review,*

Defense Electronics, Aviation Week and Space Technology, Survival, Naval War College Review, and *International Security.*

50. See " 'Common Security': A Program for Disarmament," *USA* Nos. 9 and 10 (September–October 1982) [JPRS 82551, 82773], an abridged version of the Palme Commission report; "Dokumenty: Zayavleniye komissii Pal'me," *SShA* No. 2 (February 1985); Andrey Kokoshin, "Diskussii po tsentral'nym voprosam voyennoy politiki SShA," *SShA* No. 2 (February 1985); and idem, " 'Plan Rodzhersa,' al'ternativnye kontseptsii oborony i bezopasnost' v Evrope," *SShA* No. 9 (September 1985).

51. On a pre-Gorbachev civil society, see Donna Bahry, "Society Transformed? Rethinking the Social Roots of Perestroika," *Slavic Review* 52 (Fall 1993), for example.

Chapter 5: *Open Windows, New Ideas, and the End of the Cold War*

1. See Charles Glickham, "New Directions for Soviet Foreign Policy," *Radio Liberty Research Bulletin* Supplement 2/86 (September 6, 1986); and Matthew Evangelista, "The New Soviet Approach to Security," *World Policy Journal* 3 (Fall 1986). "Glickham" was my pseudonym when I was publishing with the Radio Free Europe/Radio Liberty Research Institute.

2. On policy paradigms, see Peter Hall, "Policy Paradigms, Social Learning and the State: The Case of Economic Policymaking in Britain," *Comparative Politics* 25 (April 1993), 279.

3. In addition to the primary sources cited in chapters 3 and 4, see William Zimmerman, *Soviet Perspectives on International Relations, 1956–67* (Princeton, N.J.: Princeton University Press, 1969); and Allen Lynch, *The Soviet Study of International Relations* (New York: Cambridge University Press, 1987).

4. The basic assumptions-strategic prescriptions dichotomy draws on George Breslauer, "Ideology and Learning in Soviet Third World Policy," *World Politics* 31 (April 1987), 430–31.

5. An examination of the broader structure of the Soviet state during the early Gorbachev years (1985–88) confirms this fact. The key center of day-to-day executive decision making was the Central Committee apparatus. Approximately seventeen of its twenty departments dealt with domestic socioeconomic issues.

6. Fedor Burlatskiy, an occasional adviser to Gorbachev in the early and mid-1980s, noted this difference as well in an interview with me. For evidence of Gorbachev's centrist-conservative beliefs on economic policy throughout the years 1985–91, see James Moltz, "Divergent Learning and the Failed Politics of Soviet Economic Reform," *World Politics* 45 (January 1993).

7. On Gorbachev's early years, see Robert Kaiser, *Why Gorbachev Happened: His Triumphs and His Failure* (New York: Simon and Schuster, 1991), chapter 1. To appreciate the dominance of domestic issues in CPSU ideology, we need only compare the attention devoted to domestic versus foreign policy in the last edition of the CPSU Party Program, adopted under Gorbachev's leadership in 1986. See "Programma Kommunisticheskoy Partii Sovetskogo Soyuza (Novaya redaktsiya)," In *XXVII s'ezd Kommunisticheskoy Partii Sovetskogo Soyuza: Stenograficheskiy otchet, Tom I* (Moscow: Politizdat, 1986).

8. See Ed Hewett, *Reforming the Soviet Economy: Equality Versus Efficiency* (Washington, D.C.: Brookings Institution, 1988), chapter 7.

9. Archie Brown, "Gorbachev: New Man in the Kremlin," *Problems of Communism* 34 (May–June 1985), 14–17, has provided the most extensive documentation of these points. Vadim Pechenev, who served as a close aide to General Secretary Chernenko, claims that Gorbachev was in fact CPSU second secretary as early as February 1984. See Pechenev, "Kremlevskiye tayny: Vverkh po lestnitse, vedushchey vniz," *Literaturnaya gazeta,* January 30, 1991, p. 3.

10. For Gorbachev's orthodox commentary during this period, see his Supreme Soviet election speech on February 29, 1984; a speech in Smolensk on June 27; and his speech in Sofia, Bulgaria, on September 8, all in *M. S. Gorbachev. Izbrannye rechi i stat'i, Tom 2* (Moscow: Politizdat, 1987), pp. 17–19, 61–64, 71–73. Yet Gorbachev clearly sought an improvement in Soviet-American relations. See *M. S. Gorbachev. Izbrannye rechi i stat'i, Tom 2,* pp. 64, 73.

11. Gorbachev, *Zhivoye tvorchestvo naroda* (Moscow: Politizdat, 1984), pp. 40, 11.

12. Brown, "Gorbachev: New Man in the Kremlin," p. 16.

13. See Gorbachev, "Vystupleniye M. S. Gorbacheva v Britanskom parlamente," *Pravda,* December 19, 1984, pp. 4–5.

14. Interviews, Georgiy Arbatov and Aleksandr Yakovlev. Also see Sarah Mendelson, "Internal Battles and External Wars: Politics, Learning and the Soviet Withdrawal from Afghanistan," *World Politics* 45 (April 1993), 342; and Georgiy Arbatov, *Zatyanuvsheyesya vyzdorovleniye: Svidetel'stvo sovremennika* (Moscow: Mezhdunarodnye otnosheniya, 1991), pp. 335–36. For a study exploring the cognitive aspects of Gorbachev's learning, see Janice Gross Stein, "Political Learning by Doing: Gorbachev as Uncommitted Thinker and Motivated Learner," *International Organization* 48 (Spring 1994).

15. On these points, see Yuriy Andropov, "Otvety Yu. V. Andropova na voprosy gazety 'Pravda,'" *Kommunist* No. 16 (November 1983); Seweryn Bialer, "Danger in Moscow," *New York Review of Books,* February 16, 1984; and Myron Hedlin, "Moscow's Line on Arms Control," *Problems of Communism* 33 (May–June 1984), 20, 24–25.

16. On the critical importance of this international context in creating uncertainty in Gorbachev's foreign policy preferences, also see William Wohlforth, "Realism and the End of the Cold War," *International Security* 19 (Winter 1994/95), 109–15; and the remarks of Andrey Grachev (a former Gorbachev adviser) in John Lloyd, "Gorbachev Shivers in His Own Shadow," *Financial Times,* April 24, 1995.

17. On Yakovlev's domestic political role, see Bill Keller, "Riding Shotgun on Gorbachev's Glasnost Express: Aleksandr N. Yakovlev," *New York Times,* October 28, 1988, p. A10; and idem, "Moscow's Other Mastermind," *New York Times Magazine,* February 19, 1989.

18. See Jeff Checkel, *Aleksandr Nikolayevich Yakovlev,* Research Note (Cambridge, Mass.: MIT Center for International Studies, 1990).

19. Interview with Yakovlev. Also see Arkadiy Vaksberg, "Priglasheniye k sporu: Zametki na polyakh knigi A. N. Yakovleva 'Kakim my khotim videt' Sovetskiy Soyuz,'" *Literaturnaya gazeta,* May 15, 1991, p. 3. The directorship of IMEMO was open because Vladlen Martynov, who took over as the institute's leader in the wake of Inozemtsev's death, was officially only its acting director.

20. The following is based on interviews with Yakovlev, one of his personal aides, three deputy directors of IMEMO, one department head, two deputy department heads, the editor-in-chief of *Memo,* approximately a dozen senior researchers, and Georgiy Arbatov. For further evidence of Yakovlev's unorthodox views and behavior during these years, see Aleksandr Yakovlev, "Demokratiya, toropyas', ne proizvodit nravstvennoy selektsii," *Literaturnaya gazeta,* December 25, 1991, p. 3; and S. Chugrov, "Kniga Aleksandra Yakovleva i Lilli Marku vo Frantsii," *Memo* No. 12 (December 1991).

21. Three of the new sections appeared during 1984. One addressed global problems, while the other two were entitled "Tribune of Economists and Internationalists" and "Discussions-Debates." For examples of innovative articles appearing under these rubrics, see Yuriy Krasin, "Tribuna ekonomista i mezhdunarodnika: Sootnosheniye ideologii i politiki v revolyutsionnom dvizhenii," *Memo* No. 5 (May 1984); and Yu. Shishkov, "Tribuna ekonomista i mezhdunarodnika: K voprosu o edinstve sovremennogo vsemirnogo khozyaystva," *Memo* No. 8 (August 1984). Interviewees disagreed over the classified-research unit. Yakovlev asserted that it had been abolished, while two other senior researchers (one of whom had worked in the department) claimed that it had been reduced in size but not eliminated. One wonders, however, why it was classified in the first place. The most frequently used source in this department was *Aviation Week and Space Technology* — a popular trade weekly published in the United States.

22. For examples of Yakovlev's anti-American commentary, see Aleksandr Yakovlev, "Voprosy teorii imperializma — sopernichestvo i protivorechiya," *Pravda,* March 23, 1984, pp. 2–3; idem, "Rakovaya opukhol' imperskikh ambitsiy v yadernyy vek," *Memo* No. 1 (January 1984); and idem, *Ot Trumena do Reygana: Doktriny i real'nosti yadernogo veka* (Moscow: Molodaya gvardiya, 1985). Also see Jonathan Harris, *The Public Politics of Aleksandr Nikolaevich Yakovlev, 1983–1989,* Carl Beck Papers in Russian and East European Studies, No. 901 (Pittsburgh, Pa.: University of Pittsburgh Center for Russian and East European Studies, 1990). An example of Yakovlev's unorthodox writing during these years is "Dinamizm i konservatizm — ikh adepty," in Aleksandr Yakovlev, *Realizm — zemlya perestroyki: Izbrannye vystupleniya i stat'i* (Moscow: Politizdat, 1990), pp. 21–39, an essay first published in 1990 but written just as Yakovlev assumed the leadership of IMEMO in 1983.

23. This is my own reconstruction of Yakovlev's strategy. When I directly asked him to explain the extraordinary difference between his private behavior and public discourse of those years, Yakovlev grew quite angry and accused me of seriously misreading his published writings. After calming down a bit, he admitted that one had to "read between the lines" for his true meaning (that aggressive policies pursued by any country — and not just the United States — were wrong). My depiction of Yakovlev as politically adept benefited tremendously from interviews with institute personnel.

24. Georgiy Arbatov and Yakovlev confirmed this observation in interviews, as did a long-time personal aide to both Inozemtsev and Yakovlev. As Arbatov noted, it was important for leaders like himself to lead assertively; otherwise, his researchers "would just do the same thing over and over again."

25. See Yakovlev's comments in "Kruglyy stol *Memo:* Bor'ba za novyy mezhdunarodnyy ekonomicheskiy poryadok — itogi desyatiletiya," *Memo* No. 7 (July 1984), 101; and Yakovlev, "Istoki ugrozy i obshchestvennoye mneniye," *Memo* No. 3 (March 1985), 11.

As the 1980s progressed, Yakovlev became even more explicit on this point. See Yakovlev, "Obshchestvennye nauki na novom etape," *Pravda,* November 28, 1987, p. 3.

26. Interviews. Blagovolin describes Yakovlev as his "intellectual godfather."

27. See chapter 1 for a general discussion of the relations among organizations, their embedded ideologies, and policy entrepreneurs.

28. V. Lukov and Dmitriy Tomashevskiy, "Radi zhizni na zemle (Uroki velikoy pobedy i mirovaya politika nashikh dney)," *Memo* No. 2 (February 1983), 5; and idem, "Interesy chelovechestva i mirovaya politika," *Memo* No. 4 (April 1985). Tomashevskiy was a senior institute scholar and a former head of its Department of International Relations. As seen in earlier chapters, he had been a strong proponent of revising orthodox, class-based notions of the international system as far back as the late 1960s. On "objective categories," see Ivan Frolov, Editor, *Filosofskiy slovar'* (Moscow: Politizdat, 1986), p. 337.

29. See Oleg Bykov, "Leninskaya politika mira i ee voploshcheniye v deyatel'nosti KPSS," *Memo* No. 3 (March 1984), 23; and Vladimir Razmerov, "Zhiznennaya al'ternativa," *Memo* No. 9 (September 1984), 13. Both essays were published as lead articles. For the contributions by noninstitute analysts, see Krasin, "Tribuna ekonomista i mezhdunarodnika: Sootnosheniye ideologii i politiki v revolyutsionnom dvizhenii," pp. 87–88; and Sergey Tikhvinskiy, "Vazhneyshaya missiya nauki," *Memo* No. 4 (April 1985), 137.

30. See chapters 3 and 4 above, as well as Walter C. Clemens, Jr., *The USSR and Global Interdependence: Alternative Futures* (Washington, D.C.: American Enterprise Institute for Public Policy Research, 1978); Elizabeth Valkenier, *The Soviet Union and the Third World: An Economic Bind* (New York: Praeger, 1983), chapter 2; and Stephen Shenfield, *The Nuclear Predicament: Explorations in Soviet Ideology* (New York: Routledge and Kegan Paul, 1987), chapter 8.

31. N. Kolikov, "Za realizm i otvetstvennost' v mirovoy politike," *Memo* No. 3 (March 1983), 18–19. For Maksimova's comments, see "Vsesoyuznaya nauchnaya konferentsiya: Delo Marksa zhivet i pobezhdayet," *Memo* No. 7 (July 1983), 72–76.

32. See, respectively, V. Shemyatenkov, " 'Kholodnaya voyna' ili razryadka: Dilemmy vneshney politiki SShA," *Memo* No. 5 (May 1984), 10; and Shishkov, "Tribuna ekonomista i mezhdunarodnika: K voprosu o edinstve sovremennogo vsemirnogo khozyaystva," pp. 74, 81. According to Shishkov, his opponent was opportunistically using the tense international climate "to torpedo" the notion of a single world economy.

33. For representative discussions on the nature of security, see Kolikov, "Za realizm i otvetstvennost' v mirovoy politike," p. 18, where the author cautiously describes an "objective community of interests of international security"; Oleg Bykov, "Razum i otvetstvennost' (Imperativy yadernogo veka)," *Memo* No. 11 (November 1983), 3, where it is declared—without any elaboration—that nuclear weapons had "canceled many traditional postulates of politics and strategy"; and V. Kortunov, " 'Ogranichennaya yadernaya voyna'—strategiya global'nogo samoubiystva," *Memo* No. 4 (April 1984), 50, where only in the article's last paragraph is it noted that the interests of all states should be "mutually considered" when it comes to questions of security.

34. For the articles, see Yuriy Zhilin, "Bezopasnost' v yadernyy vek," *Rabochiy klass i sovremennyy mir* No. 2 (March–April 1984); and Georgiy Shakhnazarov, "Logika poli-

ticheskogo myshleniya v yadernyy vek," *Voprosy filosofii* No. 5 (May 1984). Zhilin headed a consultants' group in the Central Committee's International Department; Shakhnazarov was a deputy head of the Central Committee's department for relations with socialist countries. On the book, see Anatoliy Gromyko and Vladimir Lomeyko, *Novoye myshleniye v yadernyy vek* (Moscow: Mezhdunarodnye otnosheniya, 1984), chapters 9–10. Gromyko, the son of former Foreign Minister Andrey Gromyko, was an academic and diplomat who had headed the Academy of Sciences' Africa Institute since 1976. Lomeyko, in contrast, was more of a publicist. Although he held the rank of diplomat, the majority of his work had been press related — including ten years at the Novosti Press Agency.

35. Gorbachev was elected CPSU leader in March 1985.

36. These comments come in the opening moments of Gorbachev's address to the French Parliament. See Gorbachev, *M. S. Gorbachev. Izbrannye rechi i stat'i, Tom 2,* p. 460.

37. Gorbachev, "Politicheskiy doklad Tsentral'nogo Komiteta KPSS XXVII s'ezdu Kommunisticheskoy Partii Sovetskogo Soyuza," In *XXVII s'ezd Kommunisticheskoy Partii Sovetskogo Soyuza: Stenograficheskiy otchet, Tom I,* pp. 24, 39–41.

38. "Politicheskiy doklad," pp. 86–89. Several months later, while on a visit to Vladivostok, Gorbachev would even more clearly indicate the approach that lay behind the new thinking — noting, in particular, that it was "not a scheme that can be applied to any situation; rather, it is principles and a method that are guided by experience." Gorbachev, *M. S. Gorbachev. Izbrannye rechi i stat'i, Tom 4,* p. 26.

39. See "Rezolyutsii XXVII s'ezda Kommunisticheskoy Partii Sovetskogo Soyuza po politicheskomu dokladu Tsentral'nogo Komiteta KPSS," *Kommunist* No. 4 (March 1986). Also see the analysis in Glickham, "New Directions for Soviet Foreign Policy," p. 5.

40. See Gorbachev, "Vremya trebuyet novogo myshleniya," *Literaturnaya gazeta,* November 5, 1986, pp. 1–2; Anatoliy Dobrynin, "Glavnaya sotsial'naya sila sovremennosti," *Kommunist* No. 16 (November 1986), 23–24; and Yegor Ligachev, "Kursom oktyabrya, v dukhe revolyutsionnogo tvorchestva," *Pravda,* November 7, 1986, pp. 1–3, at p. 3.

41. For a discussion of the general secretary's ability to initiate foreign policy change of this sort, see chapter 2. Of course, these agenda-setting powers varied according to the issues. For example, Stephen Meyer, "The Sources and Prospects of Gorbachev's New Political Thinking on Security," *International Security* 13 (Fall 1988), notes the general secretary's weakened ability — as of the mid-1980s — to set the agenda on defense policy issues. For a study exploring the significant agenda-setting powers of Soviet leaders from a comparative-politics perspective, see Roger Cobb, Jennie Ross, and Marc Ross, "Agenda Building as a Comparative Political Process," *American Political Science Review* 70 (March 1976).

42. A central theme of Yegor Ligachev's memoirs is how Gorbachev and other reformers were able to exploit the Soviet "means of mass information" to advance their ideological and policy agenda. See Yegor Ligachev, *Zagadka Gorbacheva* (Novosibirsk: Interbuk, 1992).

43. For Gorbachev's commentary, see *M. S. Gorbachev. Izbrannye rechi i stat'i, Tom 4,*

pp. 19–33, a July 28 speech in Vladivostok; and "Rech' tovarishcha Gorbacheva M. S. na Vsesoyuznom soveshchanii zaveduyushchikh kafedrami obshchestvennykh nauk," *Partiynaya zhizn'* No. 20 (October 1986), 4–5, an October 1 speech in Moscow to an all-union meeting of social scientists. For statements by other members of the leadership, see, in addition to the sources already cited, Eduard Shevardnadze, *Za novoye myshleniye v mirovoy politike* (Moscow: Politizdat, 1986), pp. 4, 12, a September 23 speech to the United Nations General Assembly; and Aleksandr Yakovlev, "Mezhimperialisticheskiye protivorechiya: sovremennyy kontekst," *Kommunist* No. 17 (November 1986), 3. Yakovlev, whose essay ran as a lead article, had by this point left IMEMO, assuming a much more important position in the C.C. apparatus. See below.

The campaign in the central press included articles in *Komsomol'skaya pravda*, *Kommunist* and, especially, *Pravda*. See Yu. Zhdanov, "Voprosy teorii: Otstaivaya obshche-chelovecheskiye interesy," *Pravda*, January 23, 1986, p. 3; Vselovod Ovchinnikov, "Bezopasnost' v yadernyy vek," *Pravda*, March 11, 1986, p. 4; "O zhurnale *Kommunist*," *Kommunist* No. 12 (August 1986), 8–9; and "Novoye politicheskoye myshleniye v deystvii," *Kommunist* No. 13 (August 1986). Also see the various articles cited in Glickham, "New Directions for Soviet Foreign Policy."

44. Shevardnadze, "Strategiya uskoreniya — Leninizm v deystvii," *Pravda*, April 23, 1986, pp. 1–2. Indeed, in the early summer of 1986, a new unit — known as the Scientific Coordination Center — was created at the Foreign Ministry with the specific mission of coordinating academic research and leadership policy concerns. On the center, see Oleg Peresypkin, "Obsuzhdayem tezisy TsK KPSS: Nauku — na sluzhbu politike," *Pravda*, June 24, 1988, p. 5; and John Van Oudenaren, *The Role of Shevardnadze and the Ministry of Foreign Affairs in the Making of Soviet Defense and Arms Control Policy* (Santa Monica, Calif.: Rand Corporation, 1990), p. 30.

45. Anatoliy Dobrynin, "Za bez'yadernyy mir, navstrechu XXI veku," *Kommunist* No. 9 (June 1986), 26–28. For the conference proceedings, see Petr Fedoseyev, Editor, *Mir i razoruzheniye: Nauchnye issledovaniya (spetsial'nyy vypusk) — Materialy II Vsesoyuznoy konferentsii uchenykh po problemam mira i predotvrashcheniya yadernoy voyny* (Moscow: Nauka, 1986).

46. Sikkink, *Ideas and Institutions: Developmentalism in Brazil and Argentina* (Ithaca, N. Y.: Cornell University Press, 1991), pp. 2–3 and passim.

47. At the February 1986 Party Congress, Gorbachev had disparaged the aggressive intentions of the "ruling wing of the monopoly bourgeoisie" in the United States, noted the deepening of capitalism's general crisis, and decried the growing militarization of policy and thinking in the United States. See Gorbachev, "Politicheskiy doklad," pp. 30–41. Later in 1986, he still had few good things to say about capitalism, declaring at one point that a capitalist economy "will never begin to produce children's toys instead of rockets. Such is its nature." Gorbachev, *M. S. Gorbachev. Izbrannye rechi i stat'i, Tom 4*, pp. 20–21. Also see Gorbachev's harsh comments on "capitalist dilettantes" in "Rech' M. S. Gorbacheva," *Pravda*, March 31, 1987, p. 2.

48. For Gorbachev's radically different commentary, see "Oktyabr' i perestroyka: Revolyutsiya prodolzhayetsya," *Kommunist* No. 17 (November 1987), 31–36.

49. See Robert Legvold, "The Revolution in Soviet Foreign Policy," *Foreign Affairs* 68 (America and the World 1988/89).

50. See chapter 1 for a full explication of the theoretical logic here. On the autonomous role of ideas in shaping Gorbachev's emerging preferences, see, in addition to the primary-source and interview data cited below, Stein, "Political Learning by Doing"; and Lloyd, "Gorbachev Shivers in His Own Shadow."

51. Yakovlev moved to the Central Committee apparatus, becoming head of its Propaganda Department. This "promotion" may seem odd given Yakovlev's apparent success at IMEMO. Gorbachev, however, clearly wanted his close ally in a stronger bureaucratic position — where Yakovlev could help him overcome opposition to his policies in the Central Committee (which was still a key force in the political process).

52. Primakov's insider status is confirmed by his detailed knowledge of life at the institute during the 1970s. See Yevgeniy Primakov, "Uchenyy, rukovoditel', chelovek (k 70-letiyu akademika N. N. Inozemtseva)," *Memo* No. 4 (April 1991). On his scholarly credentials, see Jerry Hough, *The Struggle for the Third World: Soviet Debates and American Options* (Washington, D.C.: Brookings Institution, 1986), pp. 63, 245, 255; and Yuriy Polsky, *Soviet Research Institutes and the Formation of Foreign Policy: The Institute of the World Economy and International Relations* (Falls Church, Va.: Delphic Associates, 1987), pp. 115–16. Primakov, who was born in 1929, spent the early part of his career in the central media. After his stint at IMEMO during the mid-1970s, he moved to the Academy of Sciences' Institute of Oriental Studies, where he was director from 1977–85. See Andrey Gromyko et al., Editors, *Diplomaticheskiy slovar', Tom II* (Moscow: Nauka, 1985), pp. 421–22.

53. This occurred in the summer of 1987. In an interview with the author, Diligenskiy confirmed that he returned to IMEMO at the personal request of Primakov.

54. These political ambitions explain why Primakov left IMEMO in 1988 — to serve first on the Politburo, then on the Presidential Council (which had replaced the Politburo), and — in post-Soviet Russia — as head of the Russian Foreign Intelligence Service and then of the Foreign Ministry. The observation that he was a "tougher" leader was made by Diligenskiy. As a department head, editor of *Memo,* and friend of Primakov's, Diligenskiy was in a position to know. Other interviewees used adjectives like *energetic, active* and *very talented* to describe Primakov's leadership style.

55. Interviews with deputy institute director Igor' Gur'yev and Sergey Blagovolin. According to Gur'yev, Yakovlev made his recommendation to Gorbachev only after consulting with a number of top IMEMO scholars.

56. While not cast explicitly in institutional terms, two excellent analyses of evolving state-society relations in the USSR during this period are Gail Lapidus, "State and Society: Toward the Emergence of a Civil Society in the Soviet Union," in Seweryn Bialer, Editor, *Inside Gorbachev's Russia: Politics, Society, and Nationality* (Boulder, Colo.: Westview Press, 1989); and S. Frederick Starr, "Soviet Union: A Civil Society," *Foreign Policy* No. 70 (Spring 1988).

57. For the articles, see Yevgeniy Primakov, "Put' v budushchee," *Pravda,* January 22, 1986, p. 4; and idem, "Filosofiya bezopasnosti: XXVII s'ezd KPSS — Razrabotka vneshnepoliticheskoy strategii," *Pravda,* March 17, 1986, p. 6. The Primakov-Gorbachev ties first became evident in November 1985, when Primakov accompanied the general secretary to the Geneva Summit meeting. See Gary Lee, "Soviets Court World Press in Geneva," *Washington Post,* November 16, 1985, p. A12. Two deputy directors of IMEMO,

in separate interviews, confirm that by mid-1986 Primakov had become a key Gorbachev adviser. Given these close ties, it is not surprising that Primakov was named a candidate member of the Central Committee in March 1986.

58. See Gorbachev, "Politicheskiy doklad," pp. 30–41; and "Programma Kommunisticheskoy Partii Sovetskogo Soyuza (Novaya redaktsiya)," pp. 563–66. On Primakov, see, especially, Yevgeniy Primakov, "XXVII s'ezd KPSS i issledovaniye problem mirovoy ekonomiki i mezhdunarodnykh otnosheniy," *Memo* No. 5 (May 1986), 6–8.

59. See Primakov, "XXVII s'ezd KPSS i issledovaniye problem mirovoy ekonomiki i mezhdunarodnykh otnosheniy," pp. 6–9; idem, "Leninskiy analiz imperializma i sovremennost'," *Kommunist* No. 9 (June 1986), 104–07; idem, "Interv'yu," *Vestnik Leningradskogo Universiteta, seriya 5 (ekonomika)* Vypusk 3 (September 1986), 86; and idem, "Kapitalizm vo vzaimosvyazannom mire," *Kommunist* No. 13 (September 1987). Also see Primakov's comments in "Mezhdunarodnaya konferentsiya: Sovremennye osobennosti obshchego krizisa kapitalizma," *Memo* No. 6 (June 1987), 68–70.

60. See, especially, Primakov, "Kapitalizm vo vzaimosvyazannom mire," p. 106. Also see Primakov, "Filosofiya bezopasnosti: XXVII s'ezd KPSS — Razrabotka vneshnepoliticheskoy strategii"; and idem, "Leninskiy analiz imperializma i sovremennost'," p. 109. In one instance, Georgiy Arbatov, head of ISKAN, also addressed this issue. See Arbatov, "Militarizm i sovremennoye obshchestvo," *Kommunist* No. 2 (January 1987), 111–14.

61. On the historical context, see Primakov, "Uchenyy, rukovoditel', chelovek (k 70-letiyu akademika N. N. Inozemtseva)," pp. 106–07; and chapter 3, above.

62. The series began in issue No. 10 of *Memo* for 1986. It continued in issues 11 and 12 of that year, and in Nos. 1–4, 6, 7, and 12 of 1987. It eventually concluded in January 1989.

63. On the series, see Brian Taylor, "Perestroika and Soviet Foreign Policy Research: Rethinking the Theory of State-Monopoly Capitalism," *Millennium* 19 (Spring 1990). Also see "Obsuzhdayem preds'ezdovskiye dokumenty," *Memo* No. 2 (February 1986), 30, where the institute's collective argued for revising the Soviet definition of the capitalist military-industrial complex in a way that would narrow the number of institutions and individuals involved in it; Igor' Gur'yev, "V avangarde istorii," *Memo* No. 11 (November 1987), 5–9; A. Shapiro, "God posle istoricheskogo s'ezda," *Memo* No. 4 (April 1987), 8–9, 11–15; and "Dialog: Na poroge novogo veka," *Memo* No. 12 (December 1987), 52–57. All these articles undercut key elements of the theory of state-monopoly capitalism. For a definitive official statement of this "theory," see "Programma Kommunisticheskoy Partii Sovetskogo Soyuza (Novaya redaktsiya)," pp. 563–66.

64. On the Leninist theory of imperialism, see the entries "Imperializm," in Frolov, Editor, *Filosofskiy slovar'*, pp. 161–62; and "Militarizm," in Sergey Akhromeyev, Editor, *Voyennyy entsiklopedicheskiy slovar', Izdaniye vtoroye* (Moscow: Voyenizdat, 1986), p. 443. For the cautious advocacy, see Ivan Ivanov, "Tribuna ekonomista i mezhdunarodnika: Osnovnye priznaki imperializma i sovremennost' (na premere deyatel'nosti TNK i TNB)," *Memo* No. 2 (February 1986), 77.

65. See "Mezhdunarodnaya konferentsiya: Sovremennye osobennosti obshchego krizisa kapitalizma," *Memo* Nos. 6–8 (June–August 1987). In its length and bold willingness to challenge official orthodoxy, this report echoed the institute's 1969 roundtable on international relations. See chapter 3, above.

66. "Mezhdunarodnaya konferentsiya," *Memo* No. 6 (June 1987), 66–70.

67. See "Mezhdunarodnaya konferentsiya," *Memo* No. 7 (July 1987), 60–61; and idem, *Memo* No. 8 (August 1987), 85–86, 88.

68. There was an obvious source — Aleksandr Yakovlev — for Gorbachev's skeptical beliefs about capitalism. Yakovlev, who at this point was the general secretary's closest adviser, had consistently promoted an image of capitalism that was virtually identical to the one articulated by Gorbachev through early 1987. Compare, for example, Gorbachev's commentary with Yakovlev, "Voprosy teorii imperializma — sopernichestvo i protivorechiya." Even after Gorbachev's framework for analyzing capitalism had changed, Yakovlev continued to speak on the topic in a more pessimistic manner. See his comments in "Oktyabr', perestroyka i sovremennyy mir," *Pravda*, November 4, 1987, p. 8. When I interviewed him in mid-1992, Yakovlev still held to this deeply skeptical framework for interpreting capitalist political economy.

69. Examples of military commentary that stressed an aggressive image of capitalism are Dmitriy Yazov, *Na strazhe sotsializma i mira* (Moscow: Voyenizdat, 1987), pp. 3–4, 16, 30, 83; Makhmut Gareyev, *Sovetskaya voyennaya nauka* (Moscow: Znaniye, 1987), pp. 3–4; and Yuriy Kirshin, "Filosofiya formirovaniya bezopasnogo mira," *Voprosy filosofii* No. 4 (April 1987), 30–31.

70. Gorbachev, "Oktyabr' i perestroyka: Revolyutsiya prodolzhayetsya," pp. 31–36.

71. Soviet leaders since Khrushchev's time had suggested that imperialism's aggressiveness could be restrained only by the world socialist community. See Shenfield, *The Nuclear Predicament*, p. 57.

72. See Vladimir Lenin, "Bellicose Militarism and the Anti-Marxist Tactics of Social Democracy," in Aleksandr Yakovlev, Editor, *Capitalism at the End of the Century* (Moscow: Progress Publishers, 1988), pp. 116–17.

73. In the central press, see Valeriy Bushuyev and Nikita Maslennikov, "Vstupaya v novoye vremya: Dialog v interesakh mira i sotrudnichestva," *Kommunist* No. 18 (December 1987), 44–49; G. Tsagolov and A. Kireyev, "Bremya yadernykh dospekhov: Ekonomicheskaya tselesoobraznost' razoruzheniya," *Pravda*, January 4, 1988, p. 6; and, especially, Yuriy Krasin, "A esli bez militarizma? Mozhet li kapitalizm prisposobit'sya k bez'yadernomu miru," *Pravda*, January 28, 1988, p. 4. For the Gorbachev speech, see "Revolyutsionnoy perestroyke — ideologiyu obnovleniya," *Pravda*, February 19, 1988, pp. 1–3, at p. 3.

74. Yakovlev, "Obshchestvennye nauki na novom etape"; idem, "Glavnoye v perestroyke segodnya — prakticheskiye dela i konkretnye rezul'taty," *Partiynaya zhizn'* No. 10 (May 1987), 13; and idem, "Perestroyka i obshchestvennoye soznaniye," *Pravda*, April 10, 1987, p. 3. The information on Yakovlev's Central Committee responsibilities comes from the individual who served as his personal aide during this period.

75. Yakovlev, "Dostizheniye kachestvenno novogo sostoyaniya Sovetskogo obshchestva i obshchestvennye nauki," *Kommunist* No. 8 (May 1987), 10–11, 18, and passim. This was placed as the lead article.

76. Interview. The speech made similar points about the domestic reform process. On Zaslavskaya, see Bohdan Nahaylo, "Interview with Tat'yana Zaslavskaya," Radio Liberty *Research Bulletin* No. 365/87 (September 15, 1987), p. 8.

77. For analyses by academics, see, among many others, K. Smirnov, "Ekologiya i mir: Zametki s Moskovskogo mezhdunarodnogo foruma 'Za bez'yadernyy mir, za vyzhivaniye chelovechestva,'" *Kommunist* No. 6 (April 1987), 115–17; Georgiy Smirnov, "Tvorcheskaya teoriya razvivayushchegosya sotsializma: K vykhodu v svet trekh tomov 'Izbrannykh rechiy i statey' M. S. Gorbacheva," *Kommunist* No. 12 (August 1987), 31–32; Yu. Zhdanov, "Voprosy teorii: Klassovoye i obshchechelovecheskoye v yadernyy vek," *Pravda*, March 6, 1987, pp. 3–4; and I. Pantin, "Oktyabr' i razvitiye chelovechestva," *Pravda*, October 23, 1987, p. 4.

For elite commentary on the new thinking, see Nikolay Ryzhkov, "Leninizm — osnova teorii i politiki perestroyki: Doklad tovarishcha Ryzhkova N. I.," *Pravda*, April 23, 1987, pp. 1–3, at p. 3; Georgiy Razumovskiy, "Sovershenstvovat' podgotovku i perepodgotovku rukovodyashchikh kadrov partii," *Kommunist* No. 9 (June 1987), 10; Anatoliy Dobrynin, "Otvetstvennost' za budushchee," *Pravda*, May 5, 1987, p. 3; and Vadim Medvedev's comments in "Velikiy Oktyabr' i sovremennyy mir," *Pravda*, December 9, 1987, p. 4. All these individuals were Politburo members (candidate or full) or Central Committee secretaries.

For unsigned and hence authoritative editorials promoting the new approach to foreign policy, see "Kursom XXVII s'ezda KPSS," *Kommunist* No. 4 (March 1987), 18–19; and "K 70-letiyu velikogo Oktyabrya: Leninizm, revolyutsiya, sovremennost'," *Kommunist* No. 7 (May 1987), 59–60, 68.

78. "Ligachev Discusses Working with Gorbachev," *FBIS-SOV-87-233*, December 4, 1987, pp. 42–45 — a translation of an interview with Michel Tatu. Also see Tatu's comments as reported on the Sovset' Computer Network, December 3, 1987. Ligachev's public attack on the new thinking occurred in August 1988. See Jeff Checkel, "Gorbachev's 'New Political Thinking' and the Formation of Soviet Foreign Policy," Radio Liberty *Research Bulletin* No. 429/88 (September 23, 1988), 7–8.

79. On the Central Committee plenums, see the "Information Reports" published in the central press after each meeting. My source on the Politburo sessions is the individual who served as Yakovlev's chief aide during these years. Ligachev himself claims that it was only in the second half of 1987 that he "gradually began to find himself in disagreement with certain members of the higher political leadership." See Ligachev, *Zagadka Gorbacheva*, p. 71.

80. For the theoretical logic behind this point, see chapter 1.

81. Interviews (as in note 20). I am not arguing that Yakovlev and Primakov were the only conduits for new ideas. On more specific issues of national-security policy, Yakovlev, Primakov, and IMEMO were relatively uninfluential. See below.

82. This information comes from Sergey Blagovolin, a senior institute scholar who was close to Yakovlev and, later, to Gorbachev; it was confirmed by deputy institute director Gur'yev, as well as by Yakovlev's longtime personal aide. The first such report Blagovolin remembers preparing was in November 1983.

83. Yakovlev was my sole source for the second and third points.

84. See, especially, Dobrynin, "Za bez'yadernyy mir, navstrechu XXI veku"; and Yakovlev, "Dostizheniye kachestvenno novogo sostoyaniya Sovetskogo obshchestva i obshchestvennye nauki."

85. These were the natural scientists who worked for the Academy of Sciences' technical divisions and, in particular, the Committee of Soviet Scientists in Defense of Peace, Against the Nuclear Threat.

86. This information comes from an institute researcher recruited to work in the new unit.

87. See Aleksey Arbatov, *Bezopasnost' v yadernyy vek* (Moscow: Politizdat, 1980); idem, *Voyenno-strategicheskiy paritet i politika SShA* (Moscow: Politizdat, 1984); and idem, "Voyenno-strategicheskoye ravnovesiye i politika administratsii Reygana," *Memo* No. 10 (October 1984). Arbatov is the son of Georgiy Arbatov, head of ISKAN.

88. These observations are based on an analysis of numerous IMEMO publications, as well as interviews with three deputy directors of the institute, Sergey Blagovolin, and two researchers affiliated with Arbatov's unit. Also see chapters 3 and 4, above.

89. See Stephen Meyer, "The Sources and Prospects of Gorbachev's New Political Thinking on Security," *International Security* 13 (Fall 1988), 144–55; and R. Hyland Phillips and Jeffrey Sands, "Reasonable Sufficiency and Soviet Conventional Defense: A Research Note," *International Security* 13 (Fall 1988).

90. See Yevgeniy Primakov, "Novaya filosofiya vneshney politiki," *Pravda,* July 10, 1987, p. 4; and idem, "Kapitalizm vo vzaimosvyazannom mire," p. 109. Aside from my own reading of Primakov's motives, my analysis is based on an interview with a former researcher in Arbatov's department who later directed a Consultants' Group on international security issues in the C.C. International Department.

91. On Primakov's support of Arbatov, I have benefited from interviews with Sergey Blagovolin and a senior researcher in Arbatov's department.

92. For representative examples of the institute's distinctive approach to military and security issues, see Aleksandr Kalyadin, "Ogranicheniye yadernykh vooruzheniy i mezhdunarodnaya bezopasnost'," *Memo* No. 4 (April 1968); Nikolay Inozemtsev, Editor, *Mir i razoruzheniye: Nauchnye issledovaniya, 1980* (Moscow: Nauka, 1980); and Valeriy Abarenkov, *Politika SShA v oblasti 'kontrolya nad vooruzheniyami'* (Moscow: Nauka, 1987). For examples of Arbatov's military-technical expertise, see Aleksey Arbatov, "Glubokoye sokrashcheniye strategicheskikh vooruzheniy," *Memo* Nos. 4–5 (April–May 1988)—a two-part article; and Arbatov and Aleksandr Savel'yev, "Sistema upravleniya i svyazi kak faktor strategicheskoy stabil'nosti," *Memo* No. 12 (December 1987).

93. This context perhaps explains why the status of Arbatov's department at IMEMO declined in the early 1990s. Interviews. It also may explain why Arbatov spent an increasing amount of time abroad beginning in the late 1980s and why, in 1992, he established his own strategic-studies center at the Russian Foreign Policy Association. On the debate within the institute, see especially the polemic between Arbatov and Elgiz Pozdnyakov, a senior scholar in IMEMO's Department of International Relations. Aleksey Arbatov, "Deystvitel'no, yest' li povod dlya spora?" *Memo* No. 10 (October 1988); and Elgiz Pozdnyakov, "S kem, kak i po kakomu povodu sporit A. Arbatov?" *Memo* No. 10 (October 1988). On the ideational basis of the dispute, I have benefited from conversations with Sergey Blagovolin, Pozdnyakov, Oleg Bykov, Yuriy Fedorov and Aleksandr Savel'yev.

94. For details on the role of ISKAN and Kokoshin in these security debates, see Jeff

Checkel, "Organizational Behavior, Social Scientists and Soviet Foreign Policymaking" (Ph.D. diss., Massachusetts Institute of Technology, 1991), chapters 8–10. In the spring of 1992, Kokoshin was named a Deputy Minister of Defense of the Russian Federation.

95. James March and Johan Olsen, "The New Institutionalism: Organizational Factors in Political Life," *American Political Science Review* 78 (September 1984), 739.

96. Richard Sakwa, *Gorbachev and His Reforms, 1985–1990* (New York: Prentice Hall, 1990), chapter 5, provides a good overview of these groups and their activities. The few that did address foreign and security policy tended to focus — at least through 1990 — on problems that had an environmental, local politics dimension. One such group was the "Nevada" antinuclear association formed in the Kazakh Republic in 1989 to protest nuclear testing at the Semipalatinsk test site. See Matthew Evangelista, "The Paradox of State Strength: Transnational Relations, Domestic Structures and Security Policy in Russia and the Soviet Union," *International Organization* 49 (Winter 1995), 28–31. Also see John Lepingwell, "Soviet Early Warning Radars Debated," *Report on the USSR* 2 (August 17, 1990).

97. The following is based on information provided by a former head (1988–91) of a Consultants' Group on international security in the C.C. International Department; the interviewees listed in note 20; Meyer, "The Sources and Prospects of Gorbachev's New Political Thinking on Security"; and Mendelson, "Internal Battles and External Wars."

98. On the Politburo and Presidential Council sessions, my source is an aide to Yakovlev who attended many of these meetings. On the Geneva Summit, see Yevgeniy Primakov, "Vstrecha v verkakh: Vzglyad v proshloye i budushchee," *Pravda,* January 8, 1988, p. 4. On the Foreign Ministry speech, my source is Sergey Blagovolin, who wrote major portions of it. Parts of the speech were later published as "Vremya perestroyki," *Vestnik Ministerstva inostrannykh del SSSR* No. 1 (August 5, 1987).

99. Here, I draw most heavily on the recent work of Peter Hall. See Hall, "The Movement from Keynesianism to Monetarism: Institutional Analysis in British Economic Policy," in Frank Longstreth et al., Editors, *Structuring Politics: Historical Institutionalism in Comparative Analysis* (New York: Cambridge University Press, 1992), pp. 91–92; and idem, "Policy Paradigms, Social Learning and the State," pp. 279–81. However, the extension of the policy paradigm concept to foreign policy is my own. Hall's policy paradigm is similar in many respects to Weir's "programmatic ideas" and Sikkink's "ideologies." See Margaret Weir, *Politics and Jobs: The Boundaries of Employment Policy in the United States* (Princeton, N.J.: Princeton University Press, 1992), p. 169; and Sikkink, *Ideas and Institutions,* p. 1.

100. See, for example, Elgiz Pozdnyakov, "Natsional'nye, gosudarstvennye i klassovye interesy v mezhdunarodnykh otnosheniyakh," *Memo* No. 5 (May 1988); and Igor' Malashenko, "Interesy strany: mnimye i real'nye," *Kommunist* No. 13 (September 1989). For Western overviews, see Stephen Sestanovich, "Inventing the Soviet National Interest," *National Interest* No. 20 (Summer 1990); and Robert Legvold, "Soviet Learning in the 1980s," in George Breslauer and Philip Tetlock, Editors, *Learning in US and Soviet Foreign Policy* (Boulder, Colo.: Westview Press, 1991), pp. 713–14.

101. Interview (Yakovlev). On the ideas-behavior connection, also see Sergey Karaganov et al., "Vyzovy bezopasnosti — starye i novye," *Kommunist* No. 1 (January 1988); and Legvold, "Soviet Learning in the 1980s," pp. 714–20.

102. Wohlforth, "Realism and the End of the Cold War." Also see Daniel Deudney and G. John Ikenberry, "The International Sources of Soviet Change," *International Security* 16 (Winter 1991/92). Meyer, "The Sources and Prospects of Gorbachev's New Political Thinking on Security," presents a domestic politics explanation where it is argued that new ideas on foreign policy were only a tactical weapon, used instrumentally to regain control over the Soviet defense-policy agenda.

103. On institutionalization more generally and its importance for consolidating new ideas in policymaking, see Judith Goldstein, *Ideas, Interests and American Trade Policy* (Ithaca, N.Y.: Cornell University Press, 1993); and Weir, *Politics and Jobs.*

104. My analysis of Shevardnadze and the Foreign Ministry is based on interviews with ten former officials at the Ministry, as well as a reading of *Vestnik Ministerstva inostrannykh del SSSR,* the Ministry's journal.

Chapter 6: A Post–Cold War Cold Peace?

An earlier version of this chapter appeared as "Structure, Institutions, and Process: Russia's Changing Foreign Policy," in Karen Dawisha and Adeed Dawisha, Editors, *The Making of Foreign Policy in Russia and the New States of Eurasia* (Armonk, N.Y.: M. E. Sharpe, 1995).

1. For the epigraphs, see Leyla Boulton and John Lloyd, "Industrial Czar Puts Russia's Leader on Spot," *Financial Times,* October 29, 1992; and Steven Erlanger, "From This Boss's Seat, Yeltsin Appears Small," *New York Times,* January 8, 1993.

2. On the theoretical interest, see James Goldgeier and Michael McFaul, "A Tale of Two Worlds: Core and Periphery in the Post–Cold War World," *International Organization* 46 (Spring 1992).

3. Also see Matthew Evangelista, "The Paradox of State Strength: Transnational Relations, Domestic Structures and Security Policy in Russia and the Soviet Union," *International Organization* 49 (Winter 1995).

4. This is a proposition familiar to students of American politics, where the challenge is not so much to get a hearing for one's proposal (this is usually easy), but to insure that, once adopted, it has an enduring impact on policy. For the theoretical rationale behind such arguments, see Margaret Weir, "Ideas and Politics: The Acceptance of Keynesianism in Britain and the United States," in Peter Hall, Editor, *The Political Power of Economic Ideas: Keynesianism Across Nations* (Princeton, N.J.: Princeton University Press, 1989).

5. See Steven Erlanger, "Russian Finance Chief Tells of Enemies Within," *New York Times,* June 4, 1993.

6. See "Vystupleniye Prezidenta Rossii Borisa Yeltsina," *Rossiyskaya gazeta,* February 14, 1992; "Doklad Prezidenta Rossiyskoy Federatsii B. N. Yeltsina," *Rossiyskaya gazeta,* April 8, 1992; Andrey Kozyrev, "My vykhodim na novuyu sistemu tsennostey," *Krasnaya zvezda,* December 20, 1991; and idem, Preobrazhennaya Rossiya v novom mire," *Izvestiya,* January 2, 1992.

7. See "Rossiya i vyzovy sovremennosti," *Memo* No. 4 (April 1992).

8. This statement was made to the author in July 1992 by the official heading Foreign Ministry negotiations with Ukraine.

9. Interviews with Arbatov, Vladimir Benevolenskiy, scientific secretary at ISKAN, and Sergey Blagovolin, senior researcher and department head at IMEMO.

10. See ITAR-TASS (in Russian), June 26 and 27, 1992 — a speech by Foreign Minister Kozyrev to the Supreme Soviet concerning policy toward Serbia; Vladimir Volzhskiy, "V etoy bor'be pobediteley ne budet," *Nezavisimaya gazeta,* July 25, 1992; Robert Huber and Vladimir Savelyev, "Russian Parliament and Foreign Policy," *International Affairs* (Moscow) No. 3 (March 1993); and "Parliament Votes to Check on Foreign Ministry Work," *FBIS Central Eurasia Daily Report,* August 12, 1993.

11. See A. Sychev, "Avtor Rossiyskikh initsiativ ostayetsya inkognito," *Izvestiya,* February 8, 1992; "Doklad Prezidenta Rossiyskoy Federatsii B. N. Yeltsina," *Rossiyskaya gazeta,* April 8, 1992; Andrey Kozyrev, "Voyna i MID," *Komsomolskaya pravda,* June 9, 1992; and Mikhail Karpov, "Velikoy i samobytnoy Rossii," *Nezavisimaya gazeta,* October 28, 1992. On the U.S. case, see Stephen Krasner, *Defending the National Interest: Raw Materials Investment and US Foreign Policy* (Princeton, N.J.: Princeton University Press, 1978), chapter 3, for example.

12. The information on Yeltsin and Burbulis comes from interviews at the Foreign Ministry. For Kozyrev, see "Vystupleniye A. V. Kozyreva," *Rossiyskaya gazeta,* April 21, 1992.

13. See Vyacheslav Elagin, "Povod dlya bespokoystva," *Nezavisimaya gazeta,* November 26, 1992.

14. See Aleksandr Rahr, "Liberal-Centrist Coalition Takes Over in Russia," *RFE/RL Research Report* 1 (July 17, 1992); Aleksandr Shal'nev, "Andrey Kozyrev: 'Prezident Yeltsin i ya otvechayem za vneshnyuyu politiku Rossii,'" *Izvestiya,* January 5, 1993; "Foreign Policy Tasks of Security Council Commission Outlined," *FBIS Central Eurasia Daily Report,* February 9, 1993; and Radio Free Europe/Radio Liberty (hereafter RFE/RL) *Daily Report,* December 18, 1992, January 14, 18, and October 22, 1993. The presidential apparatus as a whole also grew considerably over the course of 1993 to more than 3,500 personnel; it now includes at least one department overseeing foreign affairs. See "Russia: Darkness in June?" *Economist,* January 29, 1994; and RFE/RL *Daily Report,* February 16, 1994.

15. For an excellent discussion of Russian institutional change as it pertains to economic policymaking, see Michael McFaul, "State Power, Institutional Change and the Politics of Privatization in Russia," *World Politics* 47 (January 1995). In spite of different theoretical approaches and issue areas, McFaul and I come to virtually identical empirical conclusions on changing institutional structures in Russia.

16. On the relation of bureaucratic politics to broader institutional context, also see Matthew Evangelista, *Innovation and the Arms Race: How the US and the Soviet Union Develop New Military Technologies* (Ithaca, N.Y.: Cornell University Press, 1988).

17. Interviews with personnel at the Russian Foreign Ministry, a former sector head at the C.C.'s International Department, Aleksandr Yakovlev's former chief aide, and Yakovlev himself.

18. See Stephen Foye, "Post-Soviet Russia: Politics and the New Russian Army," *RFE/RL Research Report* 1 (August 21, 1992); Scott McMichael, "Russia's New Military Doctrine," *RFE/RL Research Report* 1 (October 9, 1992); and Stephen Foye, "Up-

dating Russian Civil-Military Relations," *RFE/RL Research Report* 2 (November 19, 1993). For a sampling of the new Ministry's old worldview, see "Geostrategiya nas obyazyvayet," *Krasnaya zvezda,* December 4, 1992.

19. Interviews with Foreign Ministry personnel. On the council, see Andrey Kozyrev, "Raspakhivaya dver' vo vneshiy mir," *Rossiyskaya gazeta,* December 27, 1991; Mikhail Karpov, "Demokraticheskiye sily mobilizuyutsya," *Nezavisimaya gazeta,* November 28, 1992; and "Foreign Policy Council Discusses Eastern Europe Policy," *FBIS Central Eurasia Daily Report,* November 3, 1993.

20. See Kozyrev, "Dumat' o svoikh interesakh," *Izvestiya,* October 2, 1991; idem, "Preobrazhennaya Rossiya v novom mire," *Izvestiya,* January 2, 1992; and "Kozyrev Writes on Country's National Interests," *FBIS Central Eurasia Daily Report,* October 21, 1993.

21. See Andrey Kozyrev, "Preobrazheniye ili kafkianskaya metamorfoza," *Nezavisimaya gazeta,* August 20, 1992; idem, "K slovu 'patriotizm' prilagatel'nye ne nuzhny," *Krasnaya zvezda,* November 26, 1992; and Douglas Hurd and Andrey Kozyrev, "Challenge of Peacekeeping," *Financial Times,* December 14, 1993. One factor affecting the evolution of Kozyrev's beliefs was that, beginning in 1979, the Directorate of International Organizations at the Soviet Ministry was headed by Vladimir Petrovskiy, a scholar and pragmatist who became an early and outspoken advocate of Gorbachev's liberal foreign policy.

22. For full details on the debate, see Jeff Checkel, "Russian Foreign Policy: Back to the Future?" *RFE/RL Research Report* 1 (October 16, 1992); Aleksandr Rahr, " 'Atlanticists' versus 'Eurasians' in Russian Foreign Policy," *RFE/RL Research Report* 1 (May 29, 1992); and Suzanne Crow, "Competing Blueprints for Russian Foreign Policy," *RFE/RL Research Report* 1 (December 18, 1992).

23. ITAR-TASS (in Russian), June 18, 1992. Also see Aleksey Arbatov, "Russia's Foreign Policy Alternatives," *International Security* 18 (Fall 1993), 9–10.

24. Interviews at the Foreign Ministry; Yuriy Leonov, "Khorosha kontseptsiya, no vryad li osushchestvima," *Nezavisimaya gazeta,* February 20, 1992; and Interfax, February 21, 1992.

25. Interviews at the Foreign Ministry. Policy debates did occur in the former USSR. But they were restricted to a narrow set of actors and rarely entered the public domain, as such debates did in post-Soviet Russia.

26. See Konstantin Eggert, "Rossiya v roli 'Evraziyskogo zhandarma'?" *Izvestiya,* August 7, 1992; and Andranik Migranyan, "Podlinnye i mnimye orientiry vo vneshney politike," *Rossiyskaya gazeta,* August 4, 1992. Migranyan was at this point an adviser to Ambartsumov. For a sampling of Ambartsumov's views, see Yevgeniy Ambartsumov, "Sami sebya zagnali v ugol, samim iz nego i vykhodit'," *Rossiyskaya gazeta,* April 13, 1992.

27. See RFE/RL *Daily Report,* February 1, 1993 — a Yeltsin speech before the Indian Parliament. Also see Leyla Boulton, "Yeltsin Pledges Tough Foreign Policy to Please Right Wing," *Financial Times,* January 4, 1994.

28. See Mikhail Zinin, "MID nakonets-to nameren zayavit' o svoyem ponimanii vneshney politiki," *Nezavisimaya gazeta,* October 21, 1992; Mikhail Karpov, "Rossiya ne rassmatrivayet ni odno gosudarstvo kak vrazhdebnoye," *Nezavisimaya gazeta,* No-

vember 27, 1992; and "Kozyrev Offers Draft Foreign-Policy Guidelines," *Current Digest of the Post-Soviet Press* 44 (December 30, 1992), 14–16.

29. On access points more generally, see Desmond King, "The Establishment of Work-Welfare Programs in the United States and Britain: Politics, Ideas and Institutions," in Frank Longstreth et al., Editors, *Structuring Politics: Historical Institutionalism in Comparative Perspective* (New York: Cambridge University Press, 1992). McFaul, "State Power, Institutional Change and the Politics of Privatization in Russia," makes an analytic point similar to mine, arguing that the initial Gaidar-Yeltsin team attempted to implement a policy that was heavily influenced by neoliberal economic ideas, only to see them eviscerated under pressure from other parts of the state apparatus and broader social groupings.

30. Kozyrev's lack of political savvy is especially evident in "Partiya voyny nastupayet: i v Moldove, i v Gruzii, i v Rossii," *Izvestiya,* June 30, 1992 — an article that earned the Foreign Minister a public reprimand from Yeltsin. Also see Aleksandr Gol'ts, "Seans 'shokovoy diplomatii,'" *Krasnaya zvezda,* December 16, 1992. On Yeltsin's speech, see Gennadiy Charodeyev, "Yeltsin gotov otbit' ocherednuyu ataku," *Izvestiya,* October 27, 1992.

31. See Kathryn Sikkink, *Ideas and Institutions: Developmentalism in Brazil and Argentina* (Ithaca, N.Y.: Cornell University Press, 1991), chapter 5.

32. Interviews at the Foreign Ministry. Also see Checkel, "Russian Foreign Policy."

33. See note 14, above. Not surprisingly, the pattern described here of a lack of attention to capacity building is evident in other (domestic) issues areas as well. See McFaul, "State Power, Institutional Change and the Politics of Privatization in Russia."

34. See, for example, the scathing criticism in Arbatov, "Russia's Foreign Policy Alternatives." On the unprofessional and politicized foreign policy apparatus of the Soviet era, see the remarks by Andrey Kozyrev on Russian Television, December 28, 1991.

35. On the last point, see Fedor Shelov-Kovedyayev, "Nam nuzhna sil'naya, no ne imperskaya Rossiya," *Literaturnaya gazeta,* December 8, 1993. For useful overviews of the chaotic, weakly developed nature of political parties, see Leyla Boulton, "Reformers in Russia Seek New Identity," *Financial Times,* June 23, 1993; and "Can They Make a Democracy?" *Economist,* October 2, 1993.

36. For an example of Yeltsin's lack of clarity on foreign policy, see his address to the first session of the Federation Council, "Vystupleniye Prezidenta RF na otkrytii zasedaniya verkhney palaty parlamenta," *Rossiyskiye vesti,* January 12, 1994. Western observers have also noted Yeltsin's uncertainty over Russia's new international role. See John Lloyd, "Mr. Absent Without Leave," *Financial Times,* February 20, 1994; and "Russia: The Road to Ruin," *Economist,* January 29, 1994.

37. On this point more generally, see Stephan Haggard, *Pathways from the Periphery: The Politics of Growth in Newly Industrializing Countries* (Ithaca, N.Y.: Cornell University Press, 1990), chapter 2.

38. See Zhirinovskiy, "Milliard dollarov — i ya u vlasti," *Rossiya* No. 27 (1992); and Igor Torbakov, "The 'Statists' and the Ideology of Russian National Imperialism," *RFE/RL Research Report* 1 (December 11, 1992).

39. See RFE/RL *Daily Report,* January, 19 and 20, 1994 — reporting on a speech Kozyrev gave to Russian ambassadors gathered in Moscow; and Kozyrev's interview in

Segodnya, April 30, 1994, as summarized in RFE/RL *Daily Report,* May 2, 1994. Also see Leyla Boulton, "Moscow Less in Love with West: But Foreign Policy Has No Truck with Extreme Nationalism," *Financial Times,* February 3, 1994.

40. See Jack Snyder, *Myths of Empire: Domestic Politics and International Ambition* (Ithaca, N.Y.: Cornell University Press, 1991), chapter 2.

41. See Goldgeier and McFaul, "A Tale of Two Worlds."

42. For post–Cold War applications of this neorealist logic, see Christopher Layne, "The Unipolar Illusion: Why New Great Powers Will Rise," *International Security* 17 (Spring 1993); and Kenneth Waltz, "The Emerging Structure of International Politics," *International Security* 18 (Fall 1993).

43. For a more complete examination of Russia's new international environment that draws upon liberal and transnationalist research as well as realism, see Jeff Checkel, "Structure, Institutions and Process: Russia's Changing Foreign Policy," in Karen Dawisha and Adeed Dawisha, Editors, *The Making of Foreign Policy in Russia and the New States of Eurasia* (Armonk, N.Y.: M. E. Sharpe, 1995).

44. On the indeterminacy of structural explanations, also see Stephan Haggard, "Structuralism and Its Critics: Recent Progress in International Relations Theory," in Emanuel Adler and Beverly Crawford, Editors, *Progress in Postwar International Relations* (New York: Columbia University Press, 1991), chapter 11; and Richard Ned Lebow, "The Long Peace, the End of the Cold War and the Failure of Realism," *International Organization* 48 (Spring 1994).

Chapter 7: Ideas and Foreign Policy

1. On the need for a theoretical retooling in international relations, see Edward Kolodziej, "Renaissance in Security Studies? Caveat Lector!" *International Studies Quarterly* 36 (December 1992); John Lewis Gaddis, "International Relations Theory and the End of the Cold War," *International Security* 17 (Winter 1992/93); and the various contributions in Thomas Risse-Kappen and Richard Ned Lebow, Editors, *International Relations Theory and the End of the Cold War* (New York: Columbia University Press, 1995).

2. In the comparative-politics literature, see Peter Smith, "Crisis and Democracy in Latin America," *World Politics* 43 (July 1991); and Herbert Kitschelt, "Political Regime Change: Structure and Process-Driven Explanations?" *American Political Science Review* 86 (December 1992). In international relations, see Peter Haas, *Saving the Mediterranean: The Politics of International Environmental Cooperation* (New York: Columbia University Press, 1990); and, especially, the excellent discussion of interactionist theories in Richard Herrmann, "Conclusions: The End of the Cold War—What Have We Learned?" in Risse-Kappen and Lebow, Editors, *International Relations Theory and the End of the Cold War,* chapter 10.

3. Given this characterization of Yakovlev and Primakov, it is not surprising that both have played major political roles in post-Soviet Russia. Yakovlev organized a new political party and, for several years, headed the federal broadcast agency; Primakov led the federal counterintelligence unit throughout the early 1990s and became Russian Foreign Minister in early 1996.

4. On the need for a greater focus on politics in research on ideas, see Janice Gross Stein, "Ideas, Even Good Ideas, Are Not Enough: Changing Canada's Foreign and Defense Policies," *International Journal* 50 (Winter 1994–95).

5. Pure coalitional, interest-based accounts, of course, have a problem similar to my pure institutional approach: they are incomplete. See Jeffry Frieden, *Debt, Development and Democracy: Modern Political Economy and Latin America, 1965–85* (Princeton, N.J.: Princeton University Press, 1991), where the author's rigorous coalitional argument is partly undercut by neglect of institutional factors.

6. On the debate in policy studies, see "Toward Better Theories of the Policy Process," *PS: Political Science and Politics* 24 (June 1991). The policy-streams approach is elaborated in John Kingdon, *Agendas, Alternatives and Public Policy* (Boston: Little, Brown, 1984).

7. See, especially, Jack Snyder, *Myths of Empire: Domestic Politics and International Ambition* (Ithaca, N.Y.: Cornell University Press, 1991), which has been widely praised within the international-relations community. Representative is Jack Levy's review in *American Political Science Review* 86 (September 1992), 851–52. On the neglect of domestic politics, see, among many others, Thomas Risse-Kappen, "Public Opinion, Domestic Structure and Foreign Policy in Liberal Democracies," *World Politics* 43 (July 1991); and Helen Milner, "International Theories of Cooperation Among Nations: Strengths and Weaknesses (Review Article)," *World Politics* 44 (April 1992).

8. Snyder is explicit in characterizing his book as an attempt to "recapture" realism from systems-level neorealists. See Snyder, *Myths of Empire*, pp. 19–20. Although not a coalitional approach, another effort to develop a realist domestic-level explanation of state behavior is William Wohlforth, "Realism and the End of the Cold War," *International Security* 19 (Winter 1994/95). In Wohlforth's more eclectic approach, ideas are accorded a greater, but still secondary, causal role.

9. Hugh Heclo, *Modern Social Politics in Britain and Sweden: From Relief to Income Maintenance* (New Haven: Yale University Press, 1974), p. 305.

10. On the role of international institutions, see Ernst Haas, *When Knowledge Is Power: Three Models of Change in International Organizations* (Berkeley: University of California Press, 1990); Kevin Hartigan, "Matching Humanitarian Norms with Cold, Hard Interests: The Making of Refugee Policies in Mexico and Honduras," *International Organization* 46 (Summer 1992); Martha Finnemore, "International Organizations as Teachers of Norms: UNESCO and Science Policy," *International Organization* 47 (Autumn 1993); and Robert Keohane, "Contested Commitments in American Foreign Policy" — especially the section on "institutional enmeshment" (paper presented at University of Pittsburgh Colloquium on International Relations Theory, Pittsburgh, Pa., February 1994). There are at least three theoretical orientations within the literature on the new transnationalism: epistemic communities; issue networks; and work building on insights from social movement theory. For representative examples of each, see Haas, *Saving the Mediterranean;* Kathryn Sikkink, "Human Rights, Principled Issue-Networks and Sovereignty in Latin America," *International Organization* 47 (Summer 1993); and Alison Brysk, "From Above and Below: Social Movements, the International System and Human Rights in Argentina," *Comparative Political Studies* 26 (October 1993).

11. An influential work in this earlier tradition is Robert Keohane, *After Hegemony:*

Cooperation and Discord in the World Political Economy (Princeton, N.J.: Princeton University Press, 1984). Stephan Haggard and Beth Simmons, "Theories of International Regimes," *International Organization* 41 (Summer 1987), review the regime literature and critique its neglect of domestic politics.

12. As noted in chapter 1, this elite model is implicit in the epistemic approach.

13. Two important efforts at rectifying this problem are Matthew Evangelista, "The Paradox of State Strength: Transnational Relations, Domestic Structures and Security Policy in Russia and the Soviet Union," *International Organization* 49 (Winter 1995); and, more generally, Thomas Risse-Kappen, Editor, *Bringing Transnational Relations Back In: Non-State Actors, Domestic Structures and International Institutions* (Cambridge: Cambridge University Press, 1995). Also see Jeff Checkel, "International Norms and Domestic Institutions: Identity Politics in Post–Cold War Europe" (paper presented at the American Political Science Association Annual Convention, Chicago, September 1995).

14. See Peter Hall, Editor, *The Political Power of Economic Ideas: Keynesianism Across Nations* (Princeton, N.J.: Princeton University Press, 1989), pp. 386–89; idem, "Policy Paradigms, Social Learning and the State: The Case of Economic Policymaking in Britain," *Comparative Politics* 25 (April 1993); G. John Ikenberry, "Creating Yesterday's New World Order: Keynesian 'New Thinking' and the Anglo-American Postwar Settlement," in Judith Goldstein and Robert Keohane, Editors, *Ideas and Foreign Policy: Beliefs, Institutions and Political Change* (Ithaca, N.Y.: Cornell University Press, 1993), chapter 3; and Kathryn Sikkink, *Ideas and Institutions: Developmentalism in Brazil and Argentina* (Ithaca, N.Y.: Cornell University Press, 1991), p. 247. Those working within the epistemic framework also see crisis and uncertainty as crucial to the process empowering new ideas. See Peter Haas, Editor, "Knowledge, Power and International Policy Coordination," *International Organization* 46 (Winter 1992).

15. See Kingdon, *Agendas, Alternatives and Public Policy;* Hall, "Policy Paradigms, Social Learning and the State"; and John Keeler, "Opening the Window for Reform: Mandates, Crises and Extraordinary Policymaking," *Comparative Political Studies* 25 (January 1993), for example. The quote is taken from Sikkink, "Human Rights, Principled Issue-Networks and Sovereignty in Latin America," p. 438–39.

16. The quote, as well as the cognitive-political distinction are taken from Ikenberry, "Creating Yesterday's New World Order." Others stressing the dual role of ideas are Peter Hall, *Governing the Economy: The Politics of State Intervention in Britain and France* (New York: Oxford University Press, 1986), pp. 276–80; Peter Gourevitch, "Keynesian Politics: The Political Sources of Economic Policy Choices," in Hall, Editor, *The Political Power of Economic Ideas;* and Margaret Weir, *Politics and Jobs: The Boundaries of Employment Policy in the United States* (Princeton, N.J.: Princeton University Press, 1992).

17. Snyder, in developing his rational-choice framework for *Myths of Empire,* overwhelmingly emphasizes the political dimension.

18. The need to bridge the divide separating rationalist and ideas-based approaches is a central theme in John Jacobsen, "Much Ado About Ideas: The Cognitive Factor in Economic Policy," *World Politics* 47 (January 1995). Also see Judith Goldstein, *Ideas, Interests and American Trade Policy* (Ithaca, N.Y.: Cornell University Press, 1993).

19. Sikkink, *Ideas and Institutions;* and Emanuel Adler, *The Power of Ideology: The Quest for Technological Autonomy in Argentina and Brazil* (Berkeley: University of California Press, 1987).

20. See Weir, *Politics and Jobs;* and Walter Salant, "The Spread of Keynesian Doctrines and Practices in the United States," in Hall, Editor, *Political Power of Economic Ideas.*

21. Hall, "Policy Paradigms, Social Learning and the State." For additional evidence on the United States and Great Britain, see Desmond King, "The Establishment of Work-Welfare Programs in the United States and Britain: Politics, Ideas and Institutions," in Frank Longstreth et al., Editors, *Structuring Politics: Historical Institutionalism in Comparative Analysis* (New York: Cambridge University Press, 1992), which confirms many of the points made separately by Weir, Salant, and Hall on the role of ideas.

22. In some instances, these entrepreneurs may be members of larger, transnational policy networks. See Evangelista, "The Paradox of State Strength."

23. Weir, *Politics and Jobs.* On these points, also see Judith Goldstein, "Creating the GATT Rules: Politics, Institutions and American Policy," in John Ruggie, Editor, *Multilateralism Matters: The Theory and Praxis of an Institutional Form* (New York: Columbia University Press, 1993); and Aaron Friedberg, "Why Didn't the United States Become a Garrison State?" *International Security* 16 (Spring 1992).

24. Adler, *The Power of Ideology;* Hall, *Governing the Economy;* Sikkink, *Ideas and Institutions;* King, "The Establishment of Work-Welfare Programs in the United States and Britain"; and Margaret Weir, "Ideas and Politics: The Acceptance of Keynesianism in Britain and the United States," in Hall, Editor, *The Political Power of Economic Ideas,* all make a start in this direction by considering two countries each.

25. See Judith Goldstein and Robert Keohane, "Ideas and Foreign Policy: An Analytical Framework," in Goldstein and Keohane, Editors, *Ideas and Foreign Policy;* and Goldstein, *Ideas, Interests and American Trade Policy,* especially chapter 1.

26. Peter Hall and Judith Goldstein have both suggested that ideas should play an even greater role in foreign as opposed to domestic policy because of the uncertainty inherent in the former. See Hall, "Policy Paradigms, Social Learning and the State," p. 291; and Goldstein, *Ideas, Interests and American Trade Policy,* pp. 254–55.

27. Thanks to Simon Reich and Peter Katzenstein for alerting me to these distinctions. On international norms, see, especially, Finnemore, "International Organizations as Teachers of Norms"; and the Social Science Research Council project on "Norms and National Security," directed by Peter Katzenstein.

28. On the elitist emphasis in the ideas literature, also see Jacobsen, "Much Ado About Ideas." Two exceptions to this elite focus are Sikkink, *Ideas and Institutions;* and Adler, *The Power of Ideology.* Both stress the importance of broader national discourses and ideologies.

29. In the norms literature, see Peter Katzenstein, "Norms and National Security: Germany and Japan at the End of the Cold War" (Paper presented at University of Pittsburgh Colloquium on International Relations Theory, Pittsburgh, Pa., January 1995), for example.

30. See the various contributions in Longstreth et al., Editors, *Structuring Politics;* Hall, *Governing the Economy;* and Victoria Hattam, "Institutions and Political Change: Working-Class Formation in England and the United States, 1820–1896," *Politics and*

Society 20 (June 1992). For an excellent critique of this literature and its inattention to theory building, see Paul Pierson, "When Effect Becomes Cause: Policy Feedback and Political Change (Review Essay)," *World Politics* 45 (July 1993).

31. For the debate over issue area, see Matthew Evangelista, "Issue-Area and Foreign Policy Revisited," *International Organization* 43 (Winter 1989). On George's method, see Alexander George, "Case Studies and Theory Development: The Method of Structured, Focused Comparison," in Paul Lauren, Editor, *Diplomacy: New Approaches in History, Theory and Policy* (New York: Free Press, 1979).

32. Theorists of international relations are displaying increasing awareness of such domestic-international connections. See note 10, as well as recent research on "two-level games": Peter Evans et al., Editors, *Double-Edged Diplomacy: International Bargaining and Domestic Politics* (Berkeley: University of California Press, 1993).

Index

D1475328